The costs of occupational stress in terms of sickness absence, ill-health-related retirement, litigation and lost productivity are increasing, putting strain on economies across the world. The fact that health care work is inherently more stressful than many other occupations makes it vital that the problem of occupational stress among health professionals is addressed.

CBT for Occupational Stress in Health Professionals goes beyond simply defining the problem and fills a gap in the current literature by providing clear and concise individual treatment interventions. In three parts, the book covers:

- an overview of stress in the occupational context
- the standard CBT approach to assessment, formulation and treatment
- a new schema-focused approach to treating occupational stress.

The schema-focused approach presented here provides powerful tools for treating a range of work-related problems for which standard CBT approaches are ineffective. Case studies are presented throughout the book to illustrate the therapeutic approaches described.

This book will be of huge benefit to clinical and organizational psychologists, psychiatrists, mental health workers, counsellors and anyone else involved in treating occupational stress. It will also have much to offer those who manage people suffering from stress, human resource workers and those who are experiencing work-related stress.

Martin R. Bamber is a chartered consultant clinical psychologist. He presently holds the post of Head of the Primary Care and Adult Cognitive Behavioural Therapy Sections of Selby and York NHS Primary Care Trust Psychological Therapies Department. He is also a teaching fellow at the University of York and is founder and Director of MRB Clinical Psychology Services, a private practice based in York.

CBT for Occupational Stress in Health Professionals

Introducing a schema-focused approach

Martin R. Bamber

Routledge
Taylor & Francis Group

LONDON AND NEW YORK

First published 2006
by Routledge
27 Church Road, Hove, East Sussex BN3 2FA

Simultaneously published in the USA and Canada
by Routledge
270 Madison Ave, New York, NY 10016

Routledge is an imprint of the Taylor & Francis Group, an informa business

Typeset in Times by RefineCatch Ltd, Bungay, Suffolk
Printed and bound in Great Britain by
MPG Books Ltd, Bodmin, Cornwall
Paperback cover design by Design Deluxe

This publication has been produced with paper manufactured to
strict environmental standards and with pulp derived from
sustainable forests.

British Library Cataloguing in Publication Data
A catalogue record for this book is available from the British Library

Library of Congress Cataloging-in-Publication Data
CBT for occupational stress in health professionals : introducing a
schema-focussed approach / edited by Martin R. Bamber.
    p. cm
  Includes bibliographical references and index.
  ISBN 1-58391-851-5 (hbk) – ISBN 1-58391-852-3 (pbk)
  1. Medical personnel–Job stress.   2. Cognitive therapy.
  I. Bamber, Martin R.
  R690.C39 2006
  610.68'3–dc22   2006008368

ISBN13: 978-1-58391-851-7 (hbk)
ISBN13: 978-1-58391-852-4 (pbk)

ISBN10: 1-58391-851-5 (hbk)
ISBN10: 1-58391-852-3 (pbk)

This book is dedicated to my family, my wife Kathy and especially to our four wonderful children Jack, Sam, Grace and Rosie. I could not have wished for more beautiful, healthy, loving and gifted children.

Contents

List of figures and tables

Figures

Tables

About the author

Martin Bamber B.A. (Hons), R.M.N., M.A., M. Phil, D. Psychol, C. Psychol, AFBPsS is a chartered consultant clinical psychologist. He completed his clinical psychology training at the University of Edinburgh in 1989. He presently holds the post of Head of the Primary Care and Adult Cognitive Behavioural Therapy Sections of Selby and York NHS Primary Care Trust Psychological Therapies Department, UK. He is also a teaching fellow at the University of York Department of Psychology and is founder and Director of MRB Clinical Psychology Services, a private practice based in York, UK. In his previous post he worked as a clinical psychologist in occupational health for four years, during which time he had the privilege of setting up and developing an occupational health psychology service for staff employed by a number of NHS trusts in Cleveland, UK. It was also during this time that the seeds of a number of ideas presented in this book were sown. His research interests are in the fields of psychoneuroimmunology, occupational stress and innovative applications of cognitive behavioural therapy.

Dr Bamber can be contacted at the Psychological Therapies Department of Selby and York NHS Primary Care Trust, Chantry Suite, Bootham Park Hospital, York YO30 7BY, UK. Email: martin.bamber@sypct.nhs.uk

Notes on contributors

Dr Paul Blenkiron is an accredited member of the British Association for Behavioural and Cognitive Psychotherapies. He has worked as Consultant in Adult and Community Psychiatry at Bootham Park Hospital in York since 2000. He is Honorary Senior Lecturer at the Academic Department of Psychiatry and Behavioural Sciences, University of Leeds and Honorary Senior Clinical Lecturer at the Hull–York Medical School. He qualified with an honours degree in medicine and surgery from the University of Oxford in 1988, obtaining membership of the Royal College of General Practitioners in 1992, and Membership of the Royal College of Psychiatrists in 1997. In 1999 he was awarded the degree of Master of Medical Sciences in Clinical Psychiatry from Leeds University, including the Max Hamilton Prize for Mental Health Research.

Mark Latham has been a lecturer in cognitive behavioural therapy (CBT) at the Department of Health Sciences, University of York, since 2001. Before this he worked in the National Health Service for 16 years, 11 of them as a cognitive behavioural nurse therapist. He completed training in behavioural psychotherapy at the Maudsley Hospital, London, in 1991, and in cognitive therapy at the Oxford Cognitive Therapy Centre in 1996. He is an accredited member of the British Association for Behavioural and Cognitive Psychotherapies, and has extensive experience as a CBT trainer, clinical supervisor and practitioner. In his spare time he runs up and down fells and through bogs for fun!

Professor Alistair Ostell (B.Sc., D. Phil, C. Psychol, AFBPsS) is Professor of Organizational Behaviour and Health at the Bradford University School of Management, where he has been Head of the Human Resource Management and Organizational Behaviour Group, Director of the BBC executive programmes and Director of the Doctor of Business Administration programme. His research interests and publications cover four main areas: factors associated with poor health in organizations; interventions to promote health; selection, appraisal, performance management and development; and the management and evaluation of interventions in organizations. He has worked extensively with public and private sector organizations to diagnose and advise upon management and organizational problems.

Dr Jason Price is a chartered clinical psychologist currently working as a neuropsychologist at James Cook University Hospital in Middlesbrough, Cleveland. After graduating with a doctorate in clinical psychology in 2002, he began a course of specialist training in clinical neuropsychology. In addition to his interests in neuropsychology, Dr Price has also professional and research interests in psychodynamic and schema theory and therapy.

Preface

Occupational stress is costing the UK economy billions of pounds each year through sickness absence, ill-health retirement, litigation and poor work performance, and it is on the increase. A survey carried out in the UK in the year 2000 found that half a million employees were suffering from work-related stress, a rise of 30% over the decade from 1990 (Smith 2000). Given that staff account for between 50% and 80% of organizational costs (Cooper *et al.* 1996), it is clear that reducing occupational stress not only makes sense on humanitarian grounds and in terms of improving patient care but it also makes sound economic sense. The British National Health Service is both labour-intensive and one of the largest employers in Europe. Health care work is also by its very nature inherently more stressful than many other occupations. For these reasons, it is becoming increasingly evident that the problem of occupational stress among health workers needs to be addressed as a matter of urgency.

Much has been written in the literature in recent years about primary (organizational) level interventions for occupational stress, and the trend has been to move away from individual level interventions. The contribution made by complex individual factors in the development of stress reactions has been de-emphasized in favour of more simplistic explanations and overly standardized treatment interventions. There has been a lack of in-depth analysis of workers as human beings with emotions, who bring with them to the workplace their own history, past experiences, beliefs, attitudes and idiosyncratic ways of coping and behaving. The reality of course is that both individual and environmental factors play a crucial part in the development of occupational stress. Also, while much has been written in the literature defining and redefining the concept of occupational stress, and its causes and consequences, there has been relatively little written about individual treatment interventions to deal with it. This book aims to redress these imbalances in the literature by focusing more on individual treatment interventions, in the knowledge that improving the mental health of the individual will ultimately lead to a healthier and more productive organization.

This book is presented in three parts. Part 1 (Chapters 1 and 2) provides an introduction to and overview of stress in the occupational context, and its causes and consequences. A cognitive behavioural model of occupational stress based on Aaron T. Beck's seminal work on the subject (Beck 1984) is developed. Part 2 (Chapters 3–8) introduces the standard cognitive behavioural therapy (CBT) approach to assessment, formulation and the primary, secondary and tertiary interventions for treating occupational stress. While the main focus of this section is on individual CBT interventions, a chapter on organizational interventions has also been included, as an acknowledgement of the importance of primary level interventions. Case illustrations of the standard CBT approach are presented in Chapters 9, 10 and 11. It should be noted that the names and some of the details presented in all the case illustrations have of course been altered to protect the identity of those individuals involved.

Part 3 (Chapters 12–14) of the book introduces a new approach to treating occupational stress and work dysfunctions, known as the 'schema-focused' approach, which is based upon the innovative work of Jeffrey Young and colleagues at the Schema Therapy Institute in New York. Chapter 12 presents a schema-focused model of occupational stress. In Chapter 13 the model is developed further, by mapping specific work dysfunctions onto early mal-adaptive schemata (EMS) and maladaptive coping styles. Chapter 14 outlines the schema-focused approach to assessment and formulation of occupational stress and work dysfunctions and identifies a range of powerful cognitive, experiential and behavioural tools and techniques, which can be applied to treating them. This approach allows the therapist to develop more in-depth individually tailored treatment programmes and provides a powerful set of tools for treating a range of other work-related problems, especially those of an interpersonal nature, for which the standard CBT approach is ineffective. A case illustration of the model (Chapter 15) and some empirical data supporting the model (Chapter 16) are also presented.

The implications for employers and therapists of adopting a schema-focused model of occupational stress are discussed in Chapter 17. In particular, it is noted that a strength of this approach is its focus on the interpersonal. Dysfunctional patterns of relating to others are at the root of much distress, dissatisfaction and conflict in the workplace and if these sources of occu-pational stress can be successfully tackled, there are benefits for everyone involved. The schema-focused approach is not intended to rival the standard CBT approach or organizational interventions, but to complement them. While acknowledging the importance of the work environment in triggering stress, this book employs an essentially clinical approach, which addresses the dysfunctional cognitive processes and maladaptive behavioural coping strat-egies emanating from these cognitive processes. It also acknowledges the complex interactions between the cognitive, emotional, behavioural and physiological processes involved in the development of occupational stress syndromes and work dysfunctions, and provides a comprehensive range of cognitive and behavioural interventions which can be used to alleviate them.

Martin Bamber
March 2006

Acknowledgements

I would like to thank everyone who has either indirectly or directly made a contribution to the writing of this book. In particular, I would like to thank Mark Latham, Paul Blenkiron, Alistair Ostell and Jason Price for their contributions to the book. I know it was not easy to make the time to do this, given all their other commitments. I would also like to thank the publishers for giving me the opportunity to write this book, and in particular the editorial team for their support and guidance.

Part I

Introduction

Chapter 1

Defining and conceptualizing stress

Martin Bamber

I know there is no happiness for man except in pleasure and enjoyment while he lives. And when man eats and drinks and finds happiness in his work, this is a gift from God.

(Book of Ecclesiastes Chapter 3: 1–14)

INTRODUCTION

One consequence of the evolution to a more global economy is that as the competition for market share and survival increases, pressure mounts on workers to become ever more productive (Hoel *et al.* 2001). Occupational stress is an unfortunate consequence of this, affecting a growing number of people across the world (Cox *et al.* 2000). It is estimated that up to 40% of all sickness absence from work is due to stress (Confederation of British Industry [CBI] 2000; Hoel *et al.* 2001). In the UK alone this is costing employers and health insurance companies billions of pounds each year in lost productivity and health insurance claims (CBI 2000; Gordon and Risley 1999). However, the costs of stress in organizational terms are much broader than just those incurred through sickness absence. They include increased staff turnover, recruitment problems, low morale in staff, decreased productivity, poor time-keeping, impaired decision-making, increased industrial conflicts, increased accident rates, premature ill-health retirement, and costs related to redeployment, retraining, replacement, grievance procedures, and litigation (Cooper *et al.* 1996; Firth-Cozens 1993).

Health care providers around the world are subject to pressures resulting from a sharp escalation of change, growing economic pressures, technological advances, increasing patient expectations, rationing of health care, and the requirement for more evidence-based and high-quality health care, improved performance, and productivity. It is well documented that health workers experience higher levels of stress and stress-related health problems than other occupational groups (Borill *et al.* 1996, 1998; Caplan 1994; Cooper and Mitchell 1990; Dawkins *et al.* 1985; Firth 1986; Firth-Cozens

1993; Harris 1989; Moore and Cooper 1996; Rees and Cooper 1992; Rodgers 1998; Williams *et al.* 1998). Among health worker groups, those thought to be most at risk for developing chronic stress syndromes are emergency service workers and mental health professionals (Clohessy and Ehlers 1999; Furnham 1997; Moore and Cooper 1996; Rees and Cooper 1992). Ambulance personnel, for example, receive more call-outs in a year than the police and fire services combined, and also have the highest rate of retirement on physical and mental health grounds compared to all other health care staff in the UK (James and Wright 1991; Rodgers 1998).

It is estimated that we spend on average at least 100,000 hours of our lives at work (Edelmann 1993), so it is important that we find it a satisfying and rewarding place to be. However, many health professionals are not experiencing their work as satisfying. In the UK health workers are leaving the National Health Service (NHS) in record numbers and, despite the uncertainty of the job market, there are chronic recruitment and retention difficulties. For example, it is estimated that as many as 14% of the doctors who qualified in the UK in 1988 are no longer practising medicine (Medical Workforce Standing Advisory Committee 1997) and, of doctors still practising, 22% say they regret their career choice (Clack 1999). One might argue that if someone is not happy in their work, then they should find another job. However, there are numerous reasons why the solution is not that simple. A health care professional may have invested many years training, may not be trained to do any other kind of work, or cannot afford to take a drop in salary. The employee may not have any alternative employment to go to, or be tied to a particular geographical area through personal and family commitments. There are thus numerous reasons why an employee cannot simply walk away from the job, and it is the long-term exposure to these unmitigated sources of stress which can lead to harmful effects on an employee's physical and mental health. Since the NHS is one of the largest employers in Europe, it is of crucial importance that occupational stress among health workers is tackled as a matter of priority.

Traditionally, the wisdom of management theorists has been that employee casualties were an inevitable and acceptable sacrifice for organizations to make in order to remain productive and profitable, and that work organizations had no responsibility to cater for the 'neurotic tendencies' of employees (Rose 1982; Taylor 1947). However, more recently it has been recognized that addressing occupational stress in the workforce makes sense not only on humanitarian grounds but it also makes sound economic sense. The current state of thinking is that it is possible to achieve a balance between the 'costs and benefits' of work, whereby the needs of both the organization and the individual can be successfully met, allowing the individual to remain healthy and motivated in their work and at the same time allowing the organization to remain productive (Beehr and Bhagat 1985; Cooper and Payne 1988; Lowman 1997; Matteson and Ivancevich 1987; Quick and Quick 1984).

The main focus of this book is on presenting a range of detailed intervention strategies aimed at reducing occupational stress. However, before looking at these, it is important to conceptualize and define what is meant by stress.

DEFINING STRESS

Stress is a general term which refers to two distinct concepts, namely 'stressors' (environmental characteristics, or thoughts which cause an adverse reaction in the individual) and 'strain' (the individual's adverse reaction to the stressor) (Beehr and O'Hara 1987; Knapp 1988). Over the last 50 years or so, a large number of definitions of stress have been proposed (e.g., Di Martino 1992; Fontana 1997; McGrath 1970; Monet and Lazarus 1977). These definitions have focused on certain situations as being stressful, on individuals' responses to these situations or on both. Examples of stressful situations include excessive noise, heat, insufficient income, too much work, overcrowding, too little stimulation, death of a close family member, divorce or a jail sentence (Glass and Singer 1972; Grosser et al 1964; Holmes and Rahe 1967). The response-based conceptualization is typified by Selye's 'general adaptation syndrome' (Selye 1936, 1946, 1974, 1975, 1976, 1983). Selye described three stages in the body's response to stressful situations, consisting of an initial alarm reaction, an adaptive middle stage and a final stage of exhaustion.

There is now a recognition among stress researchers that situation–response-based conceptualizations of stress are insufficient to explain the mediating factors within individuals which modify their susceptibility to environmental events and the stress consequently experienced. As a result of the 'cognitive revolution' in psychology, there is a growing consensus that stress is cognitively mediated and the product of an interaction between the individual and their environment (Lazarus 1993; Lazarus and Folkman 1984; Lazarus and Launier 1978). This approach has become known as the 'transactional' conceptualization of stress and it asserts that most situations or events are not in themselves intrinsically stressful but only become stressful when an individual appraises them as such (Beck 1984, 1987; Breslau and Davis 1986; Cox 1978, 1993; Di Martino 1992; Forsythe and Compass 1987; Lazarus 1975, 1976, 1977, 1982; Lazarus and Folkman 1984; Meichenbaum 1977; Ostell 1991; Singer 1986).

A COGNITIVELY MEDIATED MODEL OF STRESS

The model of stress presented in Figure 1.1 is adapted from Beck's model of stress (Beck 1984; Beck et al. 1979, 1985; Pretzer et al. 1989). It proposes that

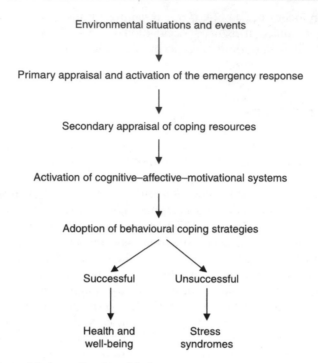

Figure 1.1 A cognitively mediated model of stress.

the way in which an individual interprets and evaluates information from the environment determines the individual's emotional and behavioural responses to it.

When an individual is under stress, information processing becomes disordered and manifests itself as distorted thinking, emotional distress and associated maladaptive patterns of behaviour. In this model, cognitions mediate directly between stressful life events and emotional distress.

Beck (1984) identified a number of steps in the model, which correspond to those presented in Figure 1.1.

Step 1: The first 'snapshot' of an event or situation

The stress reaction is triggered by specific events or situations. Beck (1984) used a camera analogy to describe an individual's construction of a particular situation or event and likened it to taking a 'snapshot'. In taking a photograph of a particular event or situation, the existing settings of the camera (lens, focus, speed and aperture settings) determine the eventual picture obtained. For example, there may be some blurring or loss of detail due to inadequate focusing, or some distortion or magnification of the picture if a wide-angle or telephoto lens has been used. In a similar way, the existing 'cognitive settings' of an individual will influence the way in which he or she perceives an event or situation. The underlying structures which determine an individual's pre-existing cognitive settings are called 'schemata' (Beck 1972, 1995, 1996; Beck *et al.* 1990; Padesky 1994). Schemata are stable structures that select and synthesize incoming information as described in the camera analogy. They provide the meaning of an event for the individual and are the starting point for triggering a subsequent sequence of cognitive, emotional, physiological and behavioural events.

Schemata are formed through early life experiences. If the individual has had a healthy and stable early environment, then these schemata are likely to be equally healthy and adaptive. However, if the individual has experienced toxic early environmental life experiences, for example abuse or trauma, or not having their physical and/or core emotional needs reliably met, then these schemata are very likely to be unhealthy and maladaptive ones. In a non-threatened state (non-stressed), these schemata are dormant and inactive but they are reactivated by specific stressful events, which thematically resemble the adverse earlier experiences upon which the schemata are based. For example, if the individual experienced significant rejection in childhood, he or she will be particularly sensitive to situations or events that signal rejection. Thus, a situation signalling rejection to this individual will result in 'hyper-activation' of that particular schema. These specific sensitivities or vulnerabilities refer to an individual's propensity to over-react to certain highly specific situations in an idiosyncratic way determined by the underlying schemata (Saul 1947).

In a non-threatened state (non-stressed), individuals may not perceive their maladaptive schemata to be plausible and can display relatively normal and adaptive information processing, emotions and behavioural responses. However, when the unhealthy schemata become hyper-activated in the way described above (when stressed), they become much more plausible, potent and dominant, and are difficult to switch off. In the example of the schema for rejection cited above, the individual begins to feel and behave as if they were in reality being rejected. Thus, schemata are considered to be at the core of the cognitive disturbance experienced in stress reactions (Beck 1967, 1972, 1976, 1996; Beck *et al.* 1990; Padesky 1994). However, it is their rigid, extreme, global nature, rather than the content of the schemata, that leads to psychopathology (Beck 1995). The initial snapshot of a situation corresponds to what Lazarus called 'primary appraisal' (Lazarus 1966, 1977; Lazarus and Folkman 1984; Lazarus and Launier 1978) and Freud (1914) called 'primitive thinking'. It is the person's initial judgement of the situation and is concerned essentially with decisions about the presence or absence of threat. The first snapshot taken thus provides information that either reinforces or modifies a pre-existing cognitive set.

Step 2: The activation of the emergency response

If the individual's initial appraisal is that there is a threat to their vital interests and there is a clear and present danger, then the 'emergency response' is activated (Beck 1984). Triggering situations include those where there is a threat to self-preservation, survival, functioning, attachments or status, such as imminent physical attack, abuse, harm or punishment, but there can also be more subtle 'social' triggers such as criticism, rejection, abandonment, deprivation, loss of social status and social exclusion (Beck 1996). One might ask why social situations should trigger the emergency response. Whilst this may be difficult to appreciate in our modern Western society and culture, it has been argued that from an evolutionary perspective, 'sociability' and being an accepted part of a social group has historically had crucial evolutionary survival value (Gilbert 1989). In more primitive societies, it not only provided protection from physical attack and support in the fulfilment of one's basic needs for food, warmth and shelter but also allowed for the formation of relationships that might ultimately lead to sexual reproduction.

Beck (1984) proposed that while the pre-existing cognitive settings are signalling a threat to one's vital self-interests, the individual is also taking a second snapshot, which is assessing their resources to cope with it. The individual will not experience stress unless he or she decides that resources are inadequate to cope with the threat. This evaluation of coping resources will be influenced by the individual's experience of previous similar situations, beliefs about him/herself and the environment, and assessment of personal or environmental resources. If the risk is appraised as being high in relation to the individual's coping resources, the emergency response is activated. This secondary appraisal plays a central role in the subsequent development of the stress reaction (Lazarus and Folkman 1984; Lazarus and Launier 1978). It is thought that both the primary and secondary appraisals are unconscious, automatic, involuntary and non-reflective processes, which take place at high speed.

Step 3: Activation of cognitive–affective–motivational systems

Once the emergency response has been elicited, normal cognitive information processing is replaced by more primitive information processing, known in psychoanalysis as 'primary process thinking' (Beck et al. 1979). In this primitive thinking mode, the individual makes more rigid, absolute, extreme, crude, simplistic, global, dichotomous, one-sided judgements. These can produce highly idiosyncratic cognitive distortions, which can ultimately become so potent that they totally dominate the individual's feelings and behaviours. Crucial cognitive functions such as objectivity and reality testing are seriously disrupted (Caplan 1981). There is also a tendency to 'frame' others who are

perceived as a threat in terms of a few simple and extreme negative characteristics (polarized thinking). This, together with a greater tendency towards
egocentricity (i.e., others do not come into the equation), can result in
increased interpersonal conflicts, as others around the stressed individual
respond negatively to their 'selfish' and 'hostile' patterns of thinking.

Secondly, behavioural inclinations are activated. These are not actual
behaviours but the precursors to action and are best described as behavioural
motivations. They are the catalysts for resulting schema-congruent emotions
and behaviours. In some situations, an individual may decide that it is in their
interests to suppress a behavioural inclination, for example by resisting the
impulse to hit someone when they are feeling angry. The intensity of a
behavioural inclination is reflected in the degree of physiological arousal that
the individual is experiencing and, if the inclination is not dissipated through
action, the individual will remain aroused. The thematic content of the triggering schema is important in determining the behavioural inclination. For
example, the perception of a situation as dangerous results in the behavioural
inclination to flee and the emotion of anxiety, whereas the perception of a
situation as friendly results in a behavioural inclination to stay and join in
and the emotion of pleasure.

An emotional response occurs in parallel to but independently of the
behavioural inclination. However, both are related to the same underlying
cognitive appraisal of the situation. If the appraisal of the situation is that
the risk is high in relation to one's coping resources, then the physiological
arousal mechanism of the 'fight/flight response' is initiated (described below
in the 'Physiology of Stress' section). If the cognitive appraisal is extreme,
then the behavioural inclination and emotional response are likely to be
equally extreme. The behavioural inclinations to flee, attack or avoid correspond to the emotions of anxiety, anger and depression, and the degree of
arousal experienced is dependent on how threatening the situation is
appraised to be by the individual.

Step 4: The adoption of behavioural strategies

A behavioural strategy is ultimately chosen to deal with the perceived threat.
The strategy adopted is thought to be a result of the interaction between
innate, stereotyped, temperamental factors and learned environmental
factors, such as specific coping strategies learned from parents or other significant care-givers in earlier life (Beck 1972, 1995, 1996; Beck *et al.* 1990;
Gilbert 1989). The main behavioural strategies are the 'fight', 'flight' and
'freeze' responses, which correspond to the emotions of anger, anxiety and
depression. If the cognitive appraisal, behavioural inclination and emotional
responses are extreme, then the behavioural strategy chosen is likely to be
equally extreme. For example, the very angry person may concede to
the behavioural inclination to hit someone, the highly anxious person may

concede to the behavioural inclination to escape from a situation or the very depressed person may concede to the behavioural inclination to stay in bed.

It is thought that the role of emotions with respect to behavioural strategies is to link the affects of pleasure and pain to behavioural outcomes. If the outcome of the behavioural strategy chosen is a positive one and the threat is removed, the individual experiences a positive emotional state of happiness or pleasure. When the behavioural strategy chosen is not successful in reducing the perceived threat, the individual stress reaction continues. These emotional mechanisms serve to reinforce successful behavioural coping strategies directed towards survival and bonding and extinguish unsuccessful ones.

Step 5: The development of stress syndromes

Prolonged exposure to situations or events perceived as threatening to one's vital self-interests and/or survival, without any successful resolution, results in the emergency response becoming chronically activated, leading to the development of stress syndromes. Also, when a schema is activated over a long period of time, the individual continues to select and process stimuli that are congruent with it and this ultimately makes it become more active. Beck (1984) identified three main stress syndromes:

- The hostility syndrome: in this syndrome, individuals are hypersensitive to events that signal restraint, trespass or assault. This behavioural coping style is characterized by the desire to counter-attack and fight the perceived challenges and affronts, and the emotional response consists of feelings ranging from mild irritation to anger and, in the extreme, full-blown rage.
- The fear syndrome: in this syndrome individuals are hypersensitive to events that signal threat or danger. This behavioural coping style is characterized by the desire to flee and escape the perceived dangers and threats and feelings of anxiety and fear.
- The depression syndrome: in this syndrome the negative cognitive triad (Beck 1976) is activated and the individual develops a negative view of self, the world and the future. This behavioural coping style is characterized by the desire to give up and surrender, and negative constructions of events and feelings ranging from mild sadness to depression and, in the extreme, abject despair and the risk of suicide.

THE PHYSIOLOGY OF STRESS

The physiological response to stress has two major components. The first is located centrally in the brain, linking a number of structures in the brain known as the limbic system (Papez 1937). This includes part of the most sophisticated and highly developed area of the brain, the cerebral cortex. The second component extends from the brain through two related branches of the nervous system called the sympathetic and parasympathetic nervous systems, and is called the autonomic nervous system, which extends to most of the important organs of the body.

The limbic system (Figure 1.2) forms a circuit linking a number of higher brain structures. It has been proposed that these structures, particularly the amygdala, form the physiological basis of the fight or flight response to stress (De Moliner and Hunsberger 1962). From the temporal lobe the hippocampus loops over the fornix to the hypothalamus, which is thought to have a major role in the production of an organized emotional response by integrating the fight or flight response with the more considered influences of the cortex, which is the thinking section of the brain. It analyses and interprets incoming information from the sense organs and also plays a part in selecting the response to that information on the basis of its personal significance to the individual based on past experiences and genetic predisposition.

The hypothalamus has two distinct segments, one concerning bodily activation to cope with environmental demands and the other concerned with the reduction of bodily activation to allow for recuperation. Continuous dominance of the arousal segment is associated with chronic anxiety; dominance of the inhibitory segments is associated with depression. These two segments are associated with the two sections of the autonomic nervous system, arousal with the sympathetic section and inhibition with the parasympathetic section. Thus the hypothalamus forms the starting point of the two sections of the

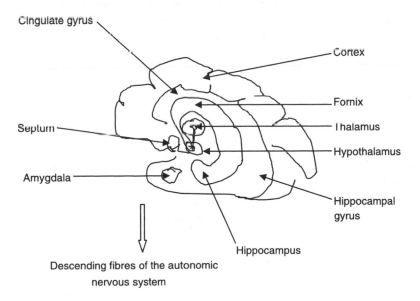

Figure 1.2 The limbic system.

autonomic nervous system. Table 1.1 outlines the main signs associated with the parasympathetic and sympathetic states.

Linked to the hypothalamus by a small stalk and connected to it by both nerves and blood vessels is the pituitary gland, which produces a number of hormones which control the activity of other glands elsewhere in the body, which themselves produce hormones. The most important of these glands are the adrenal glands, which assist the body in coping with strain by producing stress hormones. These stress hormones, in lower concentrations, have a protective effect against invasion and infection in the short term. However, if the stress is prolonged and continuous the body's ability to fight invasion and contain infection is reduced.

Neuro-endocrine systems associated with stress

Two major neuro-endocrine systems have been associated with stress. The first one is associated with acute stressful states such as fear, anger and excitement (Amkraut and Solomon 1975) and is called the sympathetic–adrenal–medullary system (SAM). SAM activation has been associated with action proneness and raised effort and it has also been described as the 'fight or flight system'. It is activated when the organism is challenged in its control of the environment, and is accompanied by the release of catecholamines (epinephrine and norepinephrine) into the bloodstream. Catecholamine output is increased in response to a challenge to perform well (Frankenhaeuser *et al.* 1980; Lundberg and Frankenhaeuser 1980).

The second neuro-endocrine system is the hypothalamic–pituitary–adrenal–cortical (HPAC) system (Asterita 1985; Cannon 1932; Cannon and de la Paz 1911; Frankenhaeuser 1983; Henry and Stephens 1977; Levine and

Table 1.1 Sympathetic and parasympathetic balance

Main signs Parasympathic state	Sympathetic state
Eyes closed	Eyes open
Pupils small	Pupils large
Nasal mucus increased	Nasal mucus decreased
Saliva produced	Dry mouth
Breathing slow	Breathing rapid
Heart rate slow	Heart rate rapid
Heart output decreased	Heart output increased
Surface blood vessels dilated	Surface blood vessels constricted
Skin hairs normal	Skin hairs erect (gooseflesh)
Dry skin	Sweating
Digestion increased	Digestion slowed
Muscles relaxed	Muscles tense
Slow metabolism	Increased metabolism

Ursin 1980; Lundberg and Frankenhaeuser 1980; Selye 1952, 1974; Ursin *et al.* 1978). The HPAC system has been described as the 'conservation – withdrawal system' and is associated with negative feelings of distress (Frankenhaeuser 1983; Lundberg and Frankenhaeuser 1980) and a withdrawal response (Henry and Stephens 1977). Activation of the HPAC system is most commonly associated with chronic stress and is thought to occur when threats are appraised as being overwhelming and the individual is appraised as not coping. It is also accompanied by depression (Gibbons 1964; Gitlin and Gerner 1986; Henry and Stephens 1977). HPAC activation results in the release of adrenocorticotrophic hormone (ACTH) and corticosteroids (cortisol in humans). Under conditions of successful coping the HPAC system is suppressed (Levine *et al.* 1979).

The development of chronic stress syndromes

Glass (1977) proposed that with brief exposure to uncontrollable stress, an acute state of hyper-responsiveness is activated. This relates to the behavioural inclinations of fight or flight, increased physiological arousal associated with the SAM system described above and the emotional responses of anger or anxiety. However, when a stress reaction continues without successful resolution for a long period of time, it is proposed that the individual moves into a chronic state of hypo-responsiveness. This relates to the behavioural inclination to freeze, decreased physiological arousal associated with the HPAC system described above and the emotional responses of hopelessness and depression. This two-stage model of the stress reaction is supported by the neurological, physiological and neuro-endocrine evidence presented above and also fits with Selye's staged conceptualization of stress (Selye 1946, 1974, 1975, 1976).

O'Leary (1990) and Henry and Stephens (1977) provided further physiological evidence to support a two-stage model of the stress reaction. O'Leary (1990) found that acute emotional states activate the SAM system and are associated with raised levels of anxiety and physiological arousal. However, Henry and Stephens (1977) found that when stressors are appraised as being uncontrollable or overwhelming, SAM activity stops and the HPAC system, which is associated with clinical depression, is activated (Gibbons 1964; Gitlin and Gerner 1986). The findings of the author that short-term acute stress is associated with anxiety, whereas chronic stress is associated with depression and emotional exhaustion, also provide support for the proposed two-stage model (Bamber 1996).

CONCLUSIONS

The financial cost of occupational stress to the nation and to employers is enormous. It has been identified as a particular problem among health workers. There is an increasing realization that it makes sense to tackle occupational stress, not just on humanitarian grounds but also on economic grounds. A review of the literature on stress reveals a growing consensus that it is a cognitively mediated interaction between the individual and the environment. A cognitively mediated model of stress has been presented in this chapter, which explains the cognitive, emotional, motivational and behavioural links between an environmental trigger and the development of stress syndromes. An overview of the literature on the physiology of stress is also provided and provides support for a two-stage model of the development of acute and chronic stress syndromes.

When reading this chapter, it would be tempting to conclude that all stress is bad for us. This is not always the case, however. Stress is a normal, natural and unavoidable part of everyday life and at moderate, optimal levels, has positive effects on motivation and the performance of tasks (for example taking an exam or a driving test). Such threats temporarily disrupt the body's equilibrium but, once the threat has passed, 'homeostasis' returns (Cannon 1929, 1935). However, prolonged exposure to unmitigated sources of stress can ultimately have harmful consequences. Given that occupational stress is potentially one of the most protracted and chronic of stressors, it is clear that this problem needs to be given priority not just on humanitarian and economic grounds but also on physical and mental health grounds.

Chapter 2

A cognitive behavioural model of occupational stress

Martin Bamber

INTRODUCTION

There are numerous models of occupational stress in the literature (e.g. Caplan 1975; Cooper 1986; Cooper and Marshall 1976; Fletcher 1988; Karasek 1979; Karasek and Theorell 1990; Ostell 1996a; Payne 1979; Warr 1987). In common with the conceptualization of stress discussed in Chapter 1, there is growing support in the literature for a 'transactional' model of occupational stress (e.g. Caplan *et al.* 1975; Fletcher 1988; Ostell 1996a; Rabin *et al.* 1999). The transactional approach proposes that most situations are not in themselves intrinsically stressful but that people distress themselves via the way in which they perceive and react to situations. This model fits well with the cognitively mediated model of stress outlined in Chapter 1, in that it emphasizes the central mediating role played by cognitive processes and behavioural coping strategies in the development of occupational stress. This is not to imply that the work environment is never to blame, or that the individual is always responsible for their own stress. Clearly there is an interaction between the individual and the work environment.

Before elaborating on a cognitive behavioural model of occupational stress, it would be helpful at this point to overview the literature on both the personal (individual) and environmental factors (in the workplace) which are believed to contribute to the development of occupational stress.

PERSONAL FACTORS

Genetic factors

It is acknowledged that, genetically, some individuals are physically stronger and intellectually more able to meet the demands which a job makes upon them (Payne 1988). It has been reported that there are sex differences in the way males and females cope with stress (Maslach and Jackson 1984). However, it is of course debatable whether this sex difference should be considered a genetic factor or a learned predisposition. Individual differences in temperament are also thought to play a part and the role of temperament is discussed in more detail in Chapter 12. For example, some individuals are by nature more timid, introverted and shy, and less sensation-seeking than others, and this may manifest itself in different ways of coping with stressful situations, such as in less assertive and more avoidant behaviours.

Acquired/learned factors

It has been suggested in the literature that age and experience are variables influencing the level of stress experienced. For example, Maslach and Jackson (1984) suggested that younger individuals are more vulnerable to stress than older individuals. Seligman (1975) argued that an individual who has more experience is less likely to suffer from stress due to 'mastery of the past' which can inoculate one against stress. Also, as already discussed in the previous chapter, the beliefs, attitudes and behavioural coping strategies that an individual learns through their early developmental life experiences can affect the way in which they perceive and react to the pressures of work. These beliefs and behaviours may be learned through the culture, goals and expectations shared by the whole population, or a sub-section of the population such as a particular social class (Machlowitz 1980). Alternatively, they may be unhealthy core schemata and maladaptive coping styles learned as a result of adverse early life experiences. Other acquired characteristics, which may influence how the individual copes with the work situation, include level of educational attainment, knowledge and skills to do the job.

Personality factors

Numerous studies have looked at the influence of personality dispositions on the level of stress experienced. For example, 'non-hardy' individuals (Kobasa 1979), those with an 'external locus of control' (Rotter 1966), those who are 'trait' anxious' (Speilberger 1972; Speilberger et al. 1988) and 'type A' personalities (Friedman and Rosenman 1974) are all more prone to stress than their hardy, internal locus of control, state anxious and type B counterparts. There is also some evidence that personality factors may affect disease through causal physiological mechanisms. For example, type A personalities show greater physiological reactivity to stressful conditions than type B personalities and are consequently at greater risk of heart disease (Barefoot et al. 1983; Dembroski et al. 1978, 1979; Hecker et al. 1988; Herd 1978; Matthews and Haynes 1986; Shekelle et al. 1983) and other diseases such as peptic ulcers, allergies and respiratory infections (Wrzesniewski et al. 1987).

ENVIRONMENTAL FACTORS

Factors in the work environment itself

Several taxonomies of stressors in the work environment can be found (e.g. Cooper and Marshall 1976; Cox 1978; Cox et al. 2000; Fletcher 1988, 1991; Warr 1987) and considerable consensus and overlap in the work stressors identified can be found. Factors such as financial remuneration, poor physical work environment, outdated technology, high workload, excessive responsibility, low social position, lack of autonomy and control, variety in job, external job demands/goals, role conflict and ambiguity, lack of support and poor career prospects have all been identified as sources of stress in the work environment (Fletcher 1988; Warr 1987).

A useful taxonomy was described by Cox et al. (2000), who identified two groups of stressful work characteristics which relate to the 'content' and 'context' of work. With respect to the content of work, Cox et al. recognized the need for a safe, supportive, comfortable, ergonomically sound work environment in which to work and the requirement for the resources and equipment to do the job effectively. The job design needs to accommodate the social and welfare needs of employees, giving them sufficient rest breaks in the shift, sociable working hours and conditions, a variety of tasks and a manageable volume of work conducted at a comfortable pace. The content of the work is considered to be an important factor in determining the level of occupational stress experienced.

With respect to the context of work, Cox et al. (2000) recognized that individuals need to have a clear understanding of the goals, norms and ideology of the organization and clarity regarding their own role and responsibilities within it. They require security of employment, fair financial remuneration, a clearly identified management structure and lines of accountability within it, clear channels of communication and regular feedback about their performance within the organization, career and promotion prospects and the appropriate training to do the job. The employee also needs to feel that they have some discretion and control over their job content, that they are part of the decision-making process and that they can influence decisions made within the organization.

Working in an organizational environment which lacks any of the content and context requirements described by Cox et al. (2000) can result in occupational stress. In health care work there is an inherent problem: many aspects of the content of the work, through their very nature, are stressful. For example, confronting human misery and suffering on a daily basis, dealing with the aftermath of accidents, death and dying, breaking bad news, supporting the relatives and families of those who are ill or dying, working with challenging behaviours such as suicide attempts, hostility, violence and aggression, and sometimes having to work with the darker side of human nature are all part and parcel of health care work.

Interpersonal causes

Occupational stress is reported to be higher in the caring professions due to the intense interpersonal nature of the work (Rees and Cooper 1992; Rodgers 1998) and, contrary to popular opinion, health workers are not always treated with the dignity and respect that one might expect from the patients that they are trying to help. Health care workers frequently have to work with challenging behaviours from difficult patients and their relatives. One study reported that 27% of health care staff surveyed had experienced violence or aggression at work in the previous year. The sources of this violence were in 80% of cases patients, and in 11% of cases carers of patients and visitors to the workplace (Bootham Park Hospital 2002). However, it is not only patients or their relatives who cause such problems. A number of recent surveys have revealed that bullying and harassment of health workers by their own colleagues is rife (Amicus 2004; Bootham Park Hospital 2002; Hoel *et al.* 2001).

Unfortunately, health care organizations have their fair share of psychologically immature and personality disordered individuals, who can wreak havoc on an organization. The problem can be magnified if such individuals are in positions of authority, since it is estimated that as much as 90% of a manager's time is spent in interpersonal contact (Stewart 1967). Divisive and disruptive behaviours such as showing favouritism, forming cliques, showing prejudice, unwarranted criticism, pulling rank, taking advantage of power, ignoring others, not allowing others to take the lead, withholding information, promoting those who are least likely to threaten a manager, refusal to negotiate, imposing decisions without discussion, criticizing subordinates publicly, the extensive use of put-downs, personal and unprovoked attacks and blaming and patronizing others are just some examples of interpersonal behaviours which cause considerable distress for employees (Edelmann 1993). Again, this is made worse if there is a power imbalance between the perpetrator and the victim (Adams 1992).

Working in health care requires the use of highly developed interpersonal skills. These include leadership and assertiveness skills, and the skills to make complex social judgements, attribute motives, make predictions about behaviours, handle angry confrontations, listen actively, break bad news, offer help and interview are essential for working in health care settings and are particularly important when working with difficult employees or patients (Edelmann 1993; Fontana 1994; Lowman 1997). A lack of the required level of social competence for dealing with the interpersonal demands of working in health care settings is thus a major source of stress, both for those who lack it and for those who are on the receiving end of socially unskilled interactions.

The home–work interface

Behaviour at work does not take place in a vacuum. It is influenced by extrinsic factors and this is known as the home–work interface (Fletcher 1991; Fontana 1997). A good marriage and social support from friends, families and relatives can act as a buffer against stress at work (Cobb 1976; Cohen and Wills 1985; House 1981). Dual careers can put considerable strain on a marriage. For example, males are expected to move readily for job transfers and promotion if they want to progress in their careers and it is traditionally expected that their family and spouse follows them. Dual careers make this more complex (Cooper 1986). Associated with dual careers is the fact that when the female's occupational prestige or income equals or exceeds that of their male spouse, this can lead to marital tensions. Sekaran (1986) suggests that women in such positions commonly try not to be 'too successful' and may even reject promotions in order to prevent such conflicts from arising. Also, despite the increase in women going out to work, responsibility for maintaining the household and child care still falls mainly on women (Ross *et al.* 1983).

A COGNITIVE BEHAVIOURAL MODEL OF OCCUPATIONAL STRESS

The model presented in Figure 2.1 translates the cognitive model of stress outlined in Chapter 1 into the work setting. It proposes that each individual employee brings with them a unique set of personal attributes and needs, temperament, beliefs and assumptions (cognitive schemata), behavioural coping strategies, physical constitution, energy level, intelligence, knowledge, skills and training to the job. In turn, the job has built in to its content and context characteristics which place demands on the employee. The model proposes that if the individual's personal attributes are sufficient to meet the demands of the job and the work environment also meets that individual's needs, the individual experiences job satisfaction, coping, positive mental health and low stress levels. However, if the individual does not have the required personal attributes or coping resources to meet the demands of the job, or the job does not meet the needs of the individual, occupational stress is likely to be experienced. The saying 'One man's meat is another man's poison' summarizes the model well, since two employees doing exactly the same job can, according to the model, appraise and experience the job in very different ways.

As a result of having very different personal characteristics, abilities, needs and coping strategies, one employee may appraise the job as being stressful but another employee may appraise it as being challenging and satisfying. So, where there is a good match between the person and their work environment

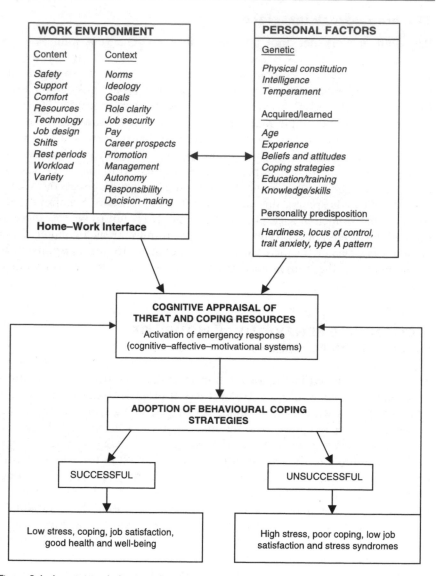

Figure 2.1 A cognitive behavioural model of occupational stress.

(i.e. a good person–environment fit), occupational stress is low, but where there is a poor match between the person and their work environment (i.e. a poor person–environment fit), occupational stress is high (Edwards and Van Harrison 1993; Furnham 1997; Furnham and Schaeffer 1984). Thus, the experience of occupational stress may reflect the characteristics of the person, the job or both (Keita and Jones 1990; Levi 1990; Lowman 1997).

THE CONSEQUENCES OF OCCUPATIONAL STRESS

The physical, psychological, behavioural and social consequences of mild to moderate levels of occupational stress are well reported (Appelberg 1996; Barling *et al.* 1993; Cooper *et al.* 1996; Earnshaw and Davidson 1994; Health and Safety Executive 1995a; Hoel *et al.* 2001; Murphy and Cooper 2000; Quick *et al.* 1992; Smith 2000; Warshaw and Messite 1996; Zaleznick *et al.* 1977) and these are briefly summarized here:

- Physical: the individual may experience somatic symptoms such as muscular pains, tremors, palpitations, diarrhoea, sweating, respiratory distress, dizziness, headaches, backache, poor sleep, loss of libido, increased heart rate, raised blood pressure, dry mouth and throat and indigestion.
- Psychological: the individual may experience feelings of unhappiness, worrying more than usual, increased irritability, and reduced job satisfaction, motivation and commitment to the organization.
- Behavioural: indicators include increased smoking, increased alcohol consumption, less attention paid to eating a healthy diet and increased use of tranquillisers.
- Social: indicators include withdrawal, strain on relationships and increased marital and family conflicts.

With more chronic (severe and prolonged) levels of occupational stress, the literature suggests that more serious physical and mental health problems can occur. Clinical levels of emotional distress such as anxiety (Beck and Emery 1985), depression (Beck *et al.* 1979; Firth-Cozens 1987; Krantz 1985) and burnout (Maslach and Jackson 1984) are some of the emotional reactions to stress. These stress syndromes can make the individual more susceptible to physical health problems. Some of the harmful physical consequences of prolonged exposure to high levels of stress are discussed below.

Fisher (1986) identified two groups of physical illnesses, which can be readily explained by the two-stage model of acute and chronic stress syndromes described in Chapter 1. The first group are related to the acute stage of the stress reaction. They are somatic illnesses caused by the struggle to gain control over stressors in the acute stage. The consequent strain placed on the physiological systems of the body can cause structural damage via somatization, for example raised blood pressure, damage to coronary arteries, gastric complaints, ulcers, muscular aches and pains, headaches and coronary heart disease (Connelly 1976; Rahe and Paasikivi 1971; Theorell and Rahe 1971, 1972). Fisher terms this 'effort distress' and links it with the sympathetic–adrenal–medullary (SAM) system.

The second group of illnesses, which are related to the chronic stage of the stress reaction, occur when the individual repeatedly fails to gain control over stressors and eventually gives up the struggle to do so. This chronic stress reaction is termed by Fisher 'distress without effort'. It is associated with activation of the hypothalamic–pituitary–adrenocortical (HPAC) system and raised cortisol levels. Raised cortisol levels in turn increase the individual's susceptibility to a whole range of immuno-incompetence-type illnesses such as colds, infections, viruses, skin complaints and allergies. Thus, it can be seen that the duration of exposure to a stressor which is perceived to be uncontrollable, or is objectively uncontrollable, plays a critical role in determining the nature of stress-induced physical health problems (Palmblad *et al.* 1975).

Fisher's two-stage model is supported by findings from the psychoneuroimmunology (PNI) literature (Ader 1981, 1987; Locke and Colligan 1986; Pelletier and Herzing 1988), which are highly suggestive of a significant association between stress and the immune response. For example, Kiecolt-Glaser *et al.* (1987) examined the effects on immunity of the chronic stress associated with caring for relatives afflicted with Alzheimer's disease. Compared to control subjects, the care-givers had higher antibody titres to Epstein Barr virus, reflecting impaired cellular immuno-competence. Other chronic stressors such as marital disharmony (Kiecolt-Glaser and Fisher 1987), separation or divorce (Kiecolt-Glaser and Fisher 1987; Kitson and Raschke 1981; Somers 1979), bereavement (Clegg 1988; Irwin *et al.* 1987; Schleifer *et al.* 1983) and loneliness (Glaser *et al.* 1985; Kiecolt-Glaser *et al.* 1984a, 1984b) have all been shown to influence immune functioning in a negative way.

Some aspects of work have been studied in more detail, such as the effects of shift work. Nakano *et al.* (1982), for example, demonstrated that T cell function is significantly more depressed in permanent night shift workers than those on permanent day shift or those who rotate over three shifts.

There is a considerable body of evidence indicating that chronic stress syndromes cause physical health problems via disabling the immune system, making the individual less able to resist opportunistic infections (Goodkin 1988; Solomon *et al.* 1987; Temoshok *et al.* 1987; Totman *et al.* 1980). Lowered lymphocyte and phagocyte responsiveness has been found in depressed individuals (Albrecht *et al.* 1985; Irwin *et al.* 1990; Kronfol and House 1989; Kronfol *et al.* 1986; Schleifer *et al.* 1985). There is also some evidence that depression increases susceptibility to diseases such as cancer (Bieliauskas and Garron 1982; Schekelle *et al.* 1981), herpes simplex virus (Glaser *et al.* 1985, 1987; Kemeny *et al.* 1989), ulcerative gingivitis (Solomon 1990) and upper respiratory tract infections (Graham *et al.* 1986; Meyer and Haggerty 1962). Many of the neurobiological processes associated with stress and depression have also been observed in anxiety and are known to influence the immune system (Locke *et al.* 1984; Stein *et al.* 1988).

CONCLUSIONS

In conclusion, there is a growing consensus that the experience of occupational stress is strongly influenced by the individual employee's perceptions of their environment. This is not to imply that working environments are always reasonable, since frequently this is not the case. It is an interaction between individual and environmental factors. This chapter has provided an overview of these factors in the causation of stress and translated the cognitively mediated model of stress outlined in Chapter 1 into the work setting. The centrality of dysfunctional cognitive mediating processes and maladaptive behavioural coping strategies in the development of occupational stress syndromes is highlighted in the cognitive behavioural model of occupational stress presented. These dysfunctional beliefs and maladaptive behavioural coping styles form the basis for the cognitive behavioural treatment interventions described later in this book.

The stress syndromes described in the model have their correlates in the diagnostic classifications found in the *Diagnostic and Statistical Treatment Manual* (DSM-IV) of the American Psychiatric Association (APA 2000). The two most common DSM-IV mental health problems seen in NHS occupational health services are anxiety and depression (Bamber 1995; McPherson 2004). Bamber estimated that anxiety in its various forms made up 25% and depression 23% of the total referrals (Bamber 1995). McPherson put the figure even higher, with anxiety at 52% and depression at 24% of the total referrals (McPherson 2004). Other less commonly referred problems included 'burnout' (15%), post-traumatic stress reactions to work-related traumas (8%) and anger management problems (5%). The majority of the remaining referrals (20%) were for interpersonal relationship difficulties experienced in the work context (Bamber 1995). McPherson's study also reported that in 21% of the total referrals, the cause appeared to be wholly related to work, with 6.5% of the total being due to post-traumatic effects of assault or accident at work. These data are consistent with the occupational stress literature, which identifies the five most common occupational stress syndromes to be anxiety in its various forms, depression, anger, post-traumatic stress and burnout. These five categories of stress syndromes form the basis for the cognitive and behavioural (CBT) treatment interventions for occupational stress syndromes proposed in Chapters 6–8 of this book.

The literature on the detrimental mental and physical health consequences of chronic stress was also reviewed in this chapter. Reading this literature on the consequences of occupational stress, one might be led to conclude that all work is bad for one's health. However, it is important to recognize that this is not always the case and there are indeed a number of positives about work, which are often overlooked. It not only provides us with the means to meet our basic physical needs (for example for food, shelter and warmth) but also our higher level needs for self-actualization, power and status (Maslow 1954).

Freud (1930, 1961) gave the work role high priority, and described a healthy personality as being one which is able to love and work productively. Conversely, unemployment is associated with a higher risk of mental and physical health problems (Arnetz *et al.* 1987; Fryer and Payne 1986; Iverson *et al.* 1987; Jackson and Warr 1987; Kessler *et al.* 1987; Moser *et al.* 1987; Warr 1987; Westin *et al.* 1988).

Part II

Standard interventions for occupational stress

Chapter 3

Assessment and treatment strategies for occupational stress

Martin Bamber

INTRODUCTION

Interventions for occupational stress can be divided up into three types, known as primary, secondary and tertiary level interventions (Cox and Cox 1993). At the primary level, the aim is to identify and reduce or eliminate the causes of stress in the working environment. However, sometimes the work environment cannot be changed since aspects of it are inherently stressful, as is often the case in health care work. The focus of secondary level interventions is thus to teach the employee coping strategies to help buffer them against an inherently stressful environment and to help them to develop the confidence to look after themselves more effectively in situations that would in actual fact be stressful for anyone. Secondary interventions include pro-actively imparting mental and physical health promotion strategies, education and the enhancement of coping skills aimed at the prevention or management of normative (sub-clinical) levels of stress in individual employees or occupational groups within the organization.

The tertiary level of intervention focuses on providing psychological therapy for those employees who are already experiencing stress syndromes which are impacting on their capacity to be productive in the work setting, or even to remain at work. In order to determine which level of intervention is most appropriate to tackle a work-related problem, a detailed assessment of the problem must first be undertaken. Unfortunately there is not at the present time any comprehensive taxonomy for occupational stress syndromes or work-related dysfunctions to assist us in this process (Lowman 1997). However, the following steps are helpful in carrying out an assessment of occupational stress and deciding upon the most appropriate level of intervention to adopt:

1 Gather information. Information can be gathered from a range of sources, including managerial and supervisor reports, work records, sickness absence statistics, disciplinary records, medical case notes and a face-to-face interview with the employee to establish the nature of the

current work-related problems and the degree to which work perform-ance is being affected. Information about the individual's personal life and background, mental and physical health history and current non-work stressors may also be of relevance in getting a detailed formulation of the employee's presenting problem and as such should form part of the interview. It may also be appropriate on occasions, as part of the assessment (with the employee's permission), to seek the views and opinions of work colleagues, peers, friends and relatives on specific matters.

2   Assess the severity of the work-related distress and disability. There is a wide range of formal psychometric tests available to assist in this process. Indeed, a whole industry has developed around the production of occu-pational and clinical assessment measures. It is recommended that self-report measures are used to measure stress, since the individual's appraisal of their situation is of primary importance in the stress reac-tion. Some of the most frequently used measures of distress include measures of anxiety such as the Beck Anxiety Inventory (Beck *et al.* 1988), measures of depression such as the Beck Depression Inventory (Beck and Steer 1987), measures of depression and anxiety such as the Hospital Anxiety and Depression Scale (Zigmond and Snaith 1983) and more general measures of mental-ill health such as the Crown–Crisp Inventory (Crown and Crisp 1979) and the General Health Questionnaire (Goldberg and Williams 1988).

Measures of coping can also be helpful in assessing occupational stress. Common measures of coping include the Ways of Coping Check-list (Folkman and Lazarus 1988), the Hassles and Uplifts Scale (Lazarus and Folkman 1989), the Multi-dimensional Coping Inventory (Endler and Parker 1990), the Moos Coping Responses Inventory (Moos 1990), the COPE scale (Carver *et al.* 1989), the Maslach Burnout Inventory (Maslach and Jackson 1986; Pines and Aronson 1981) and the Staff Burnout Scales (Jones 1980a, 1980b, 1981). There are also some com-monly used measures of personal vulnerability/resistance factors associ-ated with coping, including the Hardiness Scale (Kobasa *et al.* 1982), the Sense of Coherence Scale (Antonovsky 1979), the Locus of Control Scale (Rotter 1966; Steptoe 1983), 'Type A' behaviour scales such as the Jenkins Activity Survey (Jenkins *et al.* 1979) and measures of self esteem such as the Culture Free Self Esteem Inventory (Battle 1980).

Also commonly used are measures of work performance (Broadbent *et al.* 1982; Houston and Allt 1997; Spurgeon and Harrington 1989), job satisfaction (Brook *et al.* 1988; James and James 1989; Loher *et al.* 1985; Warr *et al.* 1979) and the Occupational Stress Indicator (Cooper *et al.* 1988).

3   Decide if the psychopathology present is a cause or a consequence of the work-related problem. This will determine the subsequent interventions

to be adopted. If the assessment identifies that the psychopathology present is a consequence of the work environment, then the focus should be on primary level interventions, aimed at reducing or eliminating stressors in the workplace. In order to make such changes the employee's manager, occupational health and/or human resources may need to become involved. This level of intervention may in itself be sufficient to alleviate the psychopathology. Primary level (organizational) interventions are described in Chapter 4 of this book.

4   Where the assessment identifies the job itself as a cause of the pathology but the options for changing the job or the working environment are limited, secondary level interventions aimed at enhancing the individual's coping skills repertoire to help buffer them against and to cope more effectively with the stressors present will be required. However, where the source of pathology is the job itself and secondary interventions are found to be ineffective in reducing or eliminating the pathology, then redeployment or a change of job may be required. In more extreme cases, complete career re-assessment and change of career may be necessary to alleviate the psychopathology. Secondary level interventions for normative levels of stress are described in Chapter 5 of this book.

5   Where psychopathology is present and the assessment identifies that it is the cause of the work-related problems, the appropriate stress-related syndrome should be treated using tertiary level psychological treatment interventions aimed at reducing or eliminating the symptoms associated with particular stress syndromes. Tertiary level treatment interventions are described in Chapters 6–8 of this book.

6   Where the work-related problems are attributable to aspects of the employee's character or personality, it is the traditional wisdom that there is little that can be done to alleviate the distress for either the individual or those with whom they are in conflict. However, exciting new developments in cognitive therapy have led to an innovative form of therapy called schema therapy, which specifically focuses on bringing about charactereological change. As far as the author is aware, this particular type of intervention is new to the field of occupational stress and has not previously been applied to occupational stress-related problems. The schema-focused approach is described in Part 3 of this book (Chapters 12–14).

The decision tree shown in Figure 3.1 summarizes the steps in the decision-making process described above and can be used to assist the therapist in deciding which intervention is most appropriate for the presenting problem.

Chapters 6–8 discuss the assessment, formulation and treatment of stress syndromes. The standard cognitive behavioural approach to therapy (CBT) is adopted, since the evidence base for the effectiveness of CBT in treating stress syndromes is strong. It is cited as the treatment of choice for a wide range of

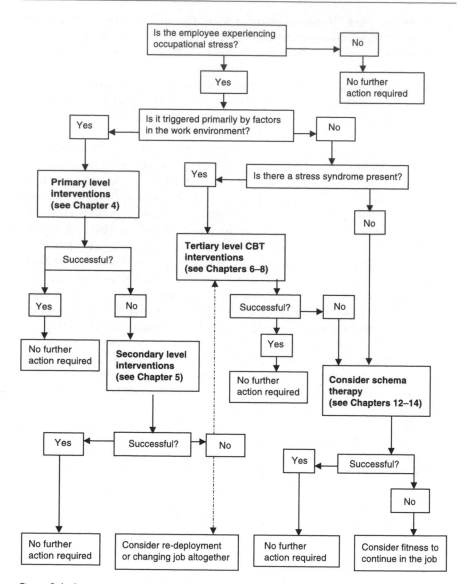

Figure 3.1 An assessment decision-making tree (derived from Lowman 1997).

disorders including depression, generalized anxiety disorder, phobias and panic disorder (see recent reviews by Department of Health 2001; National Institute for Clinical Excellence 2004b; Roth and Fonagy 1996). In order to prepare the reader for Chapters 6–8, the rest of this chapter is dedicated to describing the protocol used to deliver a course of standard CBT. In particular, it focuses on providing an overview of the parameters of CBT and how to assess, formulate and structure a course of standard CBT.

STRUCTURING A COURSE OF CBT

CBT is an active, directive, time-limited, structured approach based upon an underlying theoretical rationale that an individual's affect and behaviour are largely determined by the way in which s/he structures the world (Beck *et al.* 1979: 3). Therapy typically takes 15–20 sessions over a period of three to four months (Fennell and Teasdale 1987). Each session lasts one hour and is structured by the use of an agenda to optimize the use of time. It is problem oriented in that the therapist and patient focus on defining and solving presenting problems. The immediate target is symptom relief. Standard CBT typically deals with the here and now, without recourse to the distant past history of the patient. Rather than using psychodynamic hypothetical constructs to explain the patient's behaviour, it argues that dysfunctional behaviour is attributed to maladaptive learning, and relearning more functional behaviour is the goal of therapy. An experimental 'scientific' method is adopted and therapy involves collecting data (problems, thoughts, attitudes), formulating hypotheses, setting up experiments and evaluating results. Each clinical case is thus given the status of a single case study research design.

Homework is a core element of the CBT approach. The patient is given assignments for data collecting, verification of hypotheses and practice of cognitive skills. It is collaborative in that the patient and therapist work together to solve problems. The therapist adopts an active and directive role throughout treatment. He can be didactic sometimes but his main role is to facilitate the definition and resolution of problems. The principal therapeutic method is 'Socratic questioning', which involves asking a series of questions aimed at bringing the patient to identify underlying thoughts, perceive alternative solutions or modify opinions. The therapeutic process is not clouded in mystique. Rather it is explicit and open, with the therapist and patient sharing a common understanding of what is going on in therapy (Beck *et al.* 1979; Blackburn and Davidson 1990; Fennell 2000).

THE EIGHT STAGES OF A COURSE OF CBT

Stage 1: Assessment

There are a number of different modes of information gathering available during the assessment stage, which include the face-to-face interview, therapist- and patient-completed psychometric assessment and screening measures, direct observation by the therapist, self-monitoring by the patient and making use of written material such as the referral letter, medical records and other reports which may be made available to the therapist. A good general coverage of CBT assessment can be found in Hawton *et al.* (2000); for more specific problem types see Blackburn and Davidson (1990) and Blackburn and Twaddle (1996).

The assessment interview should elicit a brief description of the severity, frequency and duration of the presenting problems, the development of those problems and what precipitated them, and determine when they began, their time course, how long they have been going on and whether there were any previous episodes. It is also useful to identify which specific situations, people or events trigger or exacerbate the presenting problem and how it affects the patient behaviourally, emotionally, cognitively and physically. It is important to explore all of these systems in some depth, since it can be useful in measuring change later on in treatment, especially if there is a lack of 'synchrony', for example where a patient reports no change emotionally but displays clear behavioural changes (Rachman and Hodgson 1974). The symptoms reported in the interview, together with those identified by more formal psychometric assessment measures, can then be matched to the criteria outlined in diagnostic manuals such as the *DSM-IV* (American Psychiatric Association [APA] 2000) or the *ICD* (World Health Organization 1992) to define the presenting problem.

The assessment interview should also attempt to identify any factors which maintain the problem, the coping strategies used by the patient, any history of mental health problems, previous treatments, current medication and current mental state, with particular focus on assessing risk of possible harm to self or others. The assessment should aim to establish how the patient's presenting problems are affecting him/her psychosocially in the various spheres of life, including occupation, relationships, social and leisure activities, family relationships, financial situation, home situation and living conditions. Therapists tend to differ with respect to the importance that they attach to exploring the patient's personal background and history, depending on the extent to which they intend to work on the 'here and now' principle of the traditional CBT approach.

In CBT it is important to look for evidence of specific examples of faulty thinking as early as possible in the assessment process, which can be used later on in the assessment to illustrate the cognitive model. A number of techniques can be used by both the therapist and patient to explore and elicit unhelpful cognitions and behaviours (Blackburn and Davidson 1990; Kirk 2000). Blackburn and Davidson (1990) describe a number of techniques commonly used. The first one involves self-monitoring of thoughts and behaviours by the patient as part of a homework exercise. A diary can be used to establish the baseline of specific unhelpful thoughts, feelings and behaviours and the frequency, intensity, severity and duration of these.

Examples of these can then be discussed in later therapy sessions. Observation of the patient by the therapist within a session may also reveal any particularly relevant behaviours, mood shifts or the expression of strong emotions and distress, which can be explored, and the 'hot cognitions' being triggered at that moment in time can be identified.

Another useful technique commonly used is known as the 'five component model' (Greenberger and Padesky 1995). This technique involves taking a specific example from the patient's own recent experience and analysing it in terms of its components. If the patient has difficulty in identifying recent examples, then he/she can be asked to imagine situations, either real ones that have happened in the past or hypothetical ones. The use of a flip chart or white board and pen can be very helpful in conducting this exercise. This model can be used to tease out and demonstrate the links between specific thoughts, feelings, physical reactions and behaviours, and also to demonstrate the importance of situations and events in the environment which trigger these responses.

Not every patient is suitable for CBT, and it is important to establish in the assessment stage whether the patient is suitable. Some of the main criteria which make a patient suitable include 'psychologically mindedness', the ability to establish an equal, collaborative relationship, willingness to be an active participant in the therapy, 'learned resourcefulness', willingness to do homework assignments set, ability to take some responsibility in therapy and demonstrating a reasonable level of motivation. Patients with a good repertoire of cognitive and behavioural coping skills respond better to CBT than those without (Simons et al. 1985).

Other factors which need to be taken into account in assessing the patient's suitability are the length and severity of the present episode of ill health, response to previous treatment, number of previous episodes of the problem and co-existing DSM Axis II (APA 2000) problems. More severe and enduring mental health problems respond less well to a course of CBT. For example, patients with a severe depression (score on the Beck Depression Inventory of greater than 30) tend not to respond so well and if the duration of the current episode is greater than six months, their response to treatment has been found to be not so good. Also, if the patient has shown an inadequate response to previous treatment, it has been found that they are less likely to respond well to a subsequent treatment. Patients who have had more than two previous episodes of depression tend not to respond so well to treatment (Blackburn and Davidson 1990; Hawton et al. 2000).

A significant proportion of patients presenting with a DSM-IV Axis I problem have also been found to have personality disorders (Axis II problems). Such patients do not respond well to standard CBT. The Suitability for Short-term Cognitive Therapy Questionnaire (Safran and Segal 1990) is useful in helping the therapist decide whether the patient is suitable for standard CBT.

Socializing the patient to the model

There are two main tasks involved in socializing a patient to the CBT model. The first is to explain the characteristics of cognitive therapy, which are outlined earlier in this chapter. The second main task is to get the patient to begin to understand what the cognitive model is about. One specific technique, which has been extensively utilized, is known as the 'vignette' technique. These are essentially little stories which highlight the importance of cognitive interpretations. One well-known example of a vignette used by Beck (1967; 1976) is the 'cat vignette': 'It is the middle of the night and you are fast asleep. Suddenly you are woken up and startled by a loud noise downstairs. You look at your clock and it is 2 am. What thoughts are going through your head? How does it make you feel? What do actually do? Suddenly you remember that you forgot to put the cat out. You usually put the cat out because it has a tendency to climb up on furniture and knock things off. What are your thoughts? What are your feelings? What do you do?' The basic point here is that thoughts are not reality but interpretations which colour our feelings and alter our behaviours.

Stage 2: Formulation

Case formulation aims to provide a model to guide therapy and to promote understanding of the development and maintenance of the patient's problems. It is presented in terms of predisposing (developmental) factors and precipitating (triggering) factors, which are sometimes called critical incidents and maintaining factors in the 'here and now'. The model most commonly used in standard CBT is Beck's developmental cognitive model (Beck 1967, 1976), which is illustrated in Figure 3.2. It proposes that, as a result of adverse earlier life experiences, people develop dysfunctional beliefs and assumptions about themselves, others and the world around them. These beliefs and assumptions are triggered by critical incidents that are thematically similar to the early adverse experiences and, once activated, produce an upsurge of negative automatic thinking. A range of other emotional, behavioural, motivational and physical symptoms are manifested, in the way described in Chapter 1. Some examples of standard CBT formulations for specific problems can be found in Chapters 6–8 and also in the case studies illustrated by Mark Latham and Paul Blenkiron in Chapters 9–11.

Stage 3: Developing a problem list

Once the assessment and formulation has been completed it is useful to draw up a list of the problems identified by the patient. This is especially helpful when a patient has complex and multiple problems. It is also useful in summarizing the patient's problems and for the therapist to check that he/she has

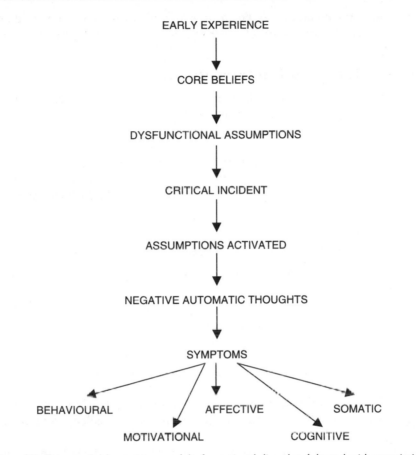

Figure 3.2 The standard cognitive model of emotional disorder. Adapted with permission from Melanie Fennell (Fennell 2000).

correctly understood and recorded the patient's problems. Where multiple and complex problems exist, it is useful to get the patient to indicate which particular problem has priority at that point in time. Obviously it is not possible to fight the battle on all fronts, and so some element of selection is necessary.

Stage 4: Treatment planning

The next step is for the therapist and patient to agree what the goals of therapy should be in relation to the problems identified on the problem list; they should also agree on the criteria of success. The goals of therapy and criteria of success should be observable, measurable, realistic and achievable ones, against which the individual's progress can be monitored. Once these have been agreed between the therapist and patient, the relevant cognitive and behavioural interventions can begin. It is helpful at this stage to write down the treatment plan on a sheet of paper and give a copy to the patient.

Stage 5: Therapeutic interventions

The format of a typical CBT therapy session is structured by an agenda. It begins with a general enquiry about the well-being of the patient and then leads on to a review of the homework set, addressing the patient's issues, the therapist's tasks for the session, setting the next homework assignment and arranging the next appointment. While this may seem obvious, it is in fact very easy to go off at a tangent in a therapy session if the agenda has not been agreed in advance, or the patient is not very focused on the problem for which they are attending.

Cognitive techniques commonly used

Beck's model (1967, 1976) identifies cognitive dysfunction at three levels, namely at the level of thought content (automatic thoughts), at the intermediate level of thought processing (systematic errors, dysfunctional assumptions) and thirdly at the deepest level, the structure of thought (schemata). Standard CBT focuses mainly on altering negative automatic thoughts and dysfunctional assumptions and to a much lesser extent on schemata (cognitive structures). It uses the variety of techniques described earlier in this chapter to elicit the raw data required for the process of restructuring cognitions. Once the patient has learned to identify and label their own negative patterns of thinking, they are taught techniques to challenge and modify them systematically.

Some of the most common cognitive distortions are outlined in the section on positive thinking in Chapter 5. A number of well-established techniques are used to challenge negative automatic thoughts. These include examining the evidence. The patient is encouraged to ask: 'What is the evidence for and against the negative thought?' 'Do the facts of the situation back up what I think, or do they contradict it?' To some extent, in this example the therapist and the patient are becoming their own lawyers and cross-examining themselves.

Another technique is to ask if there are any alternative ways of looking at the situation which are more positive. There are usually many different alternative ways to look at any experience. The therapist helps the patient brainstorm as many alternatives as they can and review the evidence for and against each, then they try to decide objectively which alternative is most likely to be correct. There are techniques which can help the patient come up with alternatives. One such technique is called the 'friend technique'. The patient is asked to consider how their best friend would react in this situation and what advice their best friend might give them if they were here now.

Alternatively, the therapist asks the patient to consider how they might advise someone else to react in this situation. Role-plays, where therapist and patient swap roles, can be an extremely useful way of exploring alternatives.

Another cognitive technique used is to look at the advantages and dis-advantages of thinking in such a negative way. The therapist and patient explore how negative thinking influences the way the individual feels and the way they behave, establishing the pros and cons of thinking in this way. They attempt to find alternative ways of thinking which reduce distress and are more helpful to the patient.

Encouraging the patient to 'check it out' can be a useful way of gathering data which disconfirm negative beliefs. This can be done by the patient asking people around them what they are thinking rather than simply 'jumping to conclusions' or 'mind reading'.

Establishing the realistic probability of each interpretation is another powerful technique for challenging negative thinking, as it does not reject the original negative interpretation, unlikely as it might be, but contrasts it with more likely interpretations. This approach trains the patient to consider thoughts as interpretations of reality rather than reality itself.

If the patient is blaming him/herself for a particular outcome, they can be taught to use the 're-attribution' technique. The re-attribution technique encourages the patient to look to external factors as causes of negative out-comes rather than internal factors or self-blame. Also, even if the individual was responsible to some extent, they need to ask: 'Are the consequences of this really as bad as they seem?' 'How might I feel about these events in one day, one week, one month or six months' time?'

Other cognitive techniques such as distraction, positive self-talk and imagery can be helpful in challenging negative thinking. Distraction tech-niques work by focusing our limited attention span on something other than the negative thoughts, such as focusing on an object in great detail, or the environment as a whole using all one's sensory modalities. Indeed any absorb-ing mental activity could be used, such as a jigsaw puzzle, a crossword, a puzzle book or other mental exercise. Thoughts can be in the form of images as well as words and the use of imagery can be a powerful intervention. These images can be of real past events such as a particularly memorable happy time, a holiday or other pleasant memory. Alternatively, the imagery can be of pleasant fantasies such as winning the lottery.

Behavioural techniques commonly used

Challenging cognitive distortions need not only take place at a cognitive level. The process can be greatly enhanced by the use of some more empirical behavioural strategies, such as conducting behavioural experiments. This involves the setting up of 'mini experiments', whereby the patient's original negative thoughts and the new alternative positive ones are treated as two possible alternative hypotheses predicting an outcome. The patient is then encouraged to test these out in a real life situation and to establish which of the two alternatives is more accurately predictive of the outcome. Similarly, experiments can be used to test out the consequences of disobeying the patient's personal rules (dysfunctional assumptions). The three other most common behavioural techniques, used particularly in the early stages of therapy, are activity scheduling, mastery and pleasure ratings and graded task assignments.

When inactivity is identified as a problem, activity scheduling is used to get the patient to be more active. The task of activity scheduling is carried out in a number of steps. The therapist begins by introducing the concept that inactivity can actually make mood worse. Very often the patient readily agrees with this, since they can identify with it in their own experience. The concepts of mastery with and without pleasure are then introduced. The patient is encouraged to rate on a 0 to 5 scale (where 0 is no mastery or pleasure and 5 is maximum mastery and/or pleasure) all the tasks they carry out as part of their daily routine. The activities that are pleasurable, as well as those which a person is good at, are thus identified. For example, the patient may be a master at ironing but find no pleasure in it at all.

The therapist then establishes what the patient is actually doing in terms of activity. This can be set as a homework task, first to ensure that the patient cannot fail at the task and second to establish the baseline level of activity upon which to build.

The starting point is usually the weekly activity schedule. If a noticeable pattern is emerging, for example if inactivity appears to be happening particularly at weekends, then the activity schedule needs to focus particularly on these high-risk times.

New activities are introduced with the aim of maximizing mastery and pleasure. Examples of this could be hobbies or other interests which the patient may have neglected. Absorbing activities which occupy mind and body, such as sports, can be particularly helpful. Those which do not require much thought can be made more absorbing and enjoyable by combining them with others, for example listening to the radio while doing housework. The patient is encouraged to rate these activities for mastery and pleasure for homework and activities can be planned a week in advance. If new pleasurable activities are introduced all in one go or too quickly, the patient may find them overwhelming. For example, a patient who used to enjoy embroidery for a hobby may feel that they do not have the concentration to be able to take it up again and do what they used to do. Thus it is important to 'grade' the task by breaking it down into smaller stages, set at a level which the patient believes to be achievable. This may be something as simple as spending five minutes doing some embroidery. Once the patient has developed more confidence, they can progress to the next stage.

Another common behavioural technique uses the 'graded exposure' hierarchy. This is used particularly where the patient is attempting to confront situations that they have previously been avoiding through fear. Together with the therapist the patient identifies and makes a comprehensive list of all the situations that are causing distress. Each situation on the list is rated on a scale from 0 to 10 (where 0 is no anxiety and 10 is maximum anxiety). Once they have all been rated, they are placed in a hierarchy, with the most difficult situations scoring highest on distress (10) at the top, then those with scores of 9, and so on right down to the lowest scores of 1 and 0 (the easiest to confront). The patient then confronts the situation lowest in the hierarchy and only moves on to confront the next situation in the hierarchy when they feel confident that they have overcome the previous one.

Sometimes an individual may be already confronting their feared situation, in which case a graded exposure hierarchy is not necessary. However, in order to help them cope with it, they may be making use of 'safety behaviours'. Safety behaviours associated with anxiety, for example, may include not drawing attention to oneself, keeping quiet in meetings, sitting near an exit or escape route or avoiding eye contact. Although the individual may feel that these safety behaviours are helping them cope, in fact they act to maintain the problem. Thus, the aim of therapy is to drop these unhelpful behaviours systematically. Again the therapist and the patient can work together to identify the safety behaviours and rate them according to how difficult the patient perceives it would be to drop them (10 is most difficult and 0 is least difficult). These are then ranked in a similar way to the graded exposure hierarchy and the patient starts by dropping the safety behaviour lowest in the hierarchy. They only move up to the next step in the hierarchy when they have successfully overcome the previous one.

Stage 6: Review and relapse prevention

The progress of therapy is reviewed at regular points throughout therapy and this may be assisted by repeated use of questionnaires, such as repeated measures on the Beck anxiety and depression scales. The patient may be encouraged to look back to old diary sheets and homework exercises to establish the degree of change that has taken place. Together, the therapist and patient can establish which goals of therapy have been achieved and the criteria of success that have been reached. The outstanding goals and criteria can then be clarified. The therapist can also check the patient's understanding, knowledge and use of the range of tools and techniques used, and the extent to which they are ready to become their own therapist can be established. Towards the end of therapy a relapse prevention exercise is introduced. This aims to ensure that the gains made in therapy are consolidated. The patient is asked to consider what gains they feel they have made in therapy, what has changed as a result of therapy, what they have learned in therapy, how they can continue to practise this in their everyday life, what their plan for self-help will be, how they might deal with set-backs, what the likely high-risk situations for relapse might be and what contingency plans they have in place to deal with such a lapse. At the final therapy session the 'pre' and 'post' measures can be compared to identify the success of the interventions employed.

Stage 7: Developing a self-help programme

This is a structured plan devised and agreed by the patient and therapist relating to what the patient will do once discharged to ensure that they continue to make progress. This may involve making sure that time is allocated on a regular basis to review progress made and set new targets. It may also include continued self-monitoring by the patient, or the continued use of all the handouts provided during the course of therapy or the use of other self-help reading materials or references given by the therapist. It could also include implementing some of the relapse prevention strategies discussed at the end of therapy.

Stage 8: Follow-up

In CBT it is desirable and is seen as part of good practice to offer follow-up sessions to the patient. This usually occurs at three months and six months after discharge. The aim is to ensure that the gains made in therapy have been maintained. If the patient has not been able to implement the self-help plan as well as anticipated, then they may require one or two 'booster' sessions, or to remain on the therapist's case load for a few months as a 'safety net'. One of the positive things about CBT is that once the skills have been learned, the patient can continue to practise them and make progress long after therapy has finished.

Chapter 4

Organizational strategies for managing stress at work

Alistair Ostell

INTRODUCTION

The focus of this chapter is upon the initiatives organizations take to manage better the damaging effects of stress in the workplace. We will first examine a model of the stress process and the implications of employee stress for employers. Some of the main changes that have occurred in the workplace that have been linked with poor health in the past few decades will be reviewed before examining the strategies and tactics organizations have adopted to develop more healthy work environments. Finally, the value of such strategies will be assessed.

THE NATURE OF 'STRESS'

Although defined variously there is a broad consensus that psychological stress is best conceptualized in *transactional* terms capturing the ways in which a person deals with the circumstances of life. A basic premise of this view is that most situations or events are not intrinsically stressful; rather, people distress themselves by the ways in which they perceive and react to situations (see Chapter 1; Cox 1978; Lazarus 1976; Ostell 1991). A transactional model of stress or health (adapted from Ostell 1996a) is presented in Figure 4.1.

The model uses three overlapping ovals to depict the transactional view. The largest oval represents a person, the central point of reference in this model. Situations to which the person has to react are portrayed by the oval on the left. They can arise from external circumstances (e.g. work, social or domestic origin) or from within the person (e.g. an individual's state of mind or health), hence the overlap of these circles. Of particular relevance for understanding occupational stress is the fact that the personal, domestic, social and work domains differ in two important respects. First, certain events and circumstances are specific to particular domains (e.g. childbearing and rearing occur primarily within the home, initially, and occupational

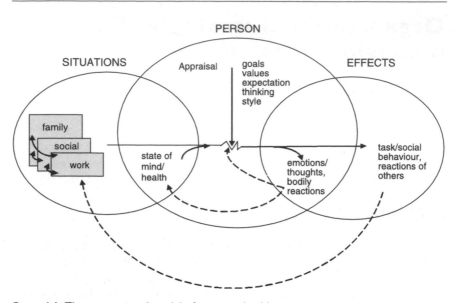

Figure 4.1 The transactional model of stress or health.

tasks are performed by most people within a work environment); second, certain values and practices tend to be specific to a particular domain so that clashes can exist between these domains (e.g. conflict between personal goals and the requirement to contribute in an appropriate way both at home and work).

Situations are not taken at face value but are appraised in terms of their significance for a person, and in terms of how to respond to them. Events or circumstances appraised as consistent with a person's values and goals, which meet expectations and offer valued opportunities, are viewed favourably, leading to positive emotions, thoughts and reactions. Conversely, situations that are appraised unfavourably tend to produce negative reactions – psychological distress (Lazarus 1976). These emotions, thoughts and bodily reactions constitute some of the effects (right oval), internal to the person, which follow from the appraisal processes. Changes also occur in the person's overt behaviour (e.g. task performance, social interaction). The broken lines indicate that these changes feed back, affecting the person's reactions and the situation to which the person is responding, thus modifying the person–situation relationship. It is because of this mutual influence and exchange between the person and situations that models of stress processes are described as transactional models.

IMPLICATIONS OF STRESS IN THE WORKPLACE FOR EMPLOYERS

The transactional perspective on stress provides an accurate and powerful understanding of the processes involved when people become distressed. Paradoxically, one consequence of this view is that when individuals become psychologically distressed at work it is easy to see them simply as causing their own distress and therefore requires them to handle their work circumstances differently, without giving thought to changing these circumstances. This is a seriously naïve view (Handy 1988) as it implicitly assumes the circumstances a person faces at work are reasonable, when this is not always true (e.g. a disaster such as a major fire or explosion; bullying behaviour or racial and sexual discrimination; unhygienic or unsafe working conditions, the inappropriate assignment of work activities/responsibilities). It is important for organizations to be able to demonstrate that their requirements of individual employees are reasonable.

The term 'reasonable' is not a matter of personal judgement with respect to stress issues but a defined legal requirement of the United Kingdom and the European Union. It is not possible to explore these issues in depth here, but it is important to appreciate several key points. Employers have a 'duty of care' to their staff, as stipulated in the Health and Safety at Work Act 1974 (Health and Safety Executive [HSE] 1995b). Failure to comply with these regulations can result in litigation against an employer. One of the first such cases in the UK, Johnstone v Bloomsbury Health Area Authority (Industrial Relations Law Reports 1991), resulted in a senior house officer receiving compensation after he crashed his car, an accident which he attributed to working excessively long hours.

The Management of Health and Safety at Work Regulations 1999 also require all employers to undertake risk assessments with respect to health and safety at work (HSE 2001). During 2004 the West Dorset Hospitals NHS Trust received an HSE 'enforcement notice' for failing to have a work-related stress policy or a risk assessment of work-related stressors.

Employees do not consistently win litigation against employers, as negligence must be proven (Income Data Services 2002: 704). Nevertheless, litigation can be very damaging for an employer in several ways. The financial costs of fighting a case, whether winning or losing, can be high and if an employer loses a case, its insurance premiums will increase. The reputation of an employer can also be tarnished through well-publicized legal cases, which is likely to make the organization less attractive to potential job applicants. Further, the impact upon existing employees can be highly disruptive, and damage employee–management relations and possibly work performance and productivity.

THE CHANGING NATURE OF WORK
AND THE WORKPLACE

The organizational context

During the 1960s and 1970s, the social and industrial climate of Britain was disturbed by worsening industrial relations and the poor productivity of British industry. This contributed to reduced competitiveness, compared with countries such as Japan and Taiwan, and the need for British companies to become more competitive, or not survive. Two strategies were adopted, one focusing essentially upon removing inefficiencies, the other on redesigning the organization, although the strategies could overlap.

Removing inefficiencies

This strategy embraced a number of diverse tactics. At the simplest level it cut costs through reducing numbers of employees by enlarging jobs (e.g. multi-tasking and multi-skilling), changing employment contracts (e.g. adopting annualized hours rather than the usual working week or shift pattern) and setting challenging performance-related-pay contracts (Ostell 1996a). These tactics introduced greater flexibility into the workforce and into patterns of employment. Another tactic was to achieve economies of scale through acquisitions and mergers (Cartwright and Cooper 1996). Once again significant numbers of employees were made redundant as functions duplicated across organizations were rationalized.

While such changes served to make some organizations more competitive, employees generally had more demanding roles, many were aggrieved by changes in their 'psychological contract' of employment (Rousseau 1995) and many experienced 'cultural confusion' in merged organizations (Cartwright and Cooper 1996), job insecurity and a sense of being 'change weary' as further changes were made if the initial ones were not successful (Worrall and Cooper 1997).

Redesigning the organization

A more radical, forward-looking approach to improving competitiveness was to redesign organizations so that they were fit to meet current and future challenges. One radical approach was to place primary emphasis upon the key processes of the organization associated with manufacturing a product or delivering a service, instead of upon its traditional, functional structure (Hammer and Champy 1993; Mintzberg and van der Heyden 1999). Support functions such as finance and human resources management were sometimes outsourced. Team working became an important feature of many of these organizations and 'high-performance work systems' and 'autonomous teams' were seen as delivering higher quality and more innovative performance than traditional approaches (Buchanan and Huczynski 2004). The more organic nature of redesigned organizations made them more interesting places to work than traditional bureaucracies and team working offered certain advantages such as mutual support when performance requirements were high.

Information technology

Developments in information technology have transformed modern organizations and the way people work. On the one hand, the availability of powerful computers now presents some workers, such as air traffic controllers, with more demanding roles in the processing of information (Hockey 2002). On the other hand, the need to have an office and desk has been replaced by people who, treating their laptop as their office, can communicate with colleagues around the globe via the internet, while moving from place to place. For such people the 'working week' has become the 'waking week' (Parker *et al.* 2001) and those working irregular hours, or moving regularly through different time zones, are prone to suffer poor health through the constant disruptions to their circadian rhythms (Folkard and Hill 2002).

Service organizations and the public sector

During the past two decades there has been a progressive reduction in the size of the British manufacturing industry, with many redundancies and the progressive development of service industries in the private sector. Front-line service roles, involving direct contact with the customer, have grown in traditional sectors such as hospitality and tourism, and more recently through the now ubiquitous call-centres. A characteristic of these jobs is the requirement for 'emotional labour', that is, the management of employees' feelings and behaviour so that they display to customers a positive and helpful approach, even though they might not be well treated in return (Hochschild 1983). Thus, these jobs are often emotionally exhausting for employees, particularly when they work long hours and deal with demanding customers. Similar problems are experienced in the public sector, particularly in education and the health, police and prison services where direct contact with pupils, patients, the public and inmates can not only be tiring but also associated with verbal abuse and even physical assault (Dickson *et al.* 1994).

Successive governments over the past 20 years have introduced into the public sector practices adopted by the private sector. Government has also imposed, top down, all kinds of performance measures upon public sector organizations, which have created greater bureaucracy, rigidity and considerable frustration for staff.

The social context

The composition and aspirations of the workforce have changed greatly in recent times. Key trends include increased numbers of women and dual-career couples, greater ethnic diversity, more educated employees and an ageing workforce (Howard 1995). Ideas about careers have also been revised with fewer employees working in a single profession or work area throughout their career. Such changes have fostered other problems. Instead of women and members of ethnic minorities being welcomed as means of enriching a workforce, they have often experienced discrimination instead (Newell 2002). Dual-career families can face difficult choices if one partner has to relocate to maintain his or her job. People also frequently have to relocate over considerable distances and across countries when finding new jobs, which often causes disruption to families and social relations (Lawler and Finegold 2000).

In summary, this far from complete review of developments in work and the workplace has attempted to outline briefly a number of the key changes that have occurred, and their implications for and in some cases their actual impact upon employee health. They provide a context for understanding the kinds of problems employers face when attempting to manage employee stress and the strategies adopted to deal with this problem.

PRIMARY INTERVENTIONS – MANAGEMENT BY DESIGN

Organizational strategies for managing occupational stress have developed in scope and effectiveness as new problems have emerged. The basic approach draws upon the tri-partite model used in preventive medicine (primary, secondary and tertiary interventions). The essential aim of primary interventions is to manage, reduce or eliminate conditions and demands that promote stress in people at work (i.e. stressor-directed); secondary interventions focus upon moderating individuals' stress reactions (i.e. response-directed) by helping individuals recognize their response to and symptoms of stress and to develop adaptive coping strategies through education and training. Tertiary interventions are symptom-directed, designed to assist in the cure and rehabilitation of stressed employees (Sutherland and Cooper 2000).

The author argues that the focus of primary interventions should not simply be stressor-directed but aim to create a 'healthy organization' – a process of management by design. This entails shaping the context, structure, policies, practices and work processes of an organization so that stressors are managed, reduced or eliminated wherever possible; conditions which are conducive to effective work performance, job satisfaction and health are created; and people who are an appropriate 'fit' to the organization are also recruited.

Primary organizational interventions can be grouped under three headings:

the macro-environment (organization-wide variables affecting the majority of employees; the micro-environment (variables with a more localized effect upon groups of employees); and recruiting people who 'fit' the job and organization. The divide between macro- and micro-environmental strategies is partly artificial as aspects of recruitment, work load and design can be organization-wide or more local in their impact. It is only possible to deal here with strategies and tactics involving the most important variables affecting employee health.

Identifying the need for primary interventions

Decisions about whether and how to modify aspects of an organization should not be taken without a firm, evidential basis for doing so, especially when an organization might be recommended to commit significant expenditure to implementing particular initiatives to manage stress.

Many companies routinely use some form of staff survey to identify employee views of and satisfaction with different aspects of the organization, including its culture, work practices, management style, reward systems and so on. While the results of such surveys can be illuminating, indicating, for example, which features of an organization are associated with low(er) job satisfaction, it is inappropriate to assume automatically that employees are also psychologically stressed. The relationship (statistical correlation) between life satisfaction and overall job satisfaction is modest, at about 0.35 (Tait et al. 1989), and a longitudinal investigation into these variables indicated that the influence of life satisfaction on job satisfaction was greater than the reverse effect (Judge and Watanabe 1993).

Evidence of low job satisfaction in staff should not be ignored. However, it is important to use properly constructed, standardized psychological tests to establish whether the psychological health of staff is affected adversely at work (cf. Bowling 1997). Diagnostic instruments, which incorporate such tests and carefully constructed measures of the characteristics of an organization (see above), are variously called stress or health audits or psychological risk assessments. These instruments should identify: whether and where 'stress problems' exist; features of the organization with which they are associated; those staff who are affected; the impact upon performance measures such as productivity and absenteeism; and how these problems can be addressed effectively for employees (Cox et al. 2000; Ostell 1996a).

Macro-environmental strategies

Organizational architecture

Critical elements in the architecture of organizations are goals, strategy, structure and culture. These are configured in particular ways in different kinds of organizations (Mintzberg 1979) so that they are internally consistent. For example, a company which aims to be pre-eminent at innovative design will adopt a more organic, adhocratic structure (in Mintzberg's terms) with a culture emphasizing flexibility, mutual working and risk taking, rather than being hierarchically organized, rule bound, driven from the top and conservative with respect to risk, characteristics of machine bureaucracies (Mintzberg 1979).

Organizations cannot be fixed entities; they have to change through time to meet the challenges of the external world. Nevertheless, as organizations change they often need to develop a new, internally consistent architecture, including a culture that promotes high levels of performance and staff commitment (Payne 2002). Culture is a complex phenomenon focused primarily around values, whereas climate refers to the psychological environment – a person's experience of those values 'in action'.

Organizational culture/climate and job future

Evidence from employee perceptions of their organization indicates that cultures associated with health are characterized by: organizational support in the form of actions taken to encourage or assist employees with their tasks and responsibilities; co-worker support (constructive, informal relations among peers); meaningful participation of employees; effective communication and information exchange; and a climate that promotes the health and safety of staff (Wilson *et al.* 2004). More importantly, the variable found to be most strongly associated with health was job future, a composite variable assessing job security, equity within the organization, the availability of learning opportunities for staff and flexible work arrangements.

It is perhaps not surprising that research into the 'Best Companies to Work For', reported in *The Sunday Times* newspaper (2004), indicates that employees rate the top companies highly on criteria such as 'well-being', 'my team', 'fair deal' and 'personal growth'.

Tactics addressing problems of culture/climate

There is not a single particular culture that is health promoting and can be adopted by all organizations, as culture will vary with the strategy and structure of an organization. However, the evidence reviewed above suggests that particular elements of cultures seem to be critical in promoting job satisfaction and health and are also associated with better work performance. Therefore efforts should focus upon incorporating these elements into an existing culture. If such elements do not 'fit' this suggests that more radical change is necessary.

Culture/climate change, focusing upon developing the above practices and behaviours, is normally addressed through formal change programmes

(Dawson 1994; Kotter 1996). Ideally, such programmes need to be initiated by top management and begin with the articulation of a mission and/or values statement, from which the nature of the desired culture can be understood. Employees typically attend workshops whose members are either drawn from across the organization or are departmentally based. These workshops explore the rationale for change, the desired culture, obstacles to change, the means of change and so on. Participants often work on specific problems regarding culture change in their organization/department using tools such as 'force-field analysis' (Robbins 1998) and identify specific mechanisms that will help inculcate culture change into the behaviour patterns of staff (e.g. establishing staff–management committees regarding new working practices). Unless the proposed changes are reinforced regularly by the behaviour of people at all levels of the organization, and forms of sanction introduced for practising contrary behaviours (e.g. bullying), long-standing change is unlikely to occur and be maintained. In the American idiom people have to 'walk the walk not just talk the talk'.

Tactics addressing problems of workload

The restructuring of organizations has frequently resulted in staff with increased workloads and unsociable work hours rather than the reverse, and in countries with de-regulated labour markets (e.g. New Zealand, United Kingdom, United States of America) work hours have been rising (Bosch 1999). To meet the demands of business many organizations have adopted compressed working weeks (e.g. 36–48 hours over three or four days) and in the mining, shipping and oil-drilling industries long work periods followed by long rest periods are employed where frequent staff change-overs would be impractical because of difficulties with travelling to remote sites (Sparkes et al. 2001). In the public service sector, research into the prolonged duty hours of trainee doctors has demonstrated that such schedules affect psychological health adversely, as well as ability to carry out simple tasks of alertness and concentration (Leonard et al. 1998; Scott 1992).

Results regarding the impact of specific strategies to minimize the effects of workload on well-being are mixed. Some people favour an extended shift because it provides longer periods at home to recuperate with family and friends, while other people are less positive. However, contemporary evidence indicates that working long hours for prolonged periods is associated with poorer health, raised sickness and absenteeism rates and lower productivity (Economic and Social Research Council 1998; Sparkes et al. 1997) and should be avoided. The costs associated with absenteeism, lower productivity and possible legal suits are likely to be more expensive for employers than the costs of reducing working hours and adopting employee-friendly schedules.

Tactics addressing learning opportunities and career development

The constant change that characterizes modern organizations means many employees lack job security and clarity about how they might develop their careers. Internal competition between employees can heighten these feelings, resulting in disenchanted and stressed employees with little commitment to an organization. Research also indicates job features lose their motivational value for employees over time so that job satisfaction decreases (Katz, 1978).

To address these issues many organizations invest heavily to provide learning opportunities and career development advice and opportunities, often through internal web sites, literature and formal advisors (*The Sunday Times* 2004). Learning opportunities include such events as training courses, secondments and sabbaticals. Mentoring, the process whereby an older more experienced employee supports/guides/counsels a younger one in better managing work life, is increasingly common (Clutterbuck 2001). Mentors are often chosen by the protégé and drawn from another department or line function. Their advisory role tends to cover two broad areas: career functions and psychosocial functions (Kram 1985).

Tactics addressing problems of equity

Adams (1965) drew attention to the significance of equity in the processes of social exchange. In organizational and social life equity is very much a matter of individual perception and determined according to the individual's goals, beliefs, values and experiences. Hence the frequently heard utterance 'It's not fair' when one person is promoted, receives a pay rise or is offered a development opportunity. Equity is not an objective state, except in relation to a particular situation when specified rules are applied, such as the fastest sprinter winning a gold medal. Nevertheless, because of the damaging effects of perceived inequity upon individual psychological health and social relations, considerable efforts have been directed toward avoiding this situation in many organizations (*The Sunday Times* 2004).

Policies designed to pre-empt inequity regarding job opportunities, promotion and pay include anti-discrimination employment policies relating to gender, ethnicity and religion. These policies have been driven largely by legislation (Willey 2003), but also by an appreciation of the negative effects upon individuals and groups of perceived inequity. A particularly pertinent issue of equity concerns harassment and bullying at work. These behaviours tend to demean the victim and are aggressive, overbearing, unnecessarily critical and intimidatory. Bullying is distinguished from harassment as it is seen to be driven by interpersonal factors, while harassment focuses upon people in particular social groups (e.g. gender, race, nationality, religion, politics); otherwise the behaviours can be very similar (Willey 2003).

Equitable behaviours of the kinds discussed clearly must become integral to an organization's values and day-to-day practices not only for legal reasons but to retain the commitment of staff.

Micro-environmental strategies

These strategies effectively 'drill down' into specific features of the work environment addressing issues of work design, flexible work arrangements and managerial style.

Work design

Recent research into work design has focused primarily upon its redesign to overcome the boring, dissatisfying and potentially damaging effects to health of job simplification, and to take account of developments in the nature of the workplace (Parker *et al.* 2001). Stimulated by the ideas of Herzberg *et al.* (1959) about work motivation, Paul and Robertson (1970) proposed the idea of job enrichment as the process of building into people's jobs greater scope for personal achievement and recognition, more challenging and responsible work, and more opportunity for advancement and personal growth.

Hackman and Oldham (1976) advanced the job characteristics model (JCM) as a way of translating ideas about job enrichment into practice. It entailed incorporating core characteristics into jobs (skill variety, task identity, task significance, autonomy and feedback), which were seen as determinants of three critical psychological states: 'experienced meaningfulness of work', 'experienced responsibility' and 'knowledge of results'. These three states were believed to promote job satisfaction, intrinsic job motivation, high performance and reduced absence and job turnover. The authors also posited that enriching jobs tended to promote improved performance more strongly in people with a desire for challenge and growth (called 'growth need strength') than in those who lacked these goals.

Parker *et al.* (2001) recently elaborated a more complex model, incorporating antecedent conditions (factors influencing the choice of work design – e.g. labour market, technology) and additional work characteristics (e.g. cognitive and emotional demands), mediating mechanisms (e.g. learning and development), outcomes (e.g. safe working, creativity) and moderating variables (e.g. tolerance for ambiguity). The model and findings relating to it are too complex to review here but indicate that a simple prescriptive model, such as JCM, while relevant, is also inadequate.

Findings indicate that the effects of job enrichment are consistently stronger for well-being, job satisfaction and motivation than for behavioural outcomes such as work performance, absence and turnover (Kelly 1992; Parker and Wall 1998).

Psychological empowerment and employee control

Other theorists take a more psychological approach to job enrichment and focus on the sense of psychological empowerment arising from job enrichment practices (Spreitzer 1995). Although there are considerable parallels with the JCM model a key difference is the emphasis upon creating motivational states that constitute psychological empowerment, rather than upon changing objective work conditions (Parker, 1998). Feelings of self-efficacy are believed to be important for health as they are associated with less compromise to the immune system during stress (Sieber *et al.* 1992). Karasek's (1979) demand–control–support model of the work environment also emphasizes employee 'control' in handling the demands of a job: high control is associated with better health even when demands are high.

The involvement of employees in finding solutions to work problems can also increase a sense of control and competence. Murphy and Hurrell (1987) describe the development of a worker–management 'stress reduction committee' as a first step in a stress management intervention. Jackson (1983) evaluated an intervention designed to reduce role ambiguity and conflict among staff in 25 outpatient clinics in hospitals in the UK through increased participation in decision-making, and demonstrated the hypothesized effects six months later.

Socio-technical systems and autonomous work groups

Many products or services can be provided only through the co-ordinated efforts of groups of people. Trist and Bamforth (1951) proposed the socio-technical systems (STS) approach to work, arguing that attention should be paid equally to the social and technical systems when designing group work. Cherns (1976) extended this approach, proposing that work systems should be minimally specified so groups could decide their own methods of working and of dealing with work variances at source in what are called autonomous work groups (AWG), or self-managed teams. The benefits arising from STS and AWG parallel those for individual work design: motivational and well-being effects are largely supported although the impact upon performance is mixed (Parker and Wall 1998).

Flexible work arrangements

As the demands of the workplace and the numbers of dual-earner and single parent families have increased, the need to find flexible work arrangements (FWA) to permit employees to juggle home and work responsibilities effectively, particularly when the care of dependents is involved, has grown. The number and diversity of FWAs is high, including job sharing, part-time working, leave of absence, flexibility regarding time and place of work, operating-from-home arrangements and compressed weeks/fortnights (Chartered Institute of Personnel and Development 2002; Department of Trade and Industry 2003).

There is not sufficient, systematic research into FWAs to be clear about their individual effectiveness, although case studies suggest the different options can work well for those who choose them (Chartered Institute of Personnel and Development 2002; Department of Trade and Industry 2003). Choice could be the critical factor as, this enables an individual to match personal circumstances with a suitable FWA. However, providing choice is not necessarily a straightforward matter. First, many small organizations might not be able to afford to support a wide range of FWAs. Second, when employees work in teams co-ordinating the choices of different individuals could be difficult. The teams might have to agree upon one option, which will mean it could be more-or-less suitable for different team members. Third, the organizational culture/climate needs actively to support these kinds of initiatives so that those who benefit are not viewed as receiving 'special treatment' compared with others.

Managerial style

Managerial style is linked with culture, as the latter often defines, implicitly or explicitly, acceptable behaviour for a person with these responsibilities. A distinction commonly made is between managers whose primary responsibilities are operational and those who have more strategic and visionary responsibilities. Kotter (1990) describes these as managerial and leadership roles, respectively, while Bass and Avolio (1990) refer to transactional and transformational leadership. In reality most managers and leaders perform both roles but to differing degrees.

From the author's perspective the significance of management/leadership with respect to issues of stress at work is that of style – the 'how', not just the 'what'. Managers must obviously perform their responsibilities competently, in a way that suits them, but they also need to both model and encourage in staff healthy ways of working and relating to others. Research into the 'Best Companies to Work For' indicates how strongly and positively managers can influence the behaviour and attitudes of staff through their managerial style (*The Sunday Times* 2004).

Recruiting employees who 'fit' the job and the organization

Traditionally, discussion of recruitment focuses upon whether a person 'fits' a job (Ostell 1996b) – that is, whether a person possesses, or has the potential to acquire, the necessary knowledge, skills and abilities to perform proficiently the activities that constitute a particular job (i.e. task performance). Borman and Motowidlo (1993) have proposed that contextual performance is also an important criterion for assessing employee behaviour. It refers to behaviour that promotes the welfare of individuals or groups (cf. 'organizational citizenship'). Thus the 'fit' of a potential employee includes both the job and the organization itself, requiring a more diverse range of criteria to be used in the selection process. Contextual performance is concerned with pro-social behaviour in organizations. A more narrowly drawn view of 'organizational fit' could relate simply to the existing culture (e.g. innovation, competitiveness and success).

There is a considerable body of research indicating that individual differences, particularly in cognitive abilities, mediate work performance, although research has demonstrated that broad measures of personality, such as 'conscientiousness', also predict job performance (Robertson and Smith 2001). It is arguable, however, that personality characteristics are more likely than cognitive ones to moderate the impact of organizational variables upon health. For example, head teachers high on absolutist thinking were more stressed by work than non-absolutist heads (Ostell and Oakland 1999); call centre customer service representatives high on conscientiousness were more emotionally exhausted when call volume was high than those low on conscientiousness (Witt *et al.* 2003). On a more positive note Kobasa (1979) demonstrated how 'hardiness' or 'resilience' (Rush *et al.* 1995) insures people against the potentially damaging effects of jobs.

The dimension of extraversion–introversion (Eysenck and Eysenck 1985) predicts whether individuals will be drawn to highly sociable environments that value self-expression, spontaneity and risk-taking (extroverts) rather than environments scoring lower on sociability and self-expression, where caution and reflectiveness are valued. Individuals will not necessarily be stressed in environments with which they do not 'fit', but if they do not feel comfortable they are less likely to feel job satisfaction, which could affect job performance adversely and lead eventually to stress.

Such findings indicate the importance of ensuring that individuals recruited to organizations possess the required cognitive abilities and personality characteristics so that they 'fit' the job and organizational culture/climate. Occupational psychologists have expended considerable effort identifying relevant personal characteristics and developing suitable assessment devices (e.g. personality inventories, interviews, work samples, assessment centres) for these purposes (Cook 1998; Robertson and Smith 2001), yet there is still considerable reliance upon just one or two assessment tools such as the application form and interview (Robertson and Makin 1986). Recent research indicates that the use of sophisticated recruitment and selection systems, utilizing a variety of assessment devices, is associated with the appropriate matching of people and jobs and high work performance (Huselid 1995).

Although advertisements and person specifications for everyday jobs often include phrases such as 'can cope with stress' and 'resilient under pressure', there are virtually no systematic evaluation data regarding whether recruits to such jobs demonstrate these qualities, nor is the topic addressed in many texts on recruitment or stress at work (Cook 1998; Cooper and Robertson 1995; Jex 1998). There is plenty of anecdotal evidence, however, regarding the value of resilience in managing organizational life (*Harvard Business Review* 2003). Given the potentially damaging consequences to an organization of recruiting an employee who is not equipped to cope with the demands of a job and suffers as a result, it is important for organizations to take this issue seriously and develop selection systems that can identify those who are likely to be at risk if appointed to potentially stressful jobs.

THE VALUE OF PRIMARY INTERVENTION STRATEGIES AND TACTICS FOR MANAGING STRESS IN ORGANIZATIONS

Primary intervention strategies and tactics can focus upon modifying or even replacing fundamental elements of organizations (individuals, groups, departments, worksites) and the ways in which they are assembled and co-ordinated (processes and procedures) and 'glued' together (goals, values, culture). They are, potentially, powerful tools for reducing or removing stress from the lives of all staff, yet the main focus of intervention strategies has been on the secondary and tertiary levels (Briner 1997), no doubt for reasons of perceived cost and difficulty, and perhaps a tendency to view employees as responsible for their own stress.

The evidence reviewed above is encouraging as it indicates that many primary interventions do have positive associations with health and well-being. Supportive climates in organizations which offer job security, learning and development opportunities and equitable treatment of staff, and do not tolerate harassment, are associated with health. Enriched jobs, opportunities to develop a sense of competence or self-efficacy at work and operating in autonomous work groups are associated with job satisfaction, motivation and well-being but less strongly with work performance measures.

These results need to be treated with some caution for four reasons. First, some data are purely correlational, indicating associations between variables, not necessarily causation or causal direction. Second, even longitudinal evaluation studies tend to be of a quasi-experimental nature because of inability to control the influence of many variables, which makes the interpretation of results difficult (Cox *et al.* 2000). Nevertheless, there are examples of well-designed studies (Jackson 1983).

Third, there are many examples of personality variables moderating systematically the impact of different interventions upon behaviour, outcomes and health. For example, 'growth need strength' and 'hardiness' emphasize that certain people are more naturally suited to particular kinds of jobs than other people. Thus, achieving a good person–job match with respect to personality can be important and organizations should avoid falling into the trap of assuming that 'one intervention fits all'.

Fourth, a related point, the everyday experience of psychological distress at work has much to do with how people perceive and respond to situations, which is in turn a reflection of personal values, experiences and goals. Consequently, no matter how imaginative and ingenious the strategies and tactics used to manage primary stressors, some individuals will always be capable of 'disturbing themselves' – the individuals who resent the success of others, drive themselves relentlessly against all advice or worry constantly about the possibility of improbable events.

The effective management of an organization entails two complementary activities: designing a strategy, structure and culture in order to pursue corporate goals; and recruiting, motivating and developing staff in pursuance of these goals. Success in the latter activity is partly dependent upon creating a healthy work environment that permits staff to pursue and achieve personal as well as corporate goals. Balancing these two activities is not always easy. Nevertheless, there is sufficient evidence from research into primary stress interventions to encourage organizations to invest in strategies that promote a healthy environment and the engagement of staff. The benefits of doing so outweigh the costs of inaction.

Chapter 5

Secondary level cognitive and behavioural interventions for normative levels of occupational stress

Martin Bamber

INTRODUCTION

Health care work by its nature is inherently stressful. Health workers frequently confront illness, death, dying, trauma, challenging behaviours, suicide, violence and a whole range of other inherently stressful situations. These situations are seen as a normal part of the job of health workers and since they cannot be removed the stress experienced is described as 'normative' stress. However, stress should not be part of a job to the extent that it causes physical or mental health problems. Where the work environment cannot be easily changed, a range of 'secondary level' cognitive and behavioural interventions can be taught to help buffer employees against normative stress at work.

A wealth of literature reports the beneficial effects of individual stress management interventions for employees (e.g. Carson and Kuipers 1998; Cooper 1999; Fontana 1997; Jones *et al.* 2003; Lehrer and Woolfolk 1993; Mimura and Griffiths 2003; Mitchell 2000; Munz *et al.* 2001; Murphy 1996; Palmer 1996; Rose *et al.* 1998; Ross and Altmaier 1994). The secondary level individual stress management interventions covered in this chapter involve teaching employees a range of cognitive and behavioural coping skills, such as how to lead a healthier lifestyle, effective time management, assertiveness training, social skills training, positive thinking, problem solving and relaxation training. These are described below.

DEVELOPING A HEALTHIER LIFESTYLE

Health promotion programmes run by workplace organizations aim to educate employees about the importance of regular exercise, healthy diet, moderation of alcohol and medication usage, stopping smoking and getting the right amount of sleep (Fontana 1997). Employees involved in such a programme showed significant reductions in weight, body fat, systolic and diastolic blood pressure, absenteeism and accidents (Smoczyk and Dedmon

1985). Many health service employers are encouraging their employees to keep fit by offering them the opportunity to join a gymnasium at reduced corporate membership rates and/or offering such facilities within the workplace itself. Access to dietary advice and support from a dietician is also often available for health care staff through their occupational health service. Also, most health care organizations provide a staff canteen in which many employees eat on a daily basis, and this provides the opportunity for the provision of a range of healthy dietary options for employees to choose from. It is recommended that an individual should drink around two litres of water a day in order to prevent dehydration from occurring and the provision of conveniently located water dispensers for employees can help prevent this from happening. Education campaigns aimed at employees about the recommended safe limits for consumption of alcohol (21 units weekly for men and 14 units weekly for women) and the harmful effects of smoking (no safe limit) can raise awareness of these issues and, where demand dictates, the provision of smoking clinics for staff can assist in helping them stop smoking. Many health care settings are now insisting on a totally smoke-free environment and this is being supported by recent Government initiatives in the UK. Advice and support on 'sleep hygiene' is also commonly available for employees who are experiencing sleep problems, through occupational health services.

DEVELOPING EFFECTIVE TIME MANAGEMENT SKILLS

Effective time management has become increasingly more important in seeking to achieve organizational objectives of efficiency and effectiveness. There is considerable evidence to suggest that poor time management is a significant problem in the workplace. For example, Christie (1984) estimated that 20% of office workers' time is lost in non-essential or wasted tasks. Mintzberg (1973) estimated that 70% of a manager's time is spent in meetings. It is questionable how much of this is wasted time. Mintzberg (1979) also reported that only 13% of mail received by managers was of specific and immediate relevance to them.

The benefits of managing time effectively include greater efficiency and effectiveness at work, higher productivity, enhanced job satisfaction, reduced stress, increased leisure time and more room for forward planning (Alexander 1992; Fontana 1993; Lakein 1984, 1991; Lee and McGrath 1995; Macan 1994, 1996; Orpen 1993; Richards 1987; Schuler 1979). Numerous time management programmes are described in the literature (e.g. Adkins 1989; Banks 2003; Davidhizar and Eshleman 2002; Fontana 1993; Lakein 1984; Lang 1992; Lomas 2000; Queen and Queen 2005; Richards 1987; Schroeder 1998). Time management involves creating more time and using time more effectively. It involves prioritizing essential above non-essential tasks, planning ahead, setting time limits, not allowing oneself to get side-tracked and giving oneself enough 'prime time' to plan and organize the working week. Some examples of behavioural changes that can be made in order to manage time more effectively include the following (Fontana 1993):

- Plan ahead. It is estimated that 1% of working time spent planning is required to produce an average saving of one hour a day (Seiwert 1991).
- Making a 'to do' list into a hierarchy can also be helpful in terms of identifying priority and non-priority tasks. Once identified, the top priority items can be tackled first and the others left till later.
- Prepare for meetings. Know what you want to get out of a meeting and what your input will be in advance of it. It is also important to agree the timing of meetings at the beginning of the meeting and stick to the agreed time limits. Stick to the agenda and ensure that you communicate clearly. If necessary, rehearse what you have to say in advance and be brisk and decisive in what you have to say in the meeting. Keep them as short as possible and once you have achieved what you want in the meeting, excuse yourself from it. Unnecessary meetings should be avoided.
- Where appropriate use the telephone, email, letters or fax instead of time-consuming meetings. Letters should be kept as brief and to the point as possible and standardized letters should be used where appropriate.
- Avoid idle chatter. While social chit-chat may be enjoyable, it can be a big time waster. Face-to-face and telephone conversations should be polite but whenever possible kept brief. Reducing a coffee break from 15 to 10 minutes and limiting social chatter in the corridor can free up a considerable block of time throughout a week. Making use of a secretary to take calls or the use of an answerphone can be helpful in protecting oneself from excessive demands in the workplace.
- Delegate certain tasks where appropriate.
- Group tasks into chunks, such as grouping all your telephone calls and doing them all in one go. Blocking out time to do this can be an efficient use of time. It may be necessary to put up a 'Do not disturb' sign when doing this.
- Practise publicly saying 'no' to requests in order not to become overloaded with work.
- It is important to avoid procrastination and delaying unpleasant tasks or decisions by doing them as far as possible when they arise. If a big task seems overwhelming then it can be broken down into several smaller more manageable chunks and each one tackled in turn.
- Choose the best time to tackle difficult tasks – our own circadian rhythms dictate that there are certain times of the day when we are at our best physically and psychologically (Halberg 1960). If we are aware of these then we can fit our schedule around them.

In summary, effective time management can result in greater productivity and reduced stress levels. It can also have longer-term benefits on psychological well-being, especially when we look back over our careers. Erikson (1968) described the concept known as 'generativity', which consists of the three factors of achievement, usefulness and creativity. Success in these areas, argued Erickson, leads to greater self-acceptance in later life, through knowing that we have made the best of our time and not wasted it. If this is not achieved, then there is a longing to 'turn back the clock' and a desire to live our time again. The main point to be made here is that life is not a 'dress rehearsal' and that time is a non-renewable and valuable resource, which we need to use to maximum effect.

ASSERTIVENESS TRAINING

There are numerous studies reporting the beneficial effects of assertiveness training (e.g. Cook 1998; Crosley 1980; Dunn and Sommer 1997; Lee and Crockett 1994; Lin *et al.* 2004) and a number of assertiveness training programmes are described in the literature (Alberti and Emmons 2001; Back and Back 1999; Bond 1988; Burnard 1992; Dickson 1986; Gambrill 1995; Paterson 2000). Assertiveness is a key skill required by health workers, in order to interact effectively with patients, peers and colleagues. It involves being able to stand up for your own rights in such a way that you do not violate the rights of another person. It is about expressing one's needs, wants, opinions, feelings and beliefs in direct, honest and appropriate ways and creating a 'win-win' situation for all involved.

There are various reasons why a person may be unassertive. These may include a lack of confidence; fear of conflict, disapproval, others becoming angry, losing one's job or failure; or the desire to be looked after and protected by others. Unassertive people often feel guilty if they refuse a request, do not realize that they have rights too and have irrational negative thoughts about themselves. They may also confuse assertiveness with aggression and equate non-assertiveness with politeness.

Unassertiveness can also have effects on others, who initially may feel sorry for the unassertive individual but ultimately it can lead to a lack of respect for them, because others do not know what that person stands for. They may begin to doubt that person's integrity, believing they say one thing and go away and do another. They may become irritated that the unassertive individual does not say what they really want. In addition, it can also have effects on the workplace organization when conflicts are not handled satisfactorily, difficult decisions are avoided, problems are left to get worse, few new decisions are made and staff lose respect for a manager who is unassertive. Assertiveness training focuses on four main areas.

Education

This involves learning to recognize the differences between assertive, unassertive and aggressive behaviours in both their verbal and non-verbal expressions. For example, aggressive verbal statements include excessive use of 'I' statements, boastfulness, sarcastic comments, putdowns, threats and blame, whereas unassertive verbal statements include long and rambling statements, permission seeking, self putdowns and excessive apologies. Assertive verbal communication involves giving clear statements which are concise and to the point, constructive advice and criticism and suggestions and not blaming others unfairly. Non-verbal communication involves facial expression, eye contact, bodily posture, personal space, tone and volume of voice and pattern (as opposed to content) of speech. Aggressive non-verbal communication involves raised eyebrows, firmly set jaw, scowling, staring eyes, finger pointing, fist thumping, upright posture, invading of personal space, hard and sharp tone of voice, abrupt speech pattern and raised voice volume (shouting). Unassertive behaviour includes avoiding eye contact, nervous and hesitant movements, hunched shoulders, 'ghost' smiles, soft and wobbly monotone voice filled with hesitation and frequent throat clearing. Assertiveness involves good but not staring eye contact, open gestures and movements, relaxed posture, steady and non-threatening facial expression and a sincere, firm and steady voice.

Knowing one's rights

Most employers recognize that employees have a number of rights and these usually form part of their contracts of employment, such as annual leave entitlement, terms of employment, sickness pay, study leave entitlement and maternity/paternity leave entitlement. Most of these are statutory rights covered by government legislation. At work these rights may extend to non-statutory rights such as the right to a job appraisal, time off in lieu, in-service training and continuing professional development without loss of pay. Also, this extends to having a right to know what is expected, to be consulted about decisions made affecting you, to refuse certain requests, make mistakes occasionally without fear of being sacked and so on. Employees also have responsibilities, such as turning up to work on time, adhering to a certain dress code, using time productively, putting mistakes right, learning from mistakes and trying not repeat them and abiding by the terms and conditions of employment. However, they also have rights as human beings, which are deemed necessary to live a decent life. These include, for example, the right to be treated with respect, to be treated as an equal, not to be bullied or harassed, to be listened to, to make mistakes from time to time, to change one's mind and to refuse an unreasonable request. Assertiveness training focuses on the rights of the individual as a human being since it is in these areas that unassertive individuals typically experience the most problems.

Developing assertive attitudes

This focuses on identifying aggressive and unassertive beliefs and attitudes and changing them to assertive ones. Examples of aggressive attitudes include, 'Aggression gets results,' 'Attack is the best from of defence,' and 'I must give as good as I get.' Examples of unassertive attitudes include, 'My opinions don't count,' 'I am not as important as others,' and 'It is safer not to challenge people.' Assertive attitudes include, for example, 'I am in control,' 'I am responsible for what happens to me,' and 'I am as good as others.' Techniques for changing unhelpful beliefs and attitudes were discussed in Chapter 3, so will not be duplicated here.

Developing assertive behaviours

The individual may define a hierarchy of behaviours which they wish to change and start off with making small changes such as, for example, making a request, refusing a request, disagreeing with someone, giving an opinion, giving praise, receiving praise and so on. They may also practise nonverbal behaviours such as good eye contact, open gestures and movements, relaxed posture and steady and non-threatening facial expression, and verbally communicating assertiveness through developing a firm and steady voice, which is warm and sincere. Role-play and rehearsal in imagination techniques can be particularly helpful when practicing assertive behaviours. The individual gradually moves up through a hierarchy of situations, confronting progressively more difficult situations. However, they do not move higher up the hierarchy until they feel that they are successful with the current task.

SOCIAL SKILLS TRAINING

It is assumed that most health care employees already possess the necessary basic social skills to do the job, otherwise they would not have got through the selection process. However, there are higher order social skills, which health workers can learn to use in their every day work, to manage their interactions with others better and get the best out of them. These include making a good first impression, holding one's own in a conversation, making appropriate self-disclosures and giving praise and encouragement. It involves the management of professional relationships, including making social judgements, attributing motives, active listening, breaking bad news and handling angry confrontations. It is also about demonstrating fairness, consistency, loyalty, warmth, honesty, openness and empathy. Surprisingly, while there is a considerable body of literature relating to evaluating social skills training for patients in forensic, learning disability and rehabilitation settings, there is relatively little relating specifically to developing social skills in health care professionals (Chant *et al.* 2002). There are, however, some useful references on the subject (e.g. Fontana 1994; Gorter and Eijkman 1997; Greco *et al.* 1998; Hollin and Trower 1988; Hulsman *et al.* 1999; Lau 2000; Lindsey *et al.* 1987; Parle *et al.* 1997; Reed 1993; Smoot and Gonzales 1995).

Fontana (1994) suggested that one needs to ask oneself some questions to establish how socially skilled one is. These include: 'Am I projecting myself in the best way?' 'Do others see me in the same way I see myself?' 'Do I know those I work with very well?' 'Am I consistent across situations and people?' 'Am I good at judging others and their motives?' 'Am I good at communicating with others?' 'Am I good at picking up subtle social signals?' 'Do I handle conflict well?' 'Am I a good listener?' If the answer to any of these is 'no', then Fontana suggests that there is work to be done. Social skills can be learned through training workshops of a practical nature and the use of role-play and/or audio or video feedback can be particularly helpful in learning social skills. These may include the following:

- Effective verbal communication skills such as the ability to not monopolize conversations, to show interest, to listen, to recognize the signals which tell us we are boring people, to recognize our annoying mannerisms and to talk at the right level for the listener.
- The ability to pick up on non-verbal cues, such as eye contact, body posture, movement and facial expressions such as nods, frowns, laughter and so on.
- Active listening skills and attending behaviours such as communicating warmth and empathy, talking in a soft voice, adopting a non-judgemental attitude, making good eye contact, using friendly facial expressions and adopting an interested posture by leaning forward with arms uncrossed. This also includes the use of listening skills such as summarizing, paraphrasing and reflecting back, which all demonstrate attending and listening.
- Awareness of appropriate physical contact. The rules of contact vary in different socio-cultural contexts and with the closeness of the relationship. The closeness of appropriate contact thus varies and the employee needs to be aware of these rules. For example, an arm on the shoulder of a distressed patient or colleague may be appropriate but an arm on the shoulder of a non-distressed patient or colleague may not be so in the context of a meeting.

The content of the workshops will vary according to the needs of specific occupational groups or the stage in one's career. For example it may be appropriate to offer workshops on 'breaking bad news' to those health professionals who are in a position whereby they deal with death and dying or to managers who are required to make people redundant. Similarly it might, for example, form part of the continuing professional development needs (CPD) of a manager to do further training in handling conflict, presentation skills, managing change and responding to grievances at an early stage in their career.

POSITIVE THINKING

The centrality of negative patterns of thinking in mental health problems and the beneficial effects of positive thinking is well reported (Beck 1967, 1976; Goodhart 1985; MacLeod et al. 1993, 1997; O'Connor and Sheehy 2000; O'Connor et al. 2000).

This strategy essentially involves teaching the individual to identify, label and challenge their negative thinking patterns, using the cognitive techniques outlined in Chapter 3. Some common examples of negative thinking include the following:

- Selective attention – the tendency to focus one's thinking on and attend only to the negative parts of one's life, while ignoring all the positive things that happen.
- Jumping to conclusions – assuming that the worst is going to happen without evidence and before it happens. This involves making negative predictions about the future such as, 'I know I'll make a mess of things,' 'I know this treatment won't work,' and so on. Also, instead of finding out what people are really thinking, the individual 'mind reads' and this is rarely successful.
- Black and white thinking – thinking in 'all or nothing' terms. The world is seen in terms of dichotomies, such as people are either all good or all bad, 100% successful or a failure, strong or weak and so on. Shades of grey do not seem to exist for black and white thinkers.
- Magnification – the tendency to exaggerate the importance of negative events and blow them out of proportion, such as, 'I got question nine wrong,' without reference to the fact that all the other answers were right, or 'Last Tuesday evening was awful,' without acknowledging that the other six days of last week were enjoyable.
- Minimization – playing down the significance of positive events and achievements, often attributing them to luck, chance or the skills of others but never one's own skills. Yet at the same time all failures are attributed to one's own incompetence (as in magnification).
- Overgeneralization – a single negative event is seen as part of a never-ending pattern of defeat. It is often accompanied by the terms 'never' or 'always': for example, 'I never have any success,' 'I always upset people.'

- Negative predictions – predicting that things will always have the worst outcome. Catastrophizing is an extreme form of this.
- Should statements – trying to motivate oneself with 'shoulds' and 'oughts' but invariably ending up feeling guilty as a result of not meeting these expectations or resentful towards others who do not meet these expectations.
- Labelling – applying a critical label to oneself instead of accurately describing the situation. Instead of saying, 'I didn't do that job as well as I might have done,' one say, 'I'm a failure.'
- Personalization – the tendency to see oneself as the cause of some negative events, for which one is not necessarily responsible. Neutral events are interpreted as having negative significance for the individual. For example, a friend cancels an evening out and you think it's because they don't like you, or your children behave badly and you think it must be your fault. Similarly, someone might snap at you and you blame yourself, thinking, 'I must have deserved it.'

This is not of course an exhaustive list and there are other examples (Burns 1990). These may be specific distortions as listed above, or may be more general pervasive themes or attitudes. Examples of such unhelpful attitudes include, 'I must please everybody all of the time,' 'Either I do everything 100% or I am a total flop,' 'It is right to feel anxious about things unknown,' 'It is easier to avoid difficulties than to face them,' 'I need someone stronger than me to rely on,' and 'I can't be happy, because of the past.' Others include, 'My value as a person depends upon what others think of me,' 'I should always be a nice person,' 'I should be able to do everything myself and to ask for help is weak,' and 'If people disagree with me, it means I am no good' (Maultsby 1975). The cognitive strategies outlined in Chapter 3 can also be applied to challenging these more general negative attitudes.

PROBLEM SOLVING

Common sense tells us that problem-solving skills are important for our daily living. To a degree we learn these skills through experience but the acquisition of these skills is very much left to chance, and a more systematic approach to problem solving can be very helpful in terms of managing stress. One such approach is that of Egan (1990). For Egan, the starting point is to get the individual to identify and describe their 'present scenario' (point A), which is the present unacceptable state of affairs or 'current mess' that they find themselves in. They are then asked to identify their 'preferred scenario' (point B) at some time point in the future and to describe what this would be like ideally. Where would the individual ideally like to be? Who with? What doing? What would they want to be different or change? What would make them feel happier about their life? It can be helpful in getting the individual started to ask them, 'If you could wake up tomorrow and everything was sorted out, what would it be like?'

The client is then asked to consider how they might get from point A to point B. They are asked to generate a whole range of options or possibilities. Some people tend to want to engage in the first option they come up with. However, they should be encouraged to explore a range of different ways in which their goal can be accomplished. One very useful technique is called 'brainstorming'. In brainstorming the individual is asked to think of as many ways of achieving the goal as possible and write these down. They are encouraged to list everything, however silly or unrealistic it might seem to them at the time. Once a range of options has been identified, each can be reviewed in turn. The 'best fit' (the best single option or combination) is then selected. 'Best' means the option which best fits the client's needs, preferences, values and resources and is the most realistic option in that it is least likely to be blocked by their environment. The individual is then helped to formulate a plan to achieve each goal, identifying shorter-term objectives on the way towards longer-term goals. The aim is thus to assist a transition from the current scenario to the preferred scenario (Egan 1990).

RELAXATION TRAINING

Informal techniques

Easton (1990) found in a survey that informal methods of relaxation were, in order of popularity: reading, watching television, playing sports, taking a bath and hobbies. It is not advisable to be too prescriptive about informal methods of relaxation, since everyone has their own unique preferences and ways of achieving them. While one individual might enjoy having a hot bath and relaxing in front of the fire with a hot cup of cocoa, another individual may indulge in a vigorous game of squash to relieve their tension.

Activities with more formal relaxation properties

Activities such as yoga, massage therapy and various forms of meditation are known to have relaxing properties and should be encouraged in the individual suffering from stress.

Formal relaxation training techniques

Some of the most well-known formal relaxation techniques originate from the behavioural tradition (Benson 1975; Jacobsen 1938; Wolpe *et al.* 1973) and cognitive manipulations (Achterberg and Lawlis 1980; Kabat-Zinn *et al.*

1985; Zahourek 1988). The beneficial effects of formal relaxation techniques are also well reported (Hosaka *et al.* 1995; Irish *et al.* 1994; Matsumoto and Smith 2001; McLean and Hakstian 1970; Sinatra 2000; Woolfolk and McNulty 1983; Yung *et al.* 2004). A number of anxiety management programmes have been reported in the literature (Davis *et al.* 1988, 2000; Van Dixhorn 2001). There are also on the market numerous self-help guides, manuals and tapes, which teach relaxation, correct breathing and cognitive techniques for relaxing (e.g. Burns 1990; Butler and Hope 1995; Kennerly 1997; Miller 1984).

Progressive muscular relaxation exercises involve teaching the individual to register the difference between tension and relaxation in various groups of muscles, so that they can learn to calm the body when they are feeling anxious. There are two reasons for relaxing in this way. First, when a person is suffering from anxiety, tension becomes such a habit that they no longer notice it. These exercises thus make them aware of the differences between tension and relaxation. Second, by tensing the muscle we also fatigue it and so make it easier to relax.

Correct breathing involves slow, deep breathing in through the nose and out through the mouth using the whole of the lungs. When people are anxious or panicky they tend to over-breathe using the upper part of the chest and bring on further unpleasant symptoms as a result of hyperventilation. The individual can learn to breathe in a more relaxed way and this can assist in the relaxation process. Breathing correctly is very important in managing anxiety.

Cognitive techniques can be very useful in helping the individual to relax mentally. These include the use of meditation and imagery techniques. Meditation can be combined with other relaxation exercises, such as correct breathing, to counter stress. The focus of meditation tends to be on reducing mental stress, essentially by teaching the individual to focus their attention on one thing such as a word, a sound or an object, and to ignore all the other 'mental chatter' that is going on in their mind. Attending to a word such as 'relax' in the mind's eye, or rhythmically humming a mantra while ignoring all other intrusive thoughts, would have the same effect. In some ways this is analogous to shutting down all the programs on a computer and putting the screen saver on! Imagery techniques ask the individual to visualize a pleasant and relaxing scene such as a beach, beautiful scenery or a happy memory from the past, and by doing so the individual brings on a relaxed state.

CONCLUSIONS

There is a wide range of cognitive and behavioural tools and techniques, which the individual can make use of in order to help them cope more effectively with work-related stress. This toolkit can help provide a buffer against the stresses inherent in the work situation. This chapter concludes with some useful tips for managing normative levels of stress, in the form of a checklist:

Checklist

1   Eat a healthy diet.
2   Watch your weight.
3   Avoid long-term use of medication.
4   Get regular exercise.
5   Get sufficient rest and sleep.
6   Keep alcohol consumption to a moderate level and do not use it as a coping strategy.
7   Identify and make use of your own informal relaxation techniques.
8   If necessary make use of more formal relaxation and meditation techniques.
9   Know your own limits and do not overstretch yourself.
10   Learn to recognize the signs of stress in yourself and your work colleagues.
11   Where appropriate learn to delegate to others.
12   Don't be a slave to approval. You can't please everybody all of the time.
13   Take rests in a busy schedule. The busier you are, the more important it is to take breaks.
14   As a general rule, try always to take lunch breaks.
15   Try to take a couple of coffee breaks throughout a shift.
16   Try to be tidy and organized in your work.
17   Plan ahead and be prepared.
18   Manage your time effectively.
19   Set aside prime time for thinking, planning and organizing.
20   Learn to pace yourself in your work and work at a pace which is comfortable for you.
21   Learn to prioritize tasks.
22   Give yourself enough time to complete tasks.
23   Set realistic goals and work towards them.
24   Develop your assertiveness skills.
25   Learn to say 'no' more often.
26   Identify the areas of weakness in your social and communication skills and work on improving these.
27   Experiment with changing working habits and schedules and adopt those which feel more comfortable to you.
28   Develop a programme of leisure activities and hobbies outside of work.
29   As far as possible, separate the home and work environments.
30   Learn to express your thoughts and feelings more skilfully to others.
31   Develop your problem-solving skills.
32   Develop a more rational approach to life.
33   Be kind and nurturing to yourself and reward your successes.

34 Try to learn from your mistakes rather than punishing yourself for them.
35 Keep work in its rightful place.
36 Establish what your priorities are in life, and stop wasting time on other things which are not important to achieving these.
37 Seek a fair mix and distribution of workload.
38 If possible, vary your work routine to avoid boredom.
39 Try not to be afraid of change. Seek change and variety in a positive way.
40 Develop a number of roles in your personal life outside of work.
41 Be realistic in your goals and don't promise what you can't deliver.
42 Be positive in your thinking.
43 Do not base your whole identity on the job that you do.
44 Accept that it is OK to be average in some things.
45 Don't procrastinate. Try to deal with difficult situations as and when they arise.
46 Confront your fears rather than avoid them and be prepared to come out of your comfort zone when doing so.
47 Learn to give, ask for and receive support more when it is required.

Chapter 6

Tertiary level cognitive behavioural interventions for work-related anxiety

Martin Bamber

INTRODUCTION

The *DSM-IV-TR* manual (American Psychiatric Association 2000) uses 'anxiety' as a general term for a range of more specific anxiety disorders, which includes panic attacks, generalized anxiety disorder, specific phobias, social phobias, obsessive compulsive disorder and post traumatic stress disorder. However there is currently no literature applying these criteria to work and career anxiety, and nothing in the *DSM-IV-TR* which relates these disorders specifically to the work situation. Thus, the present chapter extrapolates the existing classifications of anxiety to the workplace from other settings.

The literature on anxiety distinguishes two conceptually useful categories of anxiety, which can be applied to the work setting. The first is known as 'situation-specific anxiety' and is characterized by a persistent and excessive fear of specific work situations or tasks, extensive avoidance behaviours and situation-specific panic attacks. It is a 'state', which has usually developed during the course of the current episode of employment and is most commonly attributed to stressful situations or task characteristics. The second type is 'cross-situational anxiety' that affects performance across a wide range of work-related situations and tasks and is characterized by more pervasive, global, persistent and excessive anxiety and worry. It includes generalized anxiety, social anxiety and unexpected panic attacks. This kind of anxiety places greater emphasis on the personal characteristics or 'traits' of the employee in the origins of the anxiety. It is often conceptualized as an *a priori* state pre-dating the current episode of employment, which has been brought into the present job and exacerbated by the work situational or task characteristics. This distinction is not just useful for classification purposes, but is of clinical importance. Cross-situational anxiety, which is defined in the *DSM-IV-TR* as generalized anxiety disorder, is a different type of anxiety to situation-specific anxiety and requires a different treatment intervention.

It is important to mention at this point that although the origins of cross-situational anxiety may in part be rooted in personality traits, it is not the aim of the standard CBT presented in Part II of this book to attempt to modify the underlying cognitive structures associated with these traits. It is to reduce and hopefully eliminate the clinical symptoms of the presenting problem, in order to enable the employee to handle naturally occurring stressful events inherent in the work setting more productively (Lowman 1997). This is one of the main distinctions between the standard approach to CBT outlined in Part II of this book and the 'schema-focused' approach in Part III of the book, which does aim to modify trait characteristics.

In the work context, situation-specific anxieties most commonly revolve around the employee's performance on given tasks in a particular work setting (Lowman 1997) and this has been given the term 'performance anxiety'. Because it is so prevalent in work settings, the rest of this chapter is dedicated to the formulation and standard CBT treatment of situation-specific work-related performance anxiety. Chapter 7 looks at the formulation and standard CBT treatment of other forms of work-related anxiety, including cross-situational anxiety.

PERFORMANCE ANXIETY

Performance anxiety is defined as 'the experience of persisting, distressful apprehension about and/or actual impairment of performance skills in a public context, to a degree unwarranted given the individual's aptitude, training and level of preparation' (Salmon 1992: 61). Barrell et al. (1985) identified five factors that are present in the experience of performance anxiety. These are the perceived presence of significant others (an audience), the possibility of visible (public) failure, the need to avoid failure, the uncertainty of the outcome and the extent to which the task calls for focus on the self. The role of an audience is thought to be particularly important in some kinds of performance anxiety (Hartman 1984).

It is normal to experience some anxiety when our performance is under scrutiny in some way and, at low levels, it is considered to be a normal phenomenon. Many of us will have experienced anxiety, for example when taking an assessment, exam or test (test anxiety), writing a paper or report (writer's block), public speaking (public speaking anxiety), having an interview or doing a presentation in a meeting (presentation anxiety). At optimal levels the anxiety experienced helps us perform well and it is a normal and adaptive experience. However, at higher levels, anxiety can be extremely distressing and disabling for the individual.

The triggers for work-related performance anxiety could be either external or internal to the individual. External triggers usually result from the pressure to perform to certain external standards, which are defined by the workplace. Internal triggers result from the employee's perception that they are not meeting their own internally-defined standards. In individuals with a good pre-morbid history of functioning at work, it is more likely that the cause of

anxiety is primarily due to external pressures resulting from task characteristics of the job itself. However, where the anxiety is internally generated, the
cause of the anxiety is likely to be the result of more longstanding personal
characteristics, such as a lack of confidence and low self-esteem.

Examples of external anxiety-arousing work-related task characteristics
were outlined in Chapter 2 (see Figure 2.1). In the context of performance
anxiety they include task complexity, volume and pace of work, task familiar-
ity, role clarity, support, supervision, skills, knowledge, training and experience to do the job. The consequences of failure (actual or perceived) are also
an important trigger in work-related anxiety. If the consequence of failure is
public humiliation, the wrath of a bullying manager or even loss of job, then
the employee is more likely to be anxious than if the consequences are mini-
mal. The research literature supports the view that various types of work
conditions, especially interpersonal conflict, role conflict, role overload and
role ambiguity, increase the likelihood of work-related anxiety (Chen and
Spector 1991; Jex and Spector 1996; Moyle 1995; Sargent and Terry 1994;
Srivastava 1989).

At this point it is advisable to urge a note of caution before the therapist
embarks on a course of CBT with a patient who is presenting with situational
anxiety. It is important to establish before commencing therapy that every
possible environmental intervention and safeguard that can be, has been put
in place. Primary interventions of the nature described in Chapter 4 may
be more appropriate for those employees whose anxiety is due to external
pressures resulting from task characteristics of the job itself. For example,
interventions such as increasing support and supervision, reducing workload,
clarifying roles and responsibilities, making adequate resources and equipment available, updating the technology and providing the necessary education and training to do the job may successfully ameliorate the employee's
anxiety without the need for therapy. Thus, wherever possible primary
interventions should be considered before therapy is commenced.

Internal triggers for performance anxiety are rooted in dysfunctional
beliefs and attitudes that an individual holds about their work. Our Western
culture places much emphasis on being successful in one's job. While most of
us want to do a good job, many people in our society believe that the only
route to success and happiness is through doing well at work. This attitude
can create a crippling pressure to achieve and performance anxiety is a
product of it. It thus manifests itself mostly in individuals who base their
self-esteem on achievement and being successful. Situations in which these
individuals perceive their self-worth is under threat are thus experienced as
being particularly anxiety-provoking, for example if the employee perceives
their competence to be on trial, or their ability do the job is under scrutiny.
The anxiety is exacerbated when there is a significant (actual or perceived)
risk of failure and/or where there are significant negative consequences resulting from the failure. These individuals also tend to exaggerate the importance

of any one single performance to their career and so in each and every situation encountered they act as if their whole career depends on it, which makes the performance anxiety worse (Steptoe 1989).

One might imagine that performance anxiety is highest in employees with the least training, knowledge and experience. Paradoxically, this is not the case. There is a high incidence of performance anxiety in experienced professionals who have achieved high status and have considerable knowledge, skills and years of formal training to do the job (Salmon 1992). Typically, such individuals may be generally well-adjusted to their work and in interacting with their peers but experience 'stage fright' when, for example, making a presentation or talking in larger groups. It is as if the higher the individual has climbed up the career ladder, the more they fear the fall from that ladder. For example, among health professionals it is not uncommon for consultant medical staff to experience performance anxiety. There are many challenging situations that they have to face on a daily basis, which are subject to high levels of public scrutiny and provide many opportunities to expose their 'incompetence'. They are expected to stay calm, think clearly and rationally, act quickly and show their knowledge, skills and leadership in emergency 'life or death' situations on a regular basis. Such individuals live in fear of being publicly exposed as being 'incompetent' and much time is spent worrying that failure is just 'one miserable performance away'. This problem is not of course unique to the medical profession or, indeed, to any health professional whose performance is subject to public scrutiny. There is usually a fear of public humiliation and failure, together with an under-estimation by the anxious individual of their own ability to cope. Underlying this fear is often the belief that the 'real me' will be exposed as being lacking or flawed in some way and that 'Unless I impress others, they will not like or respect me.' The individual believes that they must come across as polished and perfect in their performance and frequently has quite rigid and stereotyped ideas about how they should perform in front of others.

FORMULATION OF PERFORMANCE ANXIETY

From the diagrammatic formulation outlined in Figure 6.1, it can be seen that in specific work-related situations or tasks, where the employee perceives that their performance is under scrutiny, negative cognitions are triggered regarding evaluation of their own performance and being negatively judged by others. Whether or not they are actually being scrutinized in reality is not the key issue, since it is the employee's perceptions that are important here. Examples of negative self-evaluations may be: 'I am not up to the job ... I will fail ... I will look stupid ... show myself up ... won't be able to cope ...'

Examples of cognitions of negative evaluation by others include: 'Others

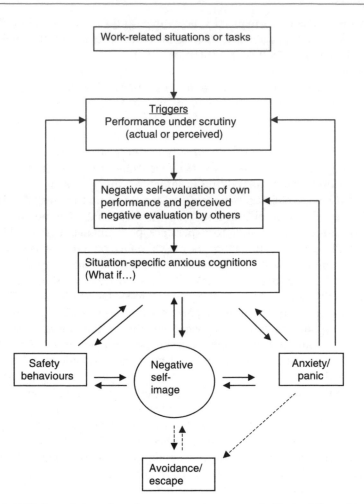

Figure 6.1 CBT formulation of performance anxiety at work (derived from Clark and Wells 1995; Wells and Matthews 1994).

will see that I am incompetent . . . think I am stupid . . . see how weak and inept I am . . .'

If the individual believes that they are being evaluated, this is sufficient to trigger performance anxiety. The anxiety is usually greater if the individual believes that the person doing the evaluation is in a position of authority such as a supervisor or manager, rather than one of their peers. Performance anxiety has cognitive, emotional, behavioural and physiological components.

From the model (Figure 6.1) it can be seen that more general negative evaluations result in situation-specific anxious cognitions. Examples include 'what if' self-statements, such as: 'What if . . . I start to shake . . . my mind goes blank . . . I look stupid . . . I come across as strange . . . I collapse in front of others . . . I start to shake . . . I blush . . . I sweat excessively . . . I stammer . . . I show myself up?'

These anxious cognitions trigger physiological and cognitive symptoms of anxiety. Examples of physical symptoms include sweating, shaking, palpitations, tension, hot flushes, nausea, dizziness, over-breathing, light-headedness and so on. Cognitive symptoms of anxiety include poor concentration, a racing mind and an increased focus of attention on oneself and one's physical symptoms.

As a result of experiencing the physiological and cognitive components of anxiety, the individual then adopts what are called 'safety behaviours'. Examples of safety behaviours include avoiding eye contact, sitting near an escape route, talking too little (or sometimes too much), talking faster, keeping quiet in meetings, folding one's arms, fidgeting, trying not to be the centre of attention and keeping out of the spotlight. The individual may avoid drinking in front of others in case they spill their drink through shaking or may wear dark clothes to hide their sweating or high-necked clothes to conceal flushing and blotches around the neck. These are all examples of safety behaviours. Anxious individuals believe that these safety behaviours are helping them cope more effectively with their anxiety but unfortunately they inadvertently have the effect of maintaining anxiety. Such individuals become pre-occupied with thoughts about their physiological arousal, ongoing performance and others' perceptions of them (Hartman 1983, 1986).

TREATING PERFORMANCE ANXIETY

The CBT formulation and treatment of performance anxiety is presented in detail in the case illustration of a medical student called 'Theresa', in Chapter 9 of this book. The reader is therefore directed to Chapter 9 for a detailed description of the treatment of a case of performance anxiety.

TREATING ASSOCIATED PANIC ATTACKS AND PHOBIC AVOIDANCE

Unfortunately, becoming anxious about one's performance creates a 'vicious cycle', since high levels of anxiety generally serve to lessen the quality of an individual's performance. The employee's line manager, supervisor or colleagues may notice that they have little to say, appear withdrawn, contribute little to meetings, volunteer infrequently or appear to have few ideas. It is thus likely that an individual with performance anxiety will receive more pressure and criticism from their line manager, supervisor or colleagues as a result of their observed performance (Collins et al. 1991; Hamilton et al. 1986). It can be seen in Figure 6.1 that the negative feedback the employee receives from the supervisor, manager or colleagues creates a negative feedback loop, which serves to increase the employee's performance anxiety. The increased anxiety further impairs the employee's performance, which in turn invites even more criticism and a downward spiral of decreasing performance, negative feedback and increasing anxiety is created.

If this downward cycle continues unabated, then the employee's anxiety can become increasingly disabling and they may begin to experience panic attacks. Ultimately, they may also start to avoid those situations that trigger the panic attacks altogether. This is known as phobic avoidance. Once the anxiety becomes phobic in intensity, the employee is usually unable to maintain their work role. As a consequence of the anxiety, panic attacks, phobic avoidance and being unable to work, the employee's self-image becomes increasingly eroded and they start to lose confidence in their ability to do the required tasks at all. Even more seriously, they may begin to doubt that they will ever be able to return to their job. Thus, it is crucially important to offer the employee who is experiencing panic attacks and/or phobic avoidance timely treatment, before the problems become chronic in nature.

Treating panic attacks

A panic attack is defined in the *DSM-IV-TR* (APA 2000: 393) as a 'discrete period in which there is a sudden onset of intense apprehension, fearfulness or terror, often associated with feelings of impending doom'. Three sub-types of panic attack are described. These are situationally bound, situationally pre-disposed and unexpected or uncued panic attacks. Situationally bound panic attacks occur immediately on exposure to, or in anticipation of, a specific situation. Situationally pre-disposed panic attacks are slightly different, in that while they are associated with a particular situation, they do not necessarily occur immediately on exposure to, or anticipation of, that situation. However, they are more likely to happen in that situation than others. Unexpected or uncued panic attacks occur in the absence of any obvious situational triggers. In the context of the work situation, the first two types are more commonly encountered and they are linked to specific triggering situations or tasks in the workplace. However, the formulation and treatment for each sub-type is similar and is described below.

In the cognitive model of panic outlined in Figure 6.2, specific work-related situations or tasks trigger the symptoms of anxiety in the employee. These include physical symptoms such as increased breathing, dizziness, blurred vision, shaking, hot flushes, sweating, tingling in the hands and feet, chest pains and palpitations, and also mental symptoms such as changes in concentration, speeding up of thoughts and changes in the focus of attention. The increased rate of breathing disrupts the balance of oxygen and carbon dioxide in the bloodstream and this causes the individual to experience

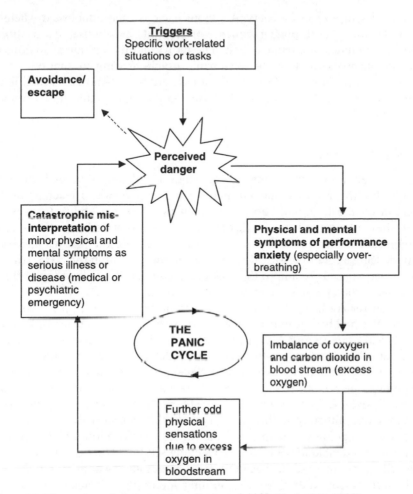

Figure 6.2 The panic cycle (adapted from Beck *et al.* 1985; Clark 1986, 1988).

further odd bodily sensations associated with hyperventilation, such as feelings of light-headedness, dizziness and faintness.

These normal physical or mental events associated with anxiety are then 'catastrophically misinterpreted' as either a medical or a psychiatric emergency (Clark 1986, 1988). For example, a mild physical symptom of anxiety such as a speeded heart rate is catastrophically interpreted as a sign of a heart attack. Or an anxious individual may catastrophically believe that mental events such as changes in concentration or speeding up of thoughts are an imminent sign of a journey into mental illness. They may worry that they are going to go berserk, collapse, faint, become incontinent, be sick or generally make a fool of themselves and look stupid in front of everyone. This 'catastrophizing' makes the individual more anxious, which in turn leads to increased symptoms of anxiety. A vicious cycle is then established whereby the individual goes through a sequence of thoughts, emotions and sensations, which culminates in a panic attack. The individual then remains anxious in that specific work situation, between panic attacks, fearing another one could happen at any time. The following is a case study of 'Andrea', which illustrates the treatment of panic attacks based on the conceptualization outlined in Figure 6.2.

A case study: Andrea

Andrea was a 43-year-old medical consultant with no previous history of mental health problems. She had many years' experience of teaching at the local medical school and had always been proud of her ability to cope. In fact, she confessed to having little time for people suffering from stress – until it happened to her. In the few months prior to her referral, Andrea had been experiencing a lot of pressure due to internal politics within the NHS Trust in which she worked. To add to the pressure, a complaint was made against her by a dissatisfied patient, which was being investigated formally. This was the last straw for Andrea, who had always been proud of her exemplary conduct record. She had been feeling particularly tense one day when teaching a group of medical students and, for the first time in her life, experienced a full-blown panic attack in front of the students. Andrea described the panic attack as the worst feeling she had ever experienced. She reported that her heart had begun pounding, she became physically weak and shaky and she experienced sensations all down her back as if needles were being stuck in her skin, a tight chest, dizziness and difficulty getting enough air. At the time she had really believed that she was going to collapse and die through suffocation. She felt so bad that she was unable to complete the teaching session. The experience eroded her self-confidence and she began to worry about having another attack.

Unfortunately, Andrea did have another severe panic attack when she was next teaching a group of medical students and after this she started to have panic attacks on a daily basis. At the time of referral she was on sick leave and was wondering if she would ever be able to return to her job again. The experience had severely eroded her self-confidence and she began to worry that she might also have panic attacks in other situations, such as when doing a crucial medical procedure, or when she was the senior person on call.

Andrea was initially not convinced that her problem was panic attacks. She was convinced that she had some serious physical illness; she was unable to believe that psychological factors could make her feel so bad. However, after a visit to her doctor and a number of physical tests had indicated that there was nothing physically wrong with her, she began to accept that her symptoms were due to anxiety. At our first session, Andrea described herself as a 'fighter' and stated that she was determined that her anxiety was 'not going to beat' her.

Treating Andrea's panic attacks

The treatment of panic attacks usually begins with educating the patient about the cognitive, emotional, physiological and behavioural symptoms of anxiety and the 'fight-flight' mechanism. However, as a medical professional Andrea already had a reasonably good understanding of the physiology of anxiety, in particular the fight-flight response and the role of adrenaline production. However, she did benefit from being educated about the CBT conceptualization (as outlined in Figure 6.2). The way in which the different components in the panic cycle interact to produce an escalation of anxiety, ultimately leading to panic attacks, was clearly new to her and she found it extremely helpful to have a framework which helped her to understand her problems better.

Andrea was then encouraged to keep a panic diary in which she identified the triggers to her panic, as well as her cognitive, behavioural and emotional responses to it. She brought these examples with her to the therapy sessions and her unhelpful patterns of thinking and behaving in response to her anxiety and panic were identified. It became clear that Andrea was catastrophically misinterpreting her symptoms of anxiety as a medical emergency. When she began to feel anxious, she believed that she was going to suffocate and die. This information allowed us to develop a conceptualization of her panic attacks. The catastrophic interpretation of her anxiety symptoms led to an increase in her anxiety, especially over-breathing. The increase in anxiety resulted in further physical sensations, especially those related to over-breathing. This escalation of symptoms then convinced Andrea that her catastrophic beliefs were about to come true and she really was going to suffocate and die.

Andrea was taught some anxiety management techniques including progressive muscular relaxation, relaxed breathing and some meditation exercises (as outlined in the section on relaxation training in Chapter 5). She was then taught some cognitive techniques for challenging her catastrophic thinking (as outlined in the section on CBT interventions in Chapters 3 and 5). These essentially focused on challenging her catastrophic belief that her anxious pattern of breathing would result in suffocation and dropping dead. With the permission of her doctor, Andrea was then encouraged to do an exercise which resulted in a re-attribution of the meaning of the symptoms for her. This entailed deliberately over-breathing. When Andrea deliberately hyperventilated, she found to her surprise that she began to experience all the symptoms she usually experienced when she had a panic attack. However, because the experiment had been conducted in the safe environment of the therapy room, she felt more able to contain the symptoms, and they did not develop into a full-blown panic attack. This exercise resulted in Andrea becoming more convinced that the CBT conceptualization of panic was correct and that if she could stop catastrophizing about her bodily symptoms, control her breathing and try to relax more, she could overcome the problem.

Andrea began practising a positive internal 'self dialogue', in which she told herself that her bodily reactions were normal ones associated with anxiety and that although they felt unpleasant, they were not harmful. She also tried not to add frightening thoughts or imagine unpleasant consequences. If she did, then she used the cognitive techniques she had been taught to challenge these anxious thoughts. She was also taught 'attention shift' exercises which encouraged her to focus her attention away from internal bodily sensations and mental events towards scanning her external environment, and away from the future of 'what might be' to the here and now of 'what is'.

Over the course of 15 sessions of CBT Andrea felt able to control her anxiety more effectively and was no longer experiencing panic attacks. She was encouraged to start confronting situations that she had previously been avoiding as a result of her panic attacks. She agreed a staged return to work with her employers and was gradually re-introduced to the teaching role. At the end of the therapy, Andrea had fully regained her confidence and was teaching medical students again. She was also made aware of the need to adopt a different attitude to her job and to make more time in her life for relaxation.

Treating phobic avoidance

Andrea, the medical consultant in the case study presented above, was determined to confront and overcome her anxiety and consequently, with a little encouragement, was able to put herself back into the situations which triggered her panic attacks in the first place. However, it is not always the case that an individual can confront their fears in this way. Frequently, once an individual has experienced a panic attack or a sequence of panic attacks in a given situation, they want to avoid that situation in case it happens to them again. Where the fear and avoidance of a specific situation becomes persistent and excessive, it is described as phobic anxiety (APA 2000).

Exposure to the phobic situation usually triggers an immediate (situationally bound) panic attack. As a result of the intense anxiety and fear that the phobic stimulus generates, it is usually avoided, or at most endured with dread. Unlike other fears, phobias are disabling and can result in significant impairment in the individual's daily routine and occupational and social functioning. In the occupational context, it can be seen from the cognitive model of panic presented in Figure 6.2 that one way of stopping the panic attacks is to avoid the specific work-related situation or tasks that trigger them. However, while it may be an option in the short term for an employee to be excused certain tasks or responsibilities, it is most unlikely that this would be seen as acceptable by an employer or by work colleagues in the longer term. Also, although avoidance gives the individual a feeling of relief in the short term, it only assists in maintaining the problem in the longer term. It is important therefore that the employee is given help to overcome their phobic avoidance at the earliest opportunity, before it becomes chronic in nature.

Phobic avoidance is best treated using the behavioural technique of systematic desensitization. Together with the therapist the patient identifies and makes a comprehensive list of all the situations being avoided. They then rate each situation in the list on a scale from 0 to 10 (where 0 is no anxiety and 10 is maximum anxiety). The situations are then placed into a hierarchy, with the most difficult situations scoring highest on distress (10) at the top, then the scores of 9, and so on right down to the lowest scores of 1 and 0 (the easiest to confront). The patient then confronts the situation lowest in the hierarchy and only moves on to confront the next step in the hierarchy when they feel confident that they have overcome the previous one. Eventually, the patient works through all the stages of this 'graded exposure' hierarchy. This exposure technique is demonstrated in the case illustration of the medical student 'Theresa' in Chapter 9, who had developed a phobia of public speaking but was able to overcome it successfully, using the techniques described.

Chapter 7

Cognitive behavioural therapy for other work-related anxiety syndromes

Martin Bamber

INTRODUCTION

Cross-situational anxiety differs from the situation-specific anxiety described in the previous chapter, in that it involves multiple anxieties and worries that affect performance across a wide range of work and non-work-related situations and tasks. Examples of cross-situational anxiety include disorders such as uncued panic attacks, agoraphobia, generalized social phobia and generalized anxiety disorder (American Psychiatric Association [APA] 2000). The treatment of panic attacks and phobias was discussed in the previous chapter. This chapter thus focuses on the formulation and treatment of generalized anxiety disorder (GAD). GAD warrants specific attention since it requires quite a different CBT treatment approach from the other forms of anxiety already mentioned. Two other anxiety syndromes which have been found to be particularly prevalent among health workers, namely post-traumatic stress disorder (PTSD) and health anxiety, are also discussed in this chapter.

GENERALIZED ANXIETY DISORDER

The *DSM-IV-TR* (APA 2000) reports that the lifetime prevalence rate of GAD in the population is 5%. It defines GAD as excessive anxiety and worry occurring on more days than not for at least six months about a number of events or activities (such as work or aspects of personal life). The person finds it difficult to control the worry and experiences at least three of the following six symptoms: restlessness or feeling keyed up and on edge, being easily fatigued, difficulty concentrating or mind going blank, irritability, muscle tension and sleep disturbance. The worry is not concerned with the anticipation of panic attacks, is not confined to features of a DSM Axis 1 disorder such as being embarrassed in public (social phobia) or having serious illness (health anxiety), does not form part of PTSD and is not due to substance effects or a medical condition.

GAD is excessive and unrealistic anxiety and worry about various multiple life circumstances such as career, finances, health of family members, household chores or job responsibilities (Clark 2000) and revolves around the themes of not being able to cope, negative evaluation by others, performance fears and somatic concerns. It can shift from one concern to another. CBT for generalized anxiety disorder has been evaluated in a number of studies and has been shown to be effective (e.g. Butler *et al.* 1987, 1991; Power *et al.* 1989). The inclusion of a cognitive component to the therapy has been demonstrated to be superior to behavioural interventions alone (Borkovec and Costello 1993) and superior to analytic therapy (Durham *et al.* 1994).

A wide range of physical symptoms are associated with GAD including muscle tension, twitching and shaking, restlessness, sweating, dry mouth, dizziness, diarrhoea, flushes and chills, nausea and the desire to urinate. In GAD chains of thoughts and images are elicited which are negatively affect-laden and relatively uncontrollable (Borkovec *et al.* 1983). They are similar in content to normal worry but more extreme, and revolve around themes of not being able to cope, negative evaluation by others, performance fears and somatic concerns, as mentioned above. Episodes of worry can consist of ruminations lasting from a few minutes to hours and in the extreme can become obsessional in nature. The cognitive model of worry (Wells 1997) distinguishes two types of worry: Type 1 and Type 2. Type 1 worries focus on external daily events such as work and also non-cognitive internal events such as bodily sensations, whereas Type 2 worries focus on the nature and occurrence of the thoughts themselves. They are basically worries about worry. For example, 'My worry will lead to insanity.'

Well's (1997) model distinguishes negative from positive Type 2 worries. Negative Type 2 worries are based on the belief that worrying is a potentially harmful activity. Examples include: 'My worry is uncontrollable,' 'Worry is harmful,' 'I could go crazy with worry,' 'My worries will take over and control me,' and 'I could enter a state of worry and never get out of it' (Wells 1997: 202). Positive Type 2 worries, however, are based on the belief that worry is a useful coping strategy. Examples of positive Type 2 worries include: 'Worrying helps me cope,' 'Worry can prevent bad things from happening,' 'It can help me solve problems,' and 'It always enables me to be ready for the worst' (Wells 1997: 203). The model asserts that the abnormal varieties of worry found in GAD are associated with a high incidence of negative Type 2 worries, in which the patient negatively appraises the activity of worrying. Unfortunately the act of worrying itself increases the individual's hypervigilance and sensitivity to threat-related information and generates an elaborate range of possible outcomes, each of which the individual can then worry about in its own right. Thus, over time the worries, and the number of scenarios about which the individual can worry, multiply.

A case illustration of GAD: The case of 'Sue'

Sue was a 31-year-old staff nurse, who had just started a new job. She described herself as a 'natural born worrier'. During the assessment it became apparent that Sue had experienced numerous previous episodes of worry, dating back to her childhood, which fulfilled the *DSM-IV-TR* criteria for GAD described earlier. For example, she had frequently worried about what other people thought about her. Would she pass her nursing exams? Would she ever get married? Would she ever start a family? Would she be able to cope with being in charge of a ward? Sue recognized that other people did not worry about things as much as she did but felt unable to control it. However, Sue's most recent episode of anxiety was triggered by starting a job as a staff nurse in a new speciality, in which she had relatively little experience and had not worked in since her training five years previously.

According to Well's (1997) cognitive model, Sue had selected worry as a coping strategy. She had some pre-existing positive Type 2 beliefs prior to starting her new job, that worry helped her cope and also prevented bad things from happening to her. Thus, as can be seen in Figure 7.1, when she started the new and challenging job, she began to worry about specific daily aspects of the job, such as how she was performing and how others perceived her performance. She also experienced some sleep disturbance and worried that if she did not get enough sleep, she would make mistakes at work. These are all examples of Type 1 worries. After a prolonged period of worrying about her achievements at work, negative Type 2 worries began to creep into Sue's mind. She began to worry that her worrying was getting out of control and that she might become ill with worry, or even have a mental breakdown.

It can be seen from Figure 7.1 that there were behavioural, cognitive, physical and emotional manifestations of GAD which served to maintain the negative Type 2 worries that Sue was experiencing. For example, in order to reduce her anxiety, Sue adopted a number of behavioural coping strategies such as reassurance-seeking, checking and avoidance. She sought reassurance that she was doing a good enough job and also started checking more in case she had made any mistakes in her work. She would if possible avoid situations and tasks which were most likely to trigger her worry. Unfortunately, these behaviours led to Sue worrying even more that she was not doing her job properly, was not coping and that her worry was out of control.

She attempted to suppress the frightening negative Type 2 thoughts she was experiencing. Unfortunately, however, this inadvertently had the opposite effect of increasing the unwanted thoughts (Clark *et al.* 1991; Wegner *et al.* 1987) and in fact strengthened her belief in the uncontrollability of her worries. The physical manifestations of anxiety and worry, which included insomnia, tension, nausea and fatigue to name a few symptoms, further convinced Sue that the worry was making her physically ill. The emotional symptoms of anxiety such as the experience of her mind racing, dissociation and

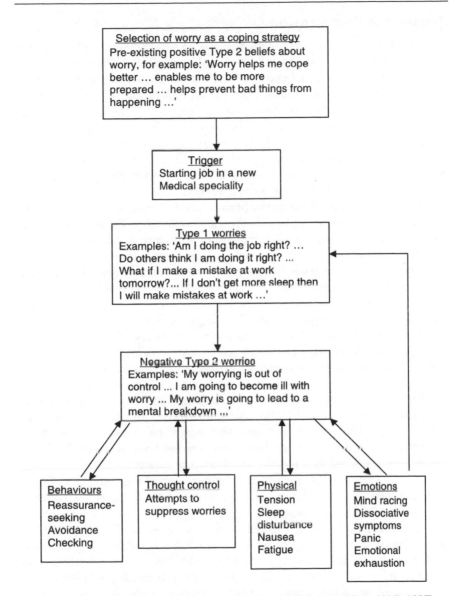

Figure 7.1 Formulation of a specific worry episode in GAD (adapted from Wells 1997).

emotional exhaustion was further evidence to Sue that she was also mentally losing control. As a consequence of catastrophising about her physical and mental symptoms, Sue began to experience panic attacks. These in turn fuelled her Type 1 and Type 2 worries, as shown in Figure 7.1. After experiencing panic attacks on a few occasions, Sue decided to seek help.

Treatment intervention

The starting point in therapy with Sue was to socialize her to the cognitive model of GAD. The idea that worry can be useful if it alerts us to a real threat, such as a hazard that needs to be removed in order to prevent someone getting injured, was introduced. The conceptualization of worry as being something normal, which we all do to some degree, was discussed. Then, the concepts of Type 1 and Type 2 worries were explained to Sue, in particular the important role of negative Type 2 worries in GAD. She was encouraged to keep a 'worry diary', in which she recorded examples of situations and events that triggered her own worry, and was helped by the therapist to distinguish her own Type 1 and Type 2 worries.

Sue was then taught a number of behavioural techniques, already described in this book, to help her manage her anxiety and worry. These included anxiety management training (as outlined in the section on relaxation training in Chapter 5). She was also encouraged to drop the reassurance and checking behaviours and confront her avoidance behaviours using a systematic desensitization hierarchy technique (as described in the section on behavioural interventions in Chapter 3). She was helped to overcome her panic attacks using the intervention techniques described in the previous chapter. In addition, Sue was taught the behavioural stimulus control technique of using 'controlled worry periods' to manage her worry, as devised by Borkovec and colleagues (1983). Essentially, this involved putting aside 30 minutes each day in the same location to worry. If she found herself worrying at other times, she had to try to postpone the worry and refocus her attention on to the 'here and now'. The worry period was used to focus on her worries and engage in problem solving to eliminate these. Sue was also taught to carry out behavioural experiments (as described in the section on behavioural interventions in Chapter 3) to test out her negative predictions of events.

Sue was then taught cognitive techniques for challenging her Type 1 worries (as described in the section on cognitive interventions in Chapters 3 and 5). In addition, she was taught some cognitive techniques specifically aimed at challenging Type 2 worries. These included challenging her belief about the uncontrollability of worrying thoughts by identifying naturally-occurring modulators of worry which interrupt or stop it, questioning the mechanism whereby worry could lead to mental breakdown, 'normalising' worry and drawing her attention to the contradictions in her beliefs – on the one hand believing that worry is a positive thing (positive Type 2 worries) and on the other hand believing it is harmful (negative Type 2 worries). A comprehensive coverage of all these cognitive techniques can be found in Wells (1997: 215–35). Other useful strategies can be found in Butler and Hope (1995: 173–91). Sue was also taught some cognitive imagery techniques. One example of this is 'boxing worries'. She was asked to imagine putting all her worries in a box, then hanging them on a tree and watching them blow away in the wind (Butler and Hope 1995: 183). Another example was asking her to place all her worries on a lily pad and then watch it float downstream. (Note that the cognitive meditation techniques described in the section on relaxation training in Chapter 5 can also be applied in this way to treat GAD.)

Over the course of 20 therapy sessions Sue learned to use a wide range of tools and techniques to manage her anxiety and worry. At the end of the therapy she reported that she felt much less anxious and was having significantly fewer worrying thoughts. While she recognized that she would never be the most relaxed person in the world, she firmly believed that she would as a result of the therapy be successfully able to prevent her worries from getting out of hand.

OTHER WORK-RELATED ANXIETY SYNDROMES

There are two other work-related anxiety syndromes which have been found to be particularly prevalent among health workers. These are post-traumatic stress disorder and health anxiety. The rest of this chapter looks at the cognitive behavioural treatment of these two anxiety syndromes.

Post-traumatic stress syndrome

The *DSM-IV-TR* manual (APA 2000) criteria for the diagnosis of post-traumatic stress disorder (PTSD) are: the person has been exposed to a traumatic event, which involved actual or threatened death or injury to the self or others; the event occasioned intense fear, helplessness or horror; the event is persistently re-experienced through intrusive recollections, dreams or reliving experiences; there is persistent avoidance of stimuli associated with the event; there are persistent symptoms of increased arousal such as sleep disturbance, exaggerated startle response or outbursts of anger; and symptoms have persisted for a period of longer than one month and cause clinically significant distress or impairment in social, occupational or other important areas of functioning. If the symptoms have persisted for less than one month, the diagnosis of acute stress disorder is given. The prevalence of PTSD in the general population is estimated to be about 1% (Helzer *et al.* 1987).

Work-related post-traumatic stress reactions among health workers can occur in response to a wide range of traumas, such as violent assault by patients, severe bullying, accidents in the workplace and witnessing horrific injury, death, dying, self-harming and suicide to name but a few examples (Balloch *et al.* 1998; Brady 1999; Budd *et al.* 1996; Einarsen *et al.* 1999; Flannery 1996; Hoel and Cooper 2000; Koss 1999; Leather *et al.* 1998; Leymann and Gustafsson 1996; Rippon 2000). Emergency workers are at particularly high risk of developing PTSD, with prevalence rates estimated to be up to 22% (Clohessy and Ehlers 1999; Grevin 1996).

Interventions for PTSD

CBT treatments for PTSD have been widely researched and experimentally validated (Foa *et al.* 1991; Follete *et al.* 1999; Horowitz 1986; Keane 1997; Kulka *et al.* 1990; Resick and Schnicke 1992; Resick *et al.* 1981). Behavioural approaches emphasize the central role of anxious arousal and phobic avoidance in the PTSD syndrome. For example, the two-factor theory (Kilpatrick *et al.* 1982) proposed that anxiety is conditioned to previously neutral cues at the time of the traumatic event. These cues then serve as subsequent triggers to the post-traumatic stress reaction. Avoidance develops in response to the anxiety and is reinforced by reduction in arousal associated with the avoidance.

There are two main cognitive approaches to treating PTSD. The first is based on the view that the traumatic event shatters previously healthy schemata related to the self, others and the world (e.g. Janoff-Bulman 1989). The second is based on the view that it is not the shattering of healthy schemata, but the re-activation of unhealthy dysfunctional schemata associated with an earlier trauma which determines vulnerability to PTSD (Dalgleish 1999; Power and Dalgleish, 1997; Williams 1999). In order to manage the complexities of treating PTSD, a phased approach has been recommended (Keane 1995; Keane *et al.* 1994; Kimble *et al.* 1999). The phases of therapy proposed are the stabilization, trauma education, stress management, trauma focused and relapse prevention phases. The interventions outlined in this section are based upon these phases.

Stabilization phase

The first phase focuses on managing the crisis and containing the associated high levels of arousal and emotional distress that have caused the patient to enter into therapy. The therapist has to be able to contain these, make the individual feel emotionally safe and manage the risk associated with strong emotional reactions such as fear, anger and shame. The role of the therapist is to provide support, ensure that the patient has the basic skills to manage the emotional aftermath of the trauma and stabilize their emotional and behavioural reactions to it. The patient may also require medication and sedation in this early stage.

Trauma educational phase

In this phase, the therapist educates the patient about post-traumatic stress reactions. This involves giving the patient information about the consequences of exposure to traumatic events and the development of PTSD symptoms.

Stress management phase

In this phase, the therapist teaches the patient skills to cope with the stress, anxiety and interpersonal difficulties they are experiencing, for example anxiety management training and breathing exercises (as outlined in Chapter 5), coping with panic attacks (as outlined in Chapter 6), sleep hygiene and other more general stress management strategies. One example of a stress management training programme that has been found to be useful at this stage is 'stress inoculation training', which teaches the individual to manage their fear and anxiety via a variety of coping skills. The individual is taught to manage physical and autonomic over-arousal through muscular relaxation, and breathing exercises. They are also taught the cognitive technique of guided self-dialogue and the behavioural techniques of covert modelling and role play (Meichenbaum and Jarenko 1983).

The trauma-focused phase

In this phase, the individual is taught specific techniques aimed at alleviating PTSD symptoms. These include changing maladaptive behaviours such as avoidance, escape and withdrawal behaviours using direct exposure techniques, which involve repeated prolonged confronting of reminders of the trauma which cause the individual distress. When exposed to stimuli associated with the trauma, the individual relives the traumatic experience and the fear associated with it. However, repeated exposure facilitates habituation of the anxiety and ultimately modifies the cognitive appraisal of the feared situations (Foa et al. 1991). Exposure to the feared stimuli is usually conducted in a graded hierarchical way (as outlined in the section on behavioural interventions in Chapter 3). If the stimuli involved are particularly distressing for the individual, it may be necessary to begin with exposure 'in imagination' and then progress to real life situations, in order to prevent the individual from being overwhelmed.

Cognitive techniques used include those outlined in the section on cognitive interventions in Chapter 3. For example, positive assumptions about one's own vulnerability, the safety of the world and the trustworthiness of others may have been shattered and need to be re-established. Also, it is not uncommon for individuals to experience what is called 'survivor guilt', in that they survived when others did not. They may have resentment towards others, who they felt did not do what they should or could have done to prevent the incident from happening. They may be ashamed that they did not do more to help others, or of their own reactions, such as putting themselves before others or behaving in a cowardly way. Cognitive techniques can be very helpful in assisting individuals with restructuring their experiences cognitively and consequently their emotional reactions to it.

Cognitive imagery techniques have also been found to be effective in treating flashbacks and intrusive images associated with PTSD (Smucker and Dancu 1999; Smucker *et al.* 1996). Typically, the individual is initially asked to imagine safe imagery, for example a pleasant memory or experience from the past, when they felt at their most relaxed, happy or secure. They are asked to imagine the experience through all sensory modalities (sight, sound, smell, touch and taste). This is known as the 'safe place', to which they can return in imagination at any time. In imagery transformation, they are then encouraged to manipulate the safe images by, for example, transforming the size, shape, colour, brightness, contrast and position of various objects in the image, altering the volume of sounds and so on.

Once the individual is able to transform images successfully, they are then asked to expose themselves to the traumatic imagery and practise transforming the distressing image into a less threatening one. This could, for example, involve turning down the brightness of the image using a dimmer switch until it disappears, introducing an object such as a cloud or a smoke screen to block out the distressing image, closing the curtains on the image or introducing something bizarre or even humorous into the image to make it feel less threatening. Imagery re-scripting may involve changing the ending or outcome and essentially re-writing the 'script' to the story, with the aim of replacing traumatic imagery with mastery imagery. The aim of this form of therapy is not to pretend or deny that the event happened but to introduce more positive and less distressing images, which enable the individual to experience less distress and cope more effectively.

Finally, there is a technique known as eye movement desensitization reprocessing or EMDR (Shapiro 1989, 1995). This technique is not described in detail here but it is mentioned because it contains cognitive and behavioural aspects, which include exposure to traumatic memories and identifying alternative cognitive appraisals of a memory. There are mixed views on the efficacy of EMDR (Poole *et al.* 1990; Richards 1999; Rosen *et al.* 1999; Shapiro and Forrest 1997) and, at the present time, 'the jury is out' as to whether or not it is an effective treatment for PTSD.

Relapse prevention and follow-up phases

In the relapse prevention phase, the individual is taught skills and strategies for dealing with a possible relapse (as outlined in the section on relapse prevention in Chapter 3). In the follow-up phase, the clinician and the patient work together to monitor the patient's functioning and provide the structure necessary for the patient to maintain the gains that have been made.

Health anxiety

Although the *DSM-IV-TR* (APA 2000) defines health anxiety as a type of somatoform disorder known as hyperchondriasis, rather than an anxiety disorder, it has been included in this chapter because it does have a number of conceptual similarities on a cognitive behavioural level to anxiety disorders. Also, in the context of this book it is termed 'health anxiety'. The main defining feature of health anxiety disorder is the belief that one has a serious disease, based on a misinterpretation of bodily symptoms, and this pre-occupation persists despite appropriate medical evaluation and reassurance which indicates that no disease is present. This preoccupation causes the individual significant distress or impairment; beliefs must be held for at least six months before a diagnosis is made. This belief is not considered to be delusional, since the individual can usually acknowledge that they may be exaggerating the extent of the feared disease, or even that there may be no disease at all. It is estimated that the prevalence of health anxiety in the general population is up to 5% (APA 2000).

Health service professionals, by the nature of their training and work, are exposed to much more information about illness and disease symptoms than the general public. For example, medical students are exposed to a broad range of symptoms of serious diseases, which can lead some more susceptible students to an excessive preoccupation with their own health (Woods *et al.* 1966). The histories of individuals who are more likely to be disposed to health anxiety often include having experienced illness or death of a family member, or being exposed to over-concerned attitudes of parents towards illness during their early developmental years. In one study, Paris and Frank (1984) found that male medical students were more likely to have experienced illness in the family during their childhood than other students. It is hypoth-esized that such experiences influence how the person perceives situations and can lead to negative core beliefs such as 'I am vulnerable to illness,' or dysfunctional attitudes such as 'People should always expect the worst when they get symptoms.'

The CBT assessment, formulation and treatment approach to health anx-iety is based upon the work of Salkovskis (1989), Warwick and Salkovskis (1990), Warwick *et al.* (1996) and Wells (1997). However, it is not discussed in this chapter since it is covered in detail in the case illustration of 'Colin' in Chapter 11 of this book.

Chapter 8

Cognitive behavioural therapy for work-related depression and other occupational stress syndromes

Martin Bamber

WORK-RELATED DEPRESSION

The *DSM-IV-TR* (American Psychiatric Association 2000) classifies depression into a number of sub-categories and distinctions are made between unipolar and bipolar, neurotic and psychotic and major depression and dysthymic disorder. These sub-categorizations provide conceptual distinctions which are clinically very helpful to the clinician trying to treat depression. When people are depressed, they feel low in mood, tearful and troubled by thoughts and feelings of low worth, guilt and self-reproach. They may be more irritable than usual, have little energy or motivation, lose interest in things that they previously enjoyed and everything seems like a big effort. They become less active, lose their appetite, experience sleep problems and sexual desire disappears. In severe cases of depression there is a risk of suicidal behaviour. In the context of this chapter, depression refers to the less severe end of the spectrum, namely non-psychotic, unipolar depression, since it is for this type of depression that cognitive behavioural therapy has been designed and extensively tested.

Depression is one of the most common workplace problems and is associated with more chronic problems in the work role than those which give rise to anxiety disorders (Firth and Britton 1989; Firth and Hardy 1992; Golding 1989; Heim 1991; Holt 1982; Phelan *et al.* 1991; Rayburn 1991; Snapp 1992; Warr 1990). Higher levels of depression have been found in the helping professions than the general public (De Leo *et al.* 1982; Firth *et al.* 1987; Holland 1985; Kahill 1988; Kalra *et al.* 1987; Krakowski 1985). CBT is the psychological treatment of choice for depression (Beck *et al.* 1979; Department of Health 2002; Firth-Cozens 1987; National Institute for Clinical Excellence 2004a; Valko and Clayton 1975). Cognitive behaviour therapy does not claim that negative thinking and unhelpful behaviour patterns are the sole cause of job-related depression, but rather that certain thoughts maintain and exacerbate it (Beck 1995).

The traditional cognitive formulation of depression (Beck 1967, 1976) is illustrated in Figure 8.1. It proposes that as a result of adverse early

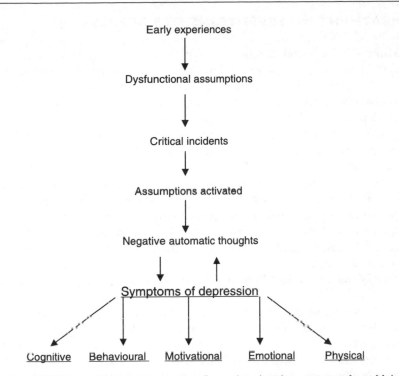

Figure 8.1 A CBT formulation of depression. Reproduced with permission from Melanie Fennell (Fennell 2000).

experiences, individuals form dysfunctional beliefs and assumptions about themselves, others and the world around them. These beliefs are used to organize perceptions and to govern and evaluate behaviour (as discussed in the cognitively mediated model of stress outlined in Chapter 1). Clinical depression does not arise from these dysfunctional assumptions alone but is triggered when critical incidents occur which mesh with the person's own unhealthy belief systems. For example, if the dysfunctional belief is that one's personal worth is entirely dependent upon success, then this could lead to depression in the face of failure; alternatively, the belief that to be loved is essential to happiness could trigger depression following rejection. Once activated, these assumptions produce an upsurge of negative automatic thoughts and unpleasant emotions, which in turn lead to the behavioural, motivational, emotional and cognitive symptoms of depression. As depression develops, a vicious cycle is formed whereby more rational thoughts are crowded out and an increasingly pervasive depressed mood develops (Fennell 2000).

TREATMENT INTERVENTIONS FOR DEPRESSION

Cognitive behavioural therapy aims to break the negative cycle described above by teaching the patient to question and challenge the negative automatic thoughts and dysfunctional assumptions upon which they are based and also identify and change the unhelpful patterns of behaviour associated with depression. The patient is taught to identify characteristic patterns of negative thinking by use of a 'thoughts diary'. The patient is then taught to challenge these negative thought patterns using specific cognitive techniques (as outlined in Chapters 3 and 5). These include looking at the evidence for and against the negative thoughts being true (rather like a jury in a court of law), coming up with more balanced and realistic alternative (less distressing) explanations for distressing situations, looking at the advantages and disadvantages of thinking in that way and challenging distortions. If patients can successfully challenge their negative automatic thoughts, they can gradually begin to feel better.

One of the main behavioural approaches used to treat depressed patients is known as 'activity scheduling'. Individuals who are depressed tend to withdraw from and stop doing the activities that previously they used to enjoy. They become unmotivated and inactive, which in turn provides even more time to ruminate on their negative thoughts. This creates a downward spiral of inactivity, which tends to make their mood even worse. Keeping an activity schedule allows the individual to structure the day better and plan a gradual increase in activity. Patients are also asked to rate these activities for 'mastery' (how good they are at it) and 'pleasure' (how much they enjoy it). By doing this, they can identify which activities they find pleasurable and satisfying and introduce more of these into the schedule.

Behavioural experiments are extremely useful when treating depressed patients, since they provide additional evidence to the patient through the process of hypothesis testing. The patient is encouraged to challenge negative predictions about future events with more positive alternative hypotheses. They are then encouraged to find out exactly what the outcome was to that given situation and how it compared with the predictions made. Invariably, because the predictions made are excessively negative and gloomy, as one would expect in depression, the outcome is more positive than the individual's predictions and can be used as evidence to disconfirm their depressive thinking patterns. Consequently, most behavioural experiments will have the effect of weakening the patient's original negative view of situations and events and at the same time strengthening alternative more positive explanations.

All of the above techniques are taught in therapy sessions and practised by the patient as homework assignments, supplemented by bibliotherapy (e.g. Burns 1990; Gilbert 1997; Greenberger and Padesky 1995). Regular assessments using measures of depression can be used to monitor progress and reinforce change. A detailed case study outlining the assessment, formulation and treatment of a patient called 'Patrick' suffering from work-related depression is presented in Chapter 10, to illustrate the approach.

THE BURNOUT SYNDROME

Burnout is a particular type of stress syndrome associated specifically with work (Cherniss 1980; Einsiedel and Tully 1981; Maslach 1976; Pines and Aronson 1981; Starrin et al. 1990). There are numerous conceptualizations and definitions of burnout in the literature on occupational stress (Cherniss 1980; Maslach 1982; Maslach and Jackson 1984; Pines and Aronson 1981). However, there is currently no *DSM* classification for the burnout syndrome. Some authors argue that burnout is basically work-related depression (Lowman 1997). However, others such as Cherniss (1980) argue that burnout differs from depression because, in classical depression, a person's symptoms appear to manifest across all situations, whereas a person who is burned out in the work sphere may function well in non-work spheres. Many conceptualizations of burnout have indicated the primacy of emotional exhaustion (Koeske and Koeske 1989; Maslach and Florian 1988; Wallace and Brinkeroff 1991). Furnham (1997: 343), for example, defines burnout as the 'outcome of physical, emotional and psychological exhaustion, which may be symptomatic of being alienated from one's work'. Whatever the stance taken, the research literature indicates that there is a considerable overlap between burnout, depression and various elements of job satisfaction and that it is related to greater absenteeism, increased staff turnover, patient abuse and detrimental effects on work performance and job commitment (Harris 1988; Jackson et al. 1987; Kahill 1988; Leiter and Maslach 1988; McGee 1989; Meier 1984; Pillemer and Bachman-Prehn 1991).

Burnout is reported to be highest in the caring professions (Ackerley et al. 1988; Borg 1990: Farber and Heifetz 1982; Matthews 1990). It is believed to be a longitudinal change process over a period of time, consisting of three stages: emotional exhaustion, depersonalization and low personal accomplishment. People entering the caring professions often do so with high ideals and a strong commitment to helping others. However, the initial idealism fades in the light of the reality of working continually with distressed and needy clients in often under-resourced services. The worker finds that the help that can be given is often limited and inadequate and begins to experience the first stage of burnout: emotional exhaustion. As feelings of emotional exhaustion set in the worker's perception of clients changes. There is a gradual withdrawal of emotional involvement with them and an increasing perception that they have caused their own difficulties and are therefore is less worthy of help. Workers often feel that they are being exploited by their clients and experience an increasing sense of depersonalization. As emotional exhaustion and negative attitudes towards clients increase, workers become increasingly dissatisfied with themselves. They begin to feel that they do not understand the clients or accomplish much in their work with them. As the feeling of low personal accomplishment takes hold, employees feel that they are not up to the job and ultimately experience a lowering of self-esteem (Golembiewski and Kim 1989; Harrison 1983; Maslach 1976; Maslach and Jackson 1984).

Some of the most common signs and symptoms of burnout include a high resistance to going to work every day, a sense of failure, anger and resentment, discouragement and indifference, isolation and withdrawal, feeling tired and exhausted all day, clock watching, loss of positive feelings towards clients, avoiding client contact, a more cynical and blaming attitude towards clients, avoiding discussion of work with colleagues, frequent colds and flu, frequent headaches, high absenteeism, poor sleep and increased use of drugs and alcohol (Cherniss 1980; Maslach 1976). Interactions of burnout with a range of other psychological variables have been reported in the literature, such as type A behaviour patterns (Burke and Greenglass 1988; Cherniss 1980; Conte *et al.* 2002; Evans *et al.* 1987; Greenglass 1990; Idemudia *et al.* 2001; Jamal 1990; Kushnir and Melamed 1991; Lavanco 1997; Mazur and Lynch 1989; Nagy and Davis 1985; Nowack 1988; Price 1982), locus of control (Ganster and Fusilier 1989; St. Yves *et al.* 1989), compulsive personality (Lemkau *et al.* 1988), hardiness (Norwack 1986; Topf 1989) and self-esteem (McCranie and Brandsma 1988).

TREATMENT INTERVENTIONS FOR BURNOUT

Some multi-modal treatments have been developed to treat the symptoms of the burnout syndrome, which incorporate both cognitive and behavioural components. These include stress reduction programmes and general stress management techniques (Bair and Greenspan 1986; Higgins 1986), physical exercise and relaxation training (Watkins 1983) and modification of patterns of over-commitment to work such as type A, obsessional and perfectionistic behaviour patterns (Burns 1999; Fontana 1997; Lowman 1997). Other interventions have focused on changing aspects of the individual's working environment (Riggar *et al.* 1984). Changing aspects of the work environment, general stress management techniques and relaxation training have been covered in Chapter 5 of this book. This section will thus focus on the modification of patterns of over-commitment to work associated with the development of the burnout syndrome.

Modifying the type A behaviour pattern

Type A behaviours include moving, walking and eating rapidly, pressured speech, emphatic gestures, always being impatient and in a hurry, trying to hurry others, finishing others' sentences for them, pretending to listen but actually thinking about something else, turning conversation to themes which have personal interest, taking on too many tasks, doing two or more things at the same time, trying to pack more and more into less and less time, making too little allowance for unforeseen events which might disrupt one's schedule and becoming frustrated and angry with others for being too slow or unmotivated. Such individuals are highly competitive and challenging, find it extremely difficult to relax and feel guilty about relaxing.

Thus, interventions for type A employees involve modifying all the above behaviours in an attempt to get the individual to behave more like a type B individual. These might include, for example, practising speaking deliberately more slowly, becoming less competitive and hostile, giving in now and again, going the long way round when travelling somewhere, hiding one's watch, scheduling a rest period in the middle of a busy day, focusing more on quality than speed or quantity, taking time to observe others and smile at them, taking time to listen to others and explore their points more, going to places where one will be made to wait, being more willing to disclose one's failures to others and giving compliments to others (Fontana 1997; Wycherley 1990). Role-play of these new behaviours and real-life behavioural experiments can be particularly helpful in this respect.

Many type A individuals argue that they just don't want to change, or that everything would be fine if other people would stop being so inefficient. Indeed, there are considerable rewards in our culture for individuals who display this type of behaviour. However, recent research has shown that type A individuals are more prone to stress-related illness and burnout than type B individuals (Cherniss 1980; Fletcher 1991; Fontana 1997; Ross and Altmaier 1994). Thus, there may be a need to educate individuals about some of the recent research findings relating to the harmful health consequences of type A behaviours, in order to increase their motivation and compliance with the therapy. Discussing the pros and cons of behavioural change is one useful way of doing this.

Modifying obsessionality

Obsessional individuals are very rigid and fixed in their thinking and uncompromising and stubborn in their behaviours. In the work context, they get stressed when the work environment does not fit round their obsessionality and spend much time and effort trying to make it do so. They attempt to control the behaviour of others, insist on rigid adherence to rules and strict standards of performance for themselves and others, are inflexible over moral or conduct issues and are highly critical and unforgiving of their own and others' mistakes. They often try to impose order on things which do not behave in a neat and orderly way, and experience considerable frustration when this is unsuccessful. They find it difficult to delegate but, if they do, they may give detailed instructions about the 'right' way to do things and expect them to be carried out to the letter. They have a low tolerance of ambiguity and find organizational change difficult to manage (Fontana 1997: 74).

It is thought that the motivation underlying obsessional behaviour is the reduction of anxiety (Andrews and Crino 1991; Naughton 1987). Jobs which are not neat and orderly, where roles are not clearly defined, where there are not clearly defined lines of accountability, where there are not clearly pre-scribed rules, policies and procedures or where change and new challenges are the norm are extremely anxiety-provoking, frustrating and stressful for these individuals. If the stress experienced continues unabated, it can ultimately lead to burnout.

Interventions for modifying obsessional behaviours involve introducing other incompatible behaviours such as listening to others' points of view more, not treating every interaction as a battle to be won, giving way and allowing others to get their own way sometimes, more compromise and con-sensus in decision-making, varying routines, doing things in a different order, not trying to be perfect all the time and delegating more. Individuals are also encouraged to get a better balance between work and home life by spending less time at work and expanding non-work-related social and leisure activ-ities. They are also encouraged to confront rather than avoid anxiety-provoking situations such as taking on new challenges, embracing change rather than shying away from it, putting themselves in situations of uncertainty and ambiguity more and learning to tolerate the distress that this causes.

Cognitive techniques are useful in challenging the rigid and dysfunctional beliefs and attitudes that these individuals hold. The techniques outlined in Chapter 3 are applicable here. The patient is helped to challenge entrenched dichotomous thinking and encouraged to see the middle ground, or the 'grey areas', more. Their rigid attitudes about unrelenting standards of perform-ance for themselves and others and moral imperatives ('shoulds') can be successfully modified using these techniques. The patient is then encouraged to adopt more healthy attitudes such as: 'It is OK not to be in control all the time,' 'I do not have to get my own way all the time,' 'Not everything fits into a neat and orderly pattern,' 'Change and uncertainty are not always a bad thing,' and 'Work is a means to an end, rather than an end in itself.' The patient is also encouraged to be less critical and more forgiving of their and others' mistakes and to adopt a more relaxed and easy-going attitude to life.

As for the type A behaviour pattern, the individual with obsessional behaviour may initially be resistive to change, since they may perceive it as a positive thing. Where this is the case, they should be encouraged to under-stand the impact of this behaviour on them personally in terms of the harm-ful consequences of the chronic stress that it causes them. It may also be useful to point out tactfully the impact that it can have on others they work with, and the problems that it can cause for the organization. A discussion of the pros and cons of changing this pattern of behaviour can be helpful in determining the motivation to change.

Modifying perfectionism

Perfectionism involves the setting of extremely high standards of performance. Two types of perfectionism have been reported. These are healthy perfectionism, where the behaviour is positively reinforced by the rewards and goals attained, and unhealthy perfectionism, where an individual is striving to prevent an unwanted outcome (such as disapproval by self or others) by a process of negative reinforcement (Slade and Owens, 1998). Unlike those with 'normal' high standards, people with unhealthy perfectionism are unable to accept even a minor flaw in their work (Hamacheck, 1978). However, perfectionists are not necessarily efficient people, since their excessive focus on getting things just right reduces their productivity. Perfectionists believe that nothing less than 100% is good enough and strive to avoid making mistakes at all costs. They adopt these unrealistic expectations not only for themselves but also for others and become irritated when others fail to meet the standards set. Because being perfect is an unachievable ideal, perfectionists are constantly giving themselves the message that they have failed and others have let them down.

Interventions for modifying perfectionism

Cognitive interventions for perfectionism include helping the patient to realize that perfectionism is an unachievable ideal, that everyone makes mistakes and that to do so is an inevitable part of being human. The advantages and disadvantages of thinking in this way are explored with the patient. In particular, the disadvantages are highlighted, in that while striving for perfection can produce some high quality work, generally it leads to constant feelings of tension and anxiety. It can also on occasions result in the patient becoming paralysed with the fear of failure, constant self-flagellation and poor relationships with others.

Alternative ways of thinking are introduced, such as: 'It is all right to make mistakes sometimes,' 'Everyone makes mistakes,' 'No-one is perfect,' 'We can learn from our mistakes,' and 'It's all right to achieve less than 100% on most occasions.' These new rules for living can then be tested out using behavioural experiments and the outcomes monitored by the patient, to use as evidence that in most situations less than perfect performance does not result in the catastrophic consequences feared. Also, the patient is encouraged to think less dichotomously and, rather than seeing situations as win–lose, good–bad or success–failure, is encouraged to see the middle ground and rate their achievements on a continuum. For example, the patient may rate their performance as 70% successful.

On a behavioural level, the patient is encouraged to focus more on activities that they enjoy, rather than only sticking to things that they are good at. An activity schedule in which they rate each activity for 'mastery' (how good they are at it) and 'pleasure' (how much enjoyment they get from it) can help the patient identify what they find pleasurable. They are encouraged to take on hobbies and interests that they enjoy and find satisfying, even if they are not very good at them. Similarly, they are encouraged to try out new activities which previously they may have avoided because of their fear of failure. Overall, the aim of therapy is to teach the patient that it is acceptable to 'accomplish less and accomplish it less perfectly' (Young *et al.* 2003: 265), that it is also acceptable to be average at something (Burns 1999) and that the feared catastrophic consequences of dropping their unrelenting standards do not materialize. The patient can also be helped to realize the benefits both socially and occupationally of adopting a more relaxed and easy-going attitude to life.

Modifying over-identification with work

Over-identification with one's job develops subtly and insidiously. Many people confess to not realizing how strong this identification has become until they are made redundant, retired or moved into a different form of employment. When these changes occur they find themselves devastated and no longer sure who they are, or what use they are to themselves or anyone else. Over-identification means that a major part of one's sense of significance and self-worth has become bound up in one's job. Briefly summarized, these individuals believe, 'My worth is my work.' Such individuals dedicate very little time to life activities and tend to see themselves personally and socially in terms of a job label. They may be obsessionals or type A individuals, or simply lonely people whose job compensates for their lack of family and friends. Alternatively, they may be insecure individuals who need their job to give them status and a sense of self-worth. Whatever the cause, they can become quite aggressive or defensive if their professional status or pride is challenged and end up having major interpersonal conflicts with work colleagues who challenge them (Fontana 1997).

Interventions for modifying over-identification with work

If the cause of over-identification is rooted in obsessionality or type A behaviour, then this needs to be treated accordingly. If the cause is loneliness, then the over-identifier needs to build more of a social life outside work. If the cause is insecurity, the over-identifier needs to develop other roles and take on other tasks in their life outside work, which provide them with other sources of status and self-worth that are totally unrelated to work. Because these individuals are more prone to becoming angry, it can be useful for them to learn the anger management strategies outlined later in this chapter. The standard cognitive techniques outlined in Chapter 3 can be employed to identify and challenge their dysfunctional beliefs and assumptions about 'one's worth is one's work' and to help them see that there are other non-work activities which can also provide a source of status, success and a sense of self-worth.

In summary, there is a wide range of treatment interventions which aim to change the dysfunctional cognitions and behaviours associated with the patterns of over-commitment, which can lead to the individual becoming burned out. However, while these standard CBT interventions have been found to be helpful when the dysfunctional beliefs and behaviours associated with burnout are flexible and of moderate severity, they have not been found to be effective with more extreme, rigid and inflexible beliefs and behavioural patterns. Unfortunately, the patterns of over-commitment described in this section are often chronic and entrenched. Where this is the case, the use of a more in-depth schema-focused approach to therapy is recommended (as outlined in Part 3 of this book). In particular, a schema-focused model of burnout and a case study illustrating the use of schema therapy to treat burnout can be found in Chapter 15.

THE HOSTILITY SYNDROME

There appears to be a low incidence of *DSM-IV-TR* (APA 2000) 'impulse control' problems among health care workers (Bamber 1995; McPherson 2004). One can speculate on possible explanations for this. Perhaps health service employees are less aggressive by temperament? However, there is no evidence to suggest that they do not experience the same cognitive and emotional manifestations of anger as anyone else. It may be that violent incidents are under-reported by employees, due to the severe sanctions imposed on those who display such behaviours, such as disciplinary action, loss of job and even criminal charges. Or perhaps health care workers have learned through their training to control their natural behavioural inclinations towards aggressive behaviour?

It is proposed that many aggressive feelings that health care workers experience, cognitively and emotionally, are channelled into alternative displacement behaviours, which collectively may be called 'letting off steam'. Examples of such displacement behaviours include banging a desk, raising one's voice, slamming a door to vent angry feelings, or the proverbial 'kicking of the cat'. They may verbalize a desire to punch someone on the nose, engage in sarcasm directed towards the perpetrator, or become increasingly cynical about their work and those they are there to help but stop short of acting out their feelings of frustration on patients.

However, of great concern is the possibility that health care workers may find more destructive outlets through which they can displace their angry feelings onto non-patients (colleagues) or others in their personal life (family, partner or children). In one's personal life this could take the form of physical abuse and domestic violence. In the workplace it could manifest itself in more subtle forms of aggressive behaviour, such as bullying, harassment, humiliation, interpersonal conflicts, passive aggression and acts of rebellion, which are more difficult to quantify. Certainly the data on bullying in the NHS, presented in the section on interpersonal causes of stress in Chapter 2 of this book, indicate that bullying and harassment are rife in the NHS and displacement provides one explanation as to why this is the case. Whatever the explanation, those suffering from the hostility syndrome experience their environment as more provoking, experience more frustration, have more arguments with their work colleagues, perceive more job stressors, experience lower job satisfaction and are more likely to engage in acts of sabotage of others' work than non-angry individuals (Spector 1998).

The experience of anger is usually triggered by the perception that one has been treated unfairly (Beck 1976; Burns 1990; Clore *et al.* 1993). It consists of cognitive, behavioural, emotional and physiological components. Physiologically one experiences a heightened state of arousal (Novaco 1978). For example, one may feel one's body tense up and experience the heart thumping. Cognitively, one demonstrates systematic biases in information processing such as extreme overgeneralization, known as 'globalizing' or 'monsterizing'. One condemns the whole person, magnifies all the negative aspects of the other person, mentally filters out all the positives and polarizes and blames the person to whom they attribute the injustice (Burns 1990: 141). The key point here is that these are distortions about the alleged perpetrator that are often very much exaggerated. Behavioural reactions may consist of physical acts of antagonism, verbal antagonism, passive aggression or avoidance (Tulloch 1991). Geen (1990) utilizes Lazarus's notions of primary and secondary appraisal (Lazarus 1966; Lazarus and Folkman 1984) to describe the cognitive mediation of a provoking event (as described in the cognitively mediated model of stress in Chapter 1) and the ultimate decision whether or not to behave in an aggressive way.

Interventions for managing anger

Most anger management training programmes teach an anger management 'package'. The interventions described in this section are derived from the work of Novaco (1975, 1978, 1993, 1994, 1997), Becker *et al.* (1997), Feindler and Ecton (1986) and Howells (1988, 1989, 1999). They consist of a number of components such as relaxation training and breathing techniques to reduce physiological arousal, and training in coping skills such as social skills, assertiveness skills, effective communication skills, negotiation skills and problem solving, which are all aimed at broadening the individual's repertoire of coping responses. These are described in Chapter 5 of this book. The use of role-play can also be extremely helpful in this context. In addition, cognitive therapy techniques are used to help the individual challenge the angry cognitions which serve to perpetuate the problem. They are taught techniques such as looking at the evidence for and against, alternative ways of seeing the situation, advantages and disadvantages and correcting distortions, as outlined in Chapter 3 of this book. Burns (1990) argues that cognitive therapy should also address the individual's dysfunctional assumptions about justice, fairness and moral codes of right and wrong, which underlie aggressive reactions.

The individual is then asked to practise these techniques in real-life situations as homework assignments, in order to consolidate the skills learned. If they still have difficulties managing their anger after going through the anger management routine, they are told to 'exit' themselves from the situation, in order to ensure that they do not act upon their aggressive inclinations, and only return to the situation once they have calmed down. They are then hopefully able to talk through it and deal with it in a more rational and objective way than they would when in a state of heightened arousal.

Chapter 9

Theresa: A case of performance anxiety

Mark Latham

INTRODUCTION

Social anxiety is a common and normal phenomenon in the majority of people, but for some it can become severe and frequent, with many social encounters being associated with fear and discomfort, and often avoided. The overriding concerns are with 'performing' in front of people and with the subsequent critical judgements that might be made by others.

The following case study is of a medical student, Theresa, who had no problems socialising with her friends or taking part in everyday social interaction, but the prospect of giving presentations during her training filled her with dread and terror, to the point where her future career was under serious threat.

DEFINITION OF THE DISORDER

The defining feature of social phobia, according to *DSM-IV-TR*, is a 'marked and persistent fear of one or more social or performance situations in which the person is exposed to unfamiliar people or to possible scrutiny by others. The individual fears that he or she will act in a way (or show anxiety symptoms) that will be humiliating or embarrassing' (American Psychiatric Association [APA] 2000: 416). As with most phobic disorders, the feared situations are either avoided or endured with great discomfort, but in social phobia the person is preoccupied with being judged by others as anxious, weak, crazy or stupid. Panic attacks may occur in social situations, or in anticipation of having to enter them, and the problem causes significant distress or impairment to the sufferer's life (APA 2000).

THE HEALTH SERVICE CONTEXT

Medical training entails students acquiring many different skills in order to qualify as doctors, and the means of assessing these skills are varied. One method is via presentation to fellow medical students. Naturally enough, many students find this an anxiety-provoking experience, but one with which they can cope and which usually gets progressively easier the more they do it.

THE COGNITIVE MODEL

The central and defining feature of social phobia is what has been termed the 'processing of self as a social object' (Wells 1997: 169). This refers to the self-consciousness that pervades it and differentiates it from other anxiety disorders. In feared situations social phobics often picture how they appear to others, assuming an 'observer' rather than a 'field' perspective (Hackmann et al. 1998; Wells et al. 1998), and seeing themselves as looking very socially incompetent, often displaying visible symptoms of anxiety, such as shaking, sweating, or blushing (Clark and Wells 1995).

Two processes then maintain and worsen this distorted self-image: internal focus of attention on physical and mental symptoms of anxiety and on anxious thoughts, and the use of safety behaviours to prevent feared consequences from coming true (Salkovskis 1991).

It is understandable that sufferers monitor their bodies for observable signs of anxiety (e.g. shaking), but this has the inevitable effect of providing confirmatory evidence of how obvious their anxiety must be to others. The same process applies to thoughts such as, 'They can see me blushing and must think I'm weak,' whereby the mere presence of the thought and the accompanying anxiety is taken as evidence of the veracity of the self-conscious image. Therefore, the internal focus of attention confirms the worst fears and also prevents any contradictory evidence being found that might suggest an alternative perspective (Wells and Papageorgiou 2001).

Anticipatory anxiety and post-event processing play a role in further maintaining social phobia (Clark and Wells 1995). When a socially anxious individual knows they are going to be in a social situation, they think about what might go wrong regarding their own performance. These forecasts of social disaster are likely to preoccupy them prior to the event, leading to an increase in anxiety, which in turn leads to further dire predictions of what will happen. Thus, a vicious cycle is set up.

Even in instances where the social event seems, at first glance, to have gone well, it is not long before the evaluation of it afterwards changes it to a social catastrophe. This is due to post-event processing, whereby details of performance are dwelt on, resulting in ever more negative conclusions.

REFERRAL

Theresa's GP referred her to the Psychotherapy Department, stating in his letter that she had been unable to complete a recent assessment in her medical training that required her to present to her peers. Her tutor suggested that she seek help. She had found propanolol medication only partially effective.

ASSESSMENT

Symptom profile

Theresa was comfortable in most informal social situations, but dreaded having to give formal presentations as part of her medical training. She experienced considerable anticipatory anxiety, often weeks in advance of the presentation, which built steadily as the event approached. Her key cognitions were all associated with how badly she would perform in front of her fellow medical students. Typical examples included: 'I'll go to pieces,' 'It'll be obvious that I'm nervous as hell,' 'They'll see me blushing,' and 'They'll think I'm pathetic.' The day before the presentation she noticed marked physiological symptoms of anxiety, particularly feeling tremulous, hot, and flushed, with a churning stomach, dry mouth, and increased heart rate. Her strategies to cope with this anxiety involved intense preparation, such as completing the presentation days or even weeks in advance, rehearsing its delivery up to a dozen times beforehand, continually making minor amendments to it, and familiarising herself with the room in which she was due to present. Usually, however, she did not go ahead with the presentation, choosing instead to avoid it by saying she was ill. She had gone through with two presentations, but had found both occasions torrid affairs. Her anxiety escalated on the day and she employed a raft of additional behaviours to try and cope. These included wearing heavy foundation make-up, drinking lots of water before and during the presentation, wearing loose-fitting clothing, keeping her hands in her pockets, and speaking very rapidly. She finished the presentation both times and then ruminated about how she had come across to her peers, concluding that the whole event had been a disaster.

History of the disorder

Theresa had several memories of incidents at primary school when she had been asked by the teacher to read out loud to the rest of the class and had experienced acute anxiety and embarrassment. When she chose medical training she had been unaware that her fears would re-surface, but the past year had become increasingly difficult and as a result she had contemplated discontinuing the course.

Personal background

She came from a Catholic family in Northern Ireland. Her father was a teacher and her mother was a part-time cleaner, and both were very supportive of Theresa's decision to become a doctor. She was the fifth of seven children and had achieved more, academically, than any of her four brothers and two sisters. She had always had plenty of friends and had been quite sporty, and she continued like this when she moved to England at 18 to start medical training. One of her older brothers had alcohol problems, and a maternal aunt had 'bad nerves', but otherwise there was no known family history of psychological problems.

Presentation

At the initial meeting Theresa was tearful when recounting her problem and sought reassurance that it was possible to change it. She was casually dressed and was engaging in her manner, showing no signs of the anxiety that plagued her in more formal social settings.

Suitability for short-term CBT

Promising prognostic indicators included her ability to identify her emotions and key cognitions readily, evidence of good alliance in and out of session, and her ability to focus. She had had the problem for many years, which did not bode so well, and her optimism and acceptance of personal responsibility for change could have been greater (Safran and Segal 1990). However, overall there was every reason to believe that CBT would have an impact on her problem.

Psychometric measures

An individualized problem definition was constructed as follows: 'Avoidance of making presentations to my peers, for fear of shaking and blushing making my anxiety obvious and them thinking that I'm pathetic.'

End-of-treatment targets were as follows:

- 'To give presentations as and when necessary in my training without rehearsing them lots of times beforehand.'
- 'Whenever I give a presentation, to refrain from carrying out a "post-mortem" afterwards.'
- 'To volunteer to be the spokesperson who feeds back after group exercises in class whenever the opportunity arises.'

Other measures used were as follows:

- Beck Depression Inventory (BDI; Beck *et al.* 1961)
- Work and Social Adjustment Scale (WSAS; Marks 1986)
- Social Phobia Rating Scale (SPRS; Wells 1997).

See Table 9.1 for Theresa's scores on these psychometric measures.

FORMULATION

Clark and Wells's (1995) cognitive model of social phobia was used as the basis for the maintenance formulation, so that symptom-focused interventions could be used to break the identified vicious cycles. Later, developmental factors were drawn out so that her underlying beliefs could be modified to reduce her vulnerability to relapse. The final version is shown in Figure 9.1. Theresa's experiences at school of having to read out loud seemed to have contributed to the development of beliefs that increased her vulnerability to social anxiety problems later ('It is awful to show anxiety in front of others'). In addition, she was acutely aware of the expectations of her parents who, although immensely supportive, were also very proud of her academic achievements in a way that she experienced as pressure to do well ('I must succeed'). Throughout her childhood she had been used to a competitive atmosphere at home and at school and, despite often outperforming others, she did not really believe that she was as able as others ('I'm not good enough').

Until she reached the point in her medical training when she had to do presentations, it had been relatively easy for her to avoid such activities, but now her underlying beliefs had been activated by this 'critical incident' (Beck *et al.* 1979).

Every time she was due to present, Theresa worried about it for weeks beforehand and anticipated how badly it would go. The consequent anxiety evoked two opposite behaviours: one was to try to avoid thinking about it and to think of excuses for not doing it, and the other was to prepare very thoroughly in order to reduce the chances of it going badly. She made predictions about how she would not cope, how visible her anxiety would be, and what others would think of her, and these led to a very strong image in her mind's eye of how she appeared to other people, particularly blushing 'as red as a post box' and looking frightened. The physiological symptoms also intensified in response to these thoughts, and served as evidence to her that her image was accurate ('I feel hot and flushed, therefore I must look bright red'). Her internal focus of attention, both on physiological feedback and anxious thoughts about evaluation by others, acted as reinforcement of the veracity of her self-conscious image.

Her anxious thoughts also led to several safety behaviours, all intended to prevent her fears from coming true. For example, heavy make-up was to conceal her blushing, loose-fitting clothes were to keep her cool, water was

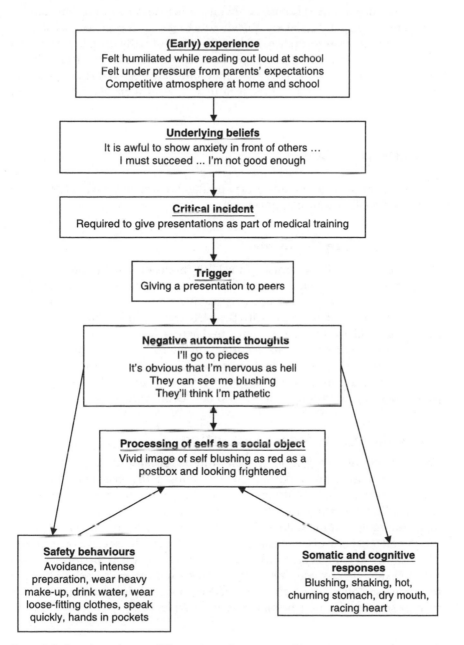

Figure 9.1 Case formulation of Theresa's performance anxiety.

to help her dry mouth, keeping her hands in her pockets to prevent shaking becoming visible, and speaking quickly was to get it all over with as soon as possible. In the short term these all had the effect of reducing her anxiety, but they had to be used each time she got anxious, so they were ineffective in the longer term and, more importantly, they prevented disconfirmation of her fears – that is, they reinforced the idea that without them she would appear more anxious.

TREATMENT PLAN

The treatment plan was broadly based on that advocated by Wells (1997) and comprised the following components.

Socialization to the model

Helping clients get a good grasp of the CBT model of social phobia and how it applies to them provides a rationale for all of the interventions that follow. While this can be done verbally, it is usually more powerful if there is an experiential element to it as well (Bennett-Levy *et al.* 2004), which often comes from behavioural experiments. In Theresa's case, it was important to illustrate the effects of focusing her attention internally, and the role of safety behaviours on her self-consciousness and on how she performed socially. The overall aim of socialising her to the model was to help her to understand the psychological processes that maintained her social phobia.

Manipulating the focus of attention

This is a crucial intervention in social phobia because it targets the attentional bias that is so important in maintaining the problem (Wells and Papageorgiou 1998). By shifting the focus of attention from an internal to an external direction, it reduces the confirmatory evidence from negative automatic thoughts and physiological symptoms, and at the same time increases the opportunity for disconfirmatory evidence from the social environment. Theresa was so preoccupied with how she was feeling when 'performing' that she rarely sought any additional information from the reactions of her peers to her presentation. This strategy needed to be implemented early on in therapy so that she could examine this extra evidence.

Thought records

Evaluation of her negative automatic thoughts could take place using 'thought records' (Greenberger and Padesky 1995). Once she had shifted her focus of attention so it was not being directed internally, she then potentially had access to external evidence that she could use to weigh up how likely it was that her feared consequence would occur – that people would notice her anxiety and judge her as pathetic.

Banning anticipatory processing

Theresa worried endlessly about all the bad things that might happen when she presented to her peers. This catastrophization increased her anxiety to the point where she found it hard to concentrate, so it was important for her to reduce this as much as possible. One strategy to help her do this was to look at the costs and benefits of worrying about it beforehand (Wells 1997: 191), while another was to complete a 'thought record'.

Dropping safety behaviours

Because of their role in preventing disconfirmation of the feared consequence, it was important that she stopped using her various safety behaviours. The best way to do this is usually through behavioural experiments that test out specific predictions about other people's reactions, or what Wells refers to as 'interrogating the environment' (Wells 1997: 191).

Video work

Unique to social phobia is the central part played by the self-conscious image one has of how one appears to others, or the 'processing of self as a social object' (Clark and Wells 1995). The biases of perception and inter-pretation that occur in social phobia mean that this image is highly likely to be negatively distorted and will not match with what others actually see. An innovative technique arising from the model is the use of video to act as an objective view of one's social performance (Bates and Clark 1998). Crucial to its success is the establishment in advance of the person's spe-cific predictions of how they will look. Theresa's image of herself blushing 'as red as a post box' and looking frightened could be modified by this means.

Banning post-mortems

Post-event processing will usually change someone's evaluation of the out-come of a social event for the worse (Clark and Wells 1995). The conclusion reached is more negative than that reached immediately after the social event and is likely to contribute to more anxiety prior to the next one. Therefore, post-event processing needs to be banned in the same way as anticipatory processing, with the rationale provided by a cost–benefit analysis, and the content being re-evaluated through use of thought records. Theresa had managed to carry out presentations only twice, but each time had ruminated afterwards at length.

Belief modification

It is often necessary to identify and start to modify underlying beliefs to help prevent relapse. These might be the rules about what is acceptable socially and/or the core beliefs that the person holds about themselves and others. Wells uses the phrase 'increasing the "bandwidth" ' to describe the process of widening the range of what we consider to be socially acceptable behaviour for ourselves (Wells 1997). Any verbal discussion is best accompanied by a behavioural experiment to test out the new, more flexible, rule. The advantage of Theresa doing this would be that the 'cost' of blushing or appearing anxious in other ways would not be as great.

PROGRESS OF THERAPY

Session 1

Socialization to the CBT model was the main aim of the first session, involving two short experiments carried out in the room. First, Theresa was asked to imagine herself in an anxiety-provoking situation and to focus on her physiological symptoms (especially feeling hot and shaky), much as she would usually in this type of situation. She rated how anxious she felt on a 0–10 scale and then was encouraged to focus even more on these symptoms. This measurement revealed, perhaps unsurprisingly, that her anxiety worsened the more she paid attention to the symptoms. She was then asked to focus her attention, in her imagination, on the room she was in, the people she was presenting to, and the material she was presenting, rather than her bodily reactions, and to rate her anxiety after a few minutes. Theresa found that her anxiety reduced, thus reinforcing the idea that her internal focus of attention was one factor maintaining her problem.

The second experiment concerned one of her safety behaviours. She was asked to read out loud a five-minute excerpt from one of her presentations at two different speeds and to rate how anxious she felt each time. She found that the faster speed of speaking actually made her more anxious than if she slowed down, thus having the opposite effect to the one she intended.

Session 2

Theresa gave a 10-minute presentation to four people (the therapist and three of his colleagues), during which she spent the first five minutes focusing her attention externally on the audience and on the content of her presentation, before switching her attention to her bodily symptoms and thoughts about how she was performing. As in the previous session, she found that when she switched her attention from an external to an internal focus, she became more anxious. Homework from this session was to note the effects of switching her attention from an internal to an external focus in a range of social situations.

Sessions 3 and 4

During the homework review she concluded that, although she had not been more than mildly anxious in any of the social situations she had encountered over the previous week, she had nevertheless discovered that her perception of events was substantially affected by whether her attention was focused externally or internally. Thought records were introduced at this session, and were used in two ways. First, Theresa used evidence that was now available to her when she focused externally, in order to re-evaluate her thoughts about how negatively others were judging her. One problem with doing this was that she did not have any actual presentations at this stage in her training in which to carry out this intervention, so it was practised in session with an audience of the therapist's work colleagues, and then repeated via imaginal scenarios as homework. Despite these limitations, it seemed to have the desired effects of reducing her anxiety and increasing her confidence. Anticipatory process-ing was also addressed by using thought records to de-catastrophize her pre-dictions about a forthcoming presentation to her peers in three weeks' time. Ideally, her use of thought records would have coincided with behavioural experiments to see what happened if she dropped her safety behaviours when presenting, but unfortunately there were no opportunities to do this between sessions.

Session 5

This was a key session in therapy because it provided Theresa with the opportunity to modify her perception of how she came across to others when presenting. To allow enough time to complete it, the session had to be extended to 90 minutes.

Another audience of the therapist's colleagues was arranged for her to practise the presentation that she was due to make to her fellow medical students in a fortnight, but this time it was also videotaped. As part of the previous week's homework, she had made predictions about how she thought she would cope and how people in the audience would react. These included that she would blush, shake, and look awkward, and that others would look embarrassed, avoid eye contact with her, and not ask any questions at the end. In addition, she agreed to start off using several safety behaviours, but then drop them one by one and note what effects this had on her anxiety.

She gave a 15-minute presentation to an audience of seven people.

Afterwards she left the room and the therapist asked the audience for specific feedback about how she had come across, video-recording their responses. The next part of the session involved a discussion between the therapist and Theresa about how she thought she had come across during the presentation. Although she did not think it had been as bad as she had originally predicted (people had appeared interested in what she was saying and had asked quite a few questions at the end), she nevertheless believed she had displayed visible signs of anxiety, including blushing and shaking, and had looked awkward. She was asked to rate how much she believed these evaluations on a 0–100 scale and then she watched the video of her presentation.

Initially, she reacted with embarrassment to seeing herself on the TV monitor, but after a short while was able to concentrate on the specific evaluations she had made. Not only was she surprised at the lack of any visible blushing or shaking, but she was also taken aback by how confident and competent she appeared. All her ratings dropped to zero as a result. This was reinforced further when she watched the feedback from the audience, who rated her ability as 'good' or 'very good' on all aspects of her presentation. Overall, they said she demonstrated a high level of skill. As homework she agreed to watch the video again, this time observing how she came across when using and then dropping her safety behaviours.

Session 6

The homework review at the beginning of this session revealed an unexpected problem. Although watching the video had helped Theresa to see how her performance got better as she dropped the safety behaviours, she had also started to ruminate about some of the more negative aspects of her performance and was thinking about her forthcoming presentation, now only six days away. She was visibly anxious as she arrived for the session, reported feeling quite despondent, and said she was contemplating not going ahead with it.

Two thought records were completed in session, one to counteract the post-mortem she had been carrying out regarding her performance in Session 5, and the other to deal with her anticipatory anxiety regarding her imminent presentation. Both produced a significant reduction in anxiety. In addition, a detailed written plan of instructions for before, during, and after the performance was completed to help 'coach' her through it, including thought records to tackle anticipatory anxiety, and refraining from safety behaviours such as rehearsing intensely. The plan reminded her that during the presentation she should speak slowly, focus on her audience, keep her hands out of her pockets, not drink too much water, and maintain an external focus of attention. It also banned post-event processing or, failing that, suggested the use of thought records to counter negative bias after the presentation. At the end of the session Theresa felt much calmer and more confident that she would cope.

Session 7

Her presentation went well and she was delighted with herself at the next session, so a considerable amount of time was spent consolidating and reinforcing the learning she had gained from the experience. She had implemented much of the plan and, although anxious, had completed the presentation without resorting to any of her safety behaviours. One strategy she had used, which had not been discussed previously, was to mention to her audience at the beginning that she was feeling a little nervous, which resulted in an almost instantaneous reduction in her anxiety. The value of this approach was discussed, and she decided to retain it as a coping tactic (Thwaite and Freeston 2005). The presentation had confirmed the value of an external focus of attention, of not using safety behaviours, and of not carrying out a post-mortem afterwards.

Theresa's spontaneous idea of informing the audience of her anxiety produced evidence that there had been a shift in one of her beliefs ('It is awful to show anxiety in front of others') and provided an opportunity to start work on modifying them. An 'assumptions flashcard' (Clark and Beck 1988) was started in session for this belief and was continued by her as homework.

Sessions 8 and 9

The last two sessions were used to continue work on her underlying beliefs and to complete a written relapse prevention plan. Another assumptions flashcard was used for the belief 'I must succeed,' including an action plan involving behavioural experiments to test out her new belief and to gather evidence. Her alternative belief to 'It is awful to show anxiety in front of others' was 'It is OK to be socially anxious sometimes because it's normal,' and her alternative to 'I must succeed' was 'It's more important to try things than to do well at them.' Some continuum work (Padesky 1994) was started on her core belief 'I'm not good enough,' and she kept a positive data log (Padesky 1994) to support her alternative core belief 'I'm OK.'

The relapse prevention plan was largely completed by Theresa as homework between Sessions 8 and 9, and included a summary of the problem, a summary of therapy, and a plan for the future, including how to deal with a setback if and when it occurred. Follow-up was arranged for six months' time.

OUTCOME

In the final session Theresa was very pleased with her progress in therapy. She had completed a second presentation to her fellow medical students and this had also gone well. She no longer dreaded the prospect of having to perform to her peers and was optimistic about continuing her medical

Table 9.1 Psychometric measures used to assess Theresa's performance anxiety

Measure	Pre	Post
Problem definition (upset) (0–8)	8	3
Problem definition (interference) (0–8)	8	2
Target 1 (0–8)	8	2
Target 2 (0–8)	8	1
Target 3 (0–8)	8	2
Beck Depression Inventory (0–63)	19	4
Work and Social Adjustment Scale (0–32)	12	4
Social Phobia Rating Scale (SPRS): Distress (0–8)	6	2
SPRS: Avoidance (0–8)	8	0
SPRS: Self-consciousness (0–8)	8	3
SPRS: Safety behaviours (0–8)	Mean = 4.6	Mean = 1.2
SPRS: Beliefs	Mean = 55%	Mean = 21%

training. The psychometric measures were completed in Session 9 and are shown in Table 9.1.

DISCUSSION

Theresa's case illustrates the successful application of a cognitive model of social phobia to performance anxiety that was very distressing and potentially career threatening. The experiments in session, especially those involving simulated presentations, allowed her to test out the role of safety behaviours and to manipulate her focus of attention. She was also encouraged to use her imagination to create the thoughts, emotions, and physiological sensations that she might get if she were to present to her peers, which was particularly helpful in ensuring she was able to complete homework relevant to what had been done in the sessions. The use of imagery techniques seems particularly appropriate for social phobia, given the central importance of self-image.

One crucial intervention was the use of video recording to modify her self-conscious image. Most people are somewhat embarrassed at seeing themselves for the first time on videotape, and Theresa was no exception. However, once she was encouraged to focus on the accuracy of her prior predictions, this technique had a profound effect on her view of how she came across to others. Access to the necessary equipment (camcorder and TV monitor) was vital in the success of this approach.

Her loss of confidence, due to an unforeseen consequence of some homework, was alarming, given that it occurred only a few days before she was due to present to her fellow medical students. Fortunately, her confidence was restored by a productive session in which she was able to draw on skills gained earlier in therapy in completing thought records, which were then consolidated by a written plan to help boost further her confidence and belief that she could cope. The problem with the homework may have been avoided if she had been given specific instructions to view the video as if she were watching 'someone towards whom she felt well disposed' (Butler and Hackmann 2004).

One important issue in the CBT treatment of anxiety disorders is whether behaviours adopted by the client are coping strategies or safety behaviours (Thwaite and Freeston 2005). What distinguishes the two is not the behaviour itself, but the function or role that it serves. In Theresa's case there were two examples that could have become safety behaviours. One was her external focus of attention, which on the face of it appears to be a good means of breaking one of the vicious cycles in the maintenance of her problem. However, if she were to use it deliberately as a means of reducing her anxiety rather than to disconfirm her beliefs about how others are judging her, then it could reinforce the problem (Butler and Hackmann 2004). Similarly, her spontaneous acknowledgement of anxiety at the beginning of the presentation had the potential to become a safety behaviour if she came to regard it as an action that she must take in order to make her feared consequence less likely to happen, rather than as a means of 'increasing the bandwidth' of socially acceptable behaviour (Wells 1997). The distinction is a relatively subtle one, but is vitally important in determining vulnerability to relapse.

Chapter 10

Patrick: A case of depression linked to perfectionism

Paul Blenkiron

INTRODUCTION

This chapter illustrates the application of the standard CBT approach to the assessment, formulation and treatment of depression in health professionals. It includes perfectionism as one important contributing cause. The case history focuses on a nurse manager called 'Patrick Grey', who was experiencing low mood due to difficulties in his job within the British National Health Service. Patrick was a 38-year-old nursing services manager who had been feeling depressed over the past year. He had not been absent from work, but contacted occupational health services because he did not feel he could cope with the pressures of his job for much longer. He was then referred to psychology services for assessment and help in the form of cognitive behaviour therapy.

ASSESSMENT

Symptom profile

He was asked to describe a recent typical example of work difficulties. In collaboration with his therapist, he produced a 'five areas' description (Greenberger and Padeskey 1995):

Situation:	Last Monday, agreed to last-minute request from nursing line manager to prepare educational talk on 'ward hygiene policy'.
Thoughts:	'I have never achieved anything,' 'No-one takes me seriously,' 'I will fail and be made redundant.'
Emotions:	Sad, frustrated, angry.
Body reactions:	Tired, no appetite, poor sleep, no sex drive.
Actions (behaviours):	Don't clarify workload with boss, miss lunch, work late, recheck talk, drink beer (three pints).

The consequences of this example were discussed. Although Patrick initially felt better for putting in the extra work preparing the talk, this was only temporary. His marriage had been adversely affected: his wife commented that he was preoccupied at home that night. He also noted that he had been tired and unable to concentrate the next day at work. Feelings of being inefficient added to his conviction about underachieving so that he became even more depressed. This account was then generalized to similar problems and by the end of the session he wrote down a problem definition: 'Difficulty coping with a belief that I am underachieving at work. I focus on current and past failures, and use these to bring myself down. As a result, I am less active at home and socially, ending up feeling depressed and cynical.'

History of the disorder

Patrick had been a diligent clinical nurse in elderly medicine, and was promoted to ward manager five years previously. Problems began after a service reorganization 12 months ago, when he was appointed to a clinical managerial post covering four elderly wards. He had also agreed to take on responsibility for implementing local trust policies and improving the computer recording of clinical information.

Despite 'giving 120%' at work, he described increasing frustration, sadness, broken sleep, reduced appetite and a lack of energy. These symptoms had only partially improved with the antidepressant fluoxetine prescribed by his general practitioner six months ago, which he continued to take. He found he was having to stay at the hospital later into the evenings to meet deadlines and avoid 'failing' at work. This had led to arguments with his wife who felt he should spend more time with their two sons, aged three and five years. Patrick also felt angry about a perceived lack of recognition of his efforts to 'stay on top' by his own line manager.

Personal background

In the second assessment session, Patrick provided details of his background. He was born and bred in Northern Ireland. He had always respected his father, 'a hard working businessman that made sacrifices' who died five years previously. He described a happy childhood in which his supportive parents paid for his private education. However, he had been affected by the death of a close school friend in a motorbike accident when he was 17. Following this he only achieved one 'A' level pass and did not feel able to fulfil his parents' expectations of a university course. Instead he saw himself as 'taking the easy option' with his career by working in office jobs for four years. He then entered nursing training, where he had progressed well since the age of 25. He moved to England and married Julie 10 years ago. Although Patrick previously enjoyed playing football, and home computing, he had found little time for these hobbies recently. He stated that his parents regarded his younger brother as having 'done very well for himself' in setting up a garage business. His only mental health history was a six-month period of taking antidepressant medication following his father's death.

Presentation

Patrick had not previously been referred for psychotherapy as he regarded himself as a 'coper'. However, he was interested in pursuing CBT after accessing a website on depression. He said he needed to 'sort this problem', and was able to see the connection between thoughts, feelings and behaviour. Patrick acknowledged that some of his coping strategies brought short-term relief but maintained the problem in the long run. He was willing to complete 'homework' between sessions and attend for CBT every one to two weeks during work time.

Suitability for short-term CBT

At his initial interview Patrick was judged as suitable for CBT, as he scored 35/50 on the Suitability for Cognitive Therapy Rating Scale (Safran and Segal 1996). This includes the following criteria:

- Able to access automatic thoughts and recognize different emotions
- Accepts personal responsibility for change
- Understands the CBT rationale
- Engages in therapeutic relationship in session
- Shows evidence of ability to establish trusting relationships out of session (e.g. wife, mother)
- Duration of the problem: at least one year
- When discussing problems, shows no evidence of 'security operations' e.g. avoiding anxiety-provoking issues, preoccupation with detail, intellectualizing
- Focality: able to describe a specific situation and define the problem
- Attitude to therapy: some initial optimism.

There were no contraindications to CBT (Blenkiron *et al.* 1999), as Patrick:

- Was not severely depressed (no significant concentration problems, psychomotor retardation or suicidal ideas)
- Appeared cognitively normal (no confusion or dementia)
- Was not misusing alcohol, caffeine or prescribed medication (e.g.

diazepam); he previously drank alcohol in excess but recently reduced this to below 21 units weekly.

Psychometric measures

Regular ratings of measures help to monitor progress and reinforce change (Hawton *et al.* 2000). Patrick rated his problem definition of perceived under-achievement at work as upsetting him 'very severely' (7 on a 0–8 scale) and interfering with his normal activities 'very often' (6).

Individualized behavioural targets were agreed early in therapy as follows:

1   Be more assertive with work colleagues: get rid of an existing responsibility before taking on any new task (rated '5' – manages 'occasionally').
2   Set boundaries for the working day:

- leave my job after an eight-hour shift, even if all tasks are not completed (rated '7' – manages 'very rarely')
- leave my briefcase at work and not take work home (rated '5' – manages occasionally)

3   Do at least one leisure activity each week involving:

- family (e.g. cinema, meal out)
- old hobbies (computer, football – both rated '0' – 'never managed').

He also completed three standardized self-report scales before and after therapy. He initially scored 28/63 (moderate depression) on the Beck Depression Inventory and 19/63 (mild anxiety) on the Beck Anxiety Inventory (Beck and Steer 1987). The Dysfunctional Attitude Scale (Weissman 1979) aims to measure beliefs that predispose to depression (e.g. black or white thinking and perfectionism). His score of 187/240 before CBT was above the typical mean for both controls (113) and depressed individuals (147).

FORMULATION

A formulation (written collaborative understanding of the problem) is normally built up over the course of therapy. Figure 10.1 illustrates the development and maintenance of Patrick's occupational difficulties using Beck's cognitive model (Beck 1976). Although the lower half of the figure (maintenance cycle) was agreed by the end of Session 2, the addition of unhelpful rules and beliefs at the top of the figure was not completed until Session 14.

EARLY EXPERIENCE
High expectations of parents (private education)
Never went to university (friend's death age 17)
Brother perceived as more successful in garage business

▼

CORE BELIEFS
I am a failure/not good enough
Others do not recognize my efforts
The world is competitive

▼

UNHELPFUL RULES (DYSFUNCTIONAL ASSUMPTIONS)
I must set myself the highest standards
If I do not do well 100% of the time then people won't respect me
I am nothing if my career is not a success
Others should always recognize my achievements

▼

TRIGGERS (CRITICAL INCIDENTS)
Father's death five years ago
Increased demands of job after promotion to nurse manager one year ago

▼

PROBLEM ACTIVATED
Feeling depressed because of a belief that I am underachieving in my job

Consequences
Try even harder at work
Raise personal standards

Situations at work
Requests to take on more projects
Meetings with line manager
Dealing with e-mails/in-tray

Results
Short term (hours):
Feeling OK: I am achieving
Longer term (months):
Family suffers
Drop hobbies e.g. football
Feel undervalued at work
Criticize myself for failing

Maintenance
cycle

Thoughts
I've never achieved anything
I will fail this time
No-one takes me seriously

Behaviours
Agree to take on more tasks
Don't clarify workload with manager
Keep sole responsibility
Don't delegate
Miss lunch, work late, drink alcohol

Emotions
Sad, frustrated, angry

Body reactions
No energy, poor appetite,
can't concentrate, broken sleep

Figure 10.1 Case formulation of Patrick's depression and perfectionism.

TREATMENT PLAN

Management of Patrick's problems followed the usual pattern of assessment (suitability, clarifying the problem, initial formulation), treatment and relapse prevention (summarizing learning, a plan to stay well and strategies for tackling future problems). The treatment phase itself comprised four overlapping stages:

1   Socialization to the model: education about the CBT approach using examples
2   Thought records: identifying and challenging negative/extreme ways of thinking using a diary (see Figure 10.2)
3   Behavioural experiments: testing out predictions using regular behavioural homework assignments that gather evidence to support or reject particular beliefs (Enright 1997)
4   Belief modification: in Patrick's case underlying unhelpful rules appeared to include high standards and fear of failure at work.

PROGRESS OF THERAPY

Patrick's suitability screening and initial assessment occurred over two sessions. He then accepted a contract for 12 weekly one-hour sessions of CBT. This was later extended by another eight sessions to a total of 20.

Sessions 1 and 2

Initial work involved education about the CBT approach, reviewing the problem definition and defining practical targets. The therapist explained that CBT was a structured treatment: each session would follow a similar format involving an introduction, setting an agenda together, and review of homework and difficulties from the previous session. The main current issues would then be addressed, followed by the setting of new homework, and ending with feedback from Patrick who would summarize the most important learning points for him. He also decided to audio-record each session and listen to it again at home. To reinforce progress, his therapist suggested that he consider reading one chapter of the self-help book *Mind Over Mood* (Greenberger and Padesky 1995) each week during therapy.

To help Patrick understand connections between his feelings, thoughts and actions a 'burglar' analogy was used. A man asleep in bed one night is woken by a crashing sound downstairs. He believes it must be a burglar. How will he feel? What will he do? But if he has a cat and remembers that he left the window open by mistake, how would he now react? This example illustrated how, according to the stoic philosopher Epictetus, 'People are disturbed not by events, but by the view they take of them' (Blenkiron *et al.* 1999: 6). Patrick was also asked to consider a situation where he is walking through the hospital when a close work colleague appears to ignore him completely. He replied that this had indeed happened to him and he took it as evidence that he had been rejected. With prompting, he was able to come up with other plausible reasons for his work friend's actions (in a hurry for a meeting, not wearing spectacles or simply did not notice him). He was encouraged to suggest other times when his thinking had been biased. He recalled receiving the result of his nursing exam by post. When he saw it was a grade 'D' he immediately threw the letter down, muttering, 'D for Dunce, D for Dismal failure.' It was only later when re-examining the letter that he noticed he had actually passed the exam, and that the 'D' stood for distinction. From this personal anecdote he concluded: 'I'm always jumping to conclusions.'

Session 3

Session 3 concentrated on the maintaining factors of his depression. Although working harder to meet deadlines produced temporary feelings of being in control, these were soon replaced by feelings of failure and a need to work even harder. This vicious circle was illustrated using a diagram (see bottom of Figure 10.1). Patrick noted how his perceptions could be likened to a 'bad hair day' metaphor (Blenkiron 2000). If a morning started badly then he saw it as filled with one problem after another as the day progressed. In this self-fulfilling prophecy, selective focusing on what was going wrong allowed negative thoughts to fuel his frustration at work. His performance fell, reinforcing his low mood, which continued into the evening at home.

Session 4

As homework Patrick had written down thoughts at times when he felt distressed. He was now encouraged to recognize and label these unhelpful styles of thinking. Typical examples included: 'The ward nurses think I'm useless' (mind reading), 'This project is going to go wrong' (fortune telling), 'It's all my fault that hospital infection rates are rising' (taking things personally), 'If I'm not 100% successful in everything that I do, then I'm a failure' (black or white thinking) and 'Bill did not attend today's meeting. I've been rejected by all my work colleagues' (jumping to conclusions).

Sessions 5–9

Use of thought records formed a key part of treatment from Session 5 onwards. Patrick was encouraged to complete a regular diary of distressing situations, mood and automatic thoughts. To develop his understanding of this approach, he first completed thought records in session with his therapist, then as written homework on his own. He later added evidence for and against the thought being true and alternative (less distressing) explanations. Patrick noted that he became quite low when identifying these thoughts and was reassured by his therapist that this was a normal reaction. Initially he found it difficult to come up with healthier, more balanced thoughts. He was therefore given the checklist below to consider when completing the diary (adapted from Beck 1995):

1   What is the evidence for and against this thought? (What makes me think the thought is true/not completely true?)
2   Is there an alternative explanation? (What's another way to look at this?)
3   Consider the outcome. (What's the worst/best that could happen? Would I still live through it? What's the most realistic outcome?)
4   Consider the effect. (What will happen if I keep telling myself the same thought?)
5   How useful is this thought? (Advantages and disadvantages) What could happen if I changed this thought?
6   Problem solving. (What practically can I do now about this thought espe- cially if realistic or true?)
7   Double standard: What would I say to . . . (a specific friend) if they were in this situation? What would I have said to myself 10 years ago? If different, what makes me so special compared to everyone else?

Eventually, Patrick was able to challenge negative thoughts not only on paper (Figure 10.2) but also in his head at times when he felt depressed. For example:

Situation:	Fed up as I haven't cleared my in-tray paperwork and it is now 6pm.
Thoughts:	I should be able to carry a full workload and deal with all my responsibilities. I am failing.
Alternative thoughts:	It would be nice if I could finish off two tasks at once but this simply isn't realistic. I will accomplish more if I give more time to myself. I will only fail if I maintain the same old pace of work and self-expectation.

Sessions 10–11

Patrick reviewed his progress regarding his initial practical targets and agreed to test the consequences using behavioural experiments. The first target involved saying 'no' to new work unless he had removed an existing responsibility. After Session 10 he was asked by his manager to review ward security policy, and he explained that he was still implementing the hygiene project. He predicted that his manager would be angry and would discipline him in writing. However, he was surprised to find that his manager respected and

Day and time	Situation	Feelings (% level of Intensity)	Thoughts	Evidence supporting thoughts	Evidence against thoughts being true	Alternative (balanced) thoughts	Re-rate feelings
Tuesday 6pm	At work, reading emails, no replies to my request for feedback on my hygiene policy document	Depressed 90% Annoyed 50%	My work is poor, I've failed I should have spent more time on the policy No-one recognizes my efforts or takes me seriously	My manager did not comment on my ideas I only checked the policy twice I feel like I've failed	Everyone is busy, they may not have had time to reply John (ward nurse) did thank me for my talk on the subject No-one has ever said that my work is sub-standard (I'm mind reading)	Just because I feel I've failed does not mean it's true Even if the policy contained flaws, this doesn't mean all my work is useless I will request feedback at my appraisal Given the deadline, I am satisfied with the result	Depressed 60% Annoyed 10%

Figure 10.2 Example of a thought record.

supported his position. Patrick could cite no evidence that others perceived him as a failure because of this.

His second target involved setting only a reasonable amount of work to do each day (going home on time even if some tasks remained unfinished). However, he had not made any progress towards this. In Session 11, Patrick admitted he was still fearful of the consequences of failing to complete all outstanding tasks to the highest standard.

Session 12 (review)

Patrick now reported significantly less depression and frustration regarding work. However, he still felt that by prioritizing tasks, trying to leave on time and accepting minor flaws in his performance, he was 'taking the easy way out' and 'underachieving' in his career. He also believed he had let down his therapist by not performing homework tasks to a sufficiently high standard and would be discharged at that point. For example, he had not brought the thought diary to Session 12 because he could not come up with any evidence to support the idea that he had failed at work. He saw this as an inability to do CBT homework 'properly' and meet the standard required. These issues were discussed and clarified as examples of Patrick mirroring his perceived lack of achievement at work within therapy itself. He was subsequently offered eight further sessions to examine unhelpful rules for living centred on his perfectionist beliefs.

Sessions 13 and 14

Patrick worked to identify common themes from thought records and his previous responses in the Dysfunctional Attitudes Scale. He concluded that high expectations from his parents, but no praise, helped explain his core belief about not being 'good enough'. Compensatory rules including 'If I do not do well 100% of the time then people won't respect me' and 'Others should always recognize my achievements' were added to complete his formulation (top of Figure 10.1).

As homework he listed the advantages and disadvantages of setting very high standards for himself at work. He identified a feeling of fulfilment and greater respect for his achievements from colleagues as the main advantages but also recognized drawbacks, including 'the faster I run the harder it is to stop', 'further to fall if I fail', 'a sense of underachieving' and 'professional burnout'.

He remained fearful about lowering self-expectations to reduce work stress. His therapist asked him to suggest occupations for which consistently high standards are essential (Patrick suggested being a proofreader or bomb disposal expert) and compare these with the majority of jobs where it is not important to get things precisely right. He was then asked to consider how others managed at his place of work. He noted that many did not seem to share his own highly conscientious approach and yet he had never concluded that they were failing in their jobs. Patrick acknowledged that he held double standards, such as encouraging colleagues to take adequate lunch breaks, when he felt he should lead others by example. He also realized that he was happy to adopt a lower standard outside of work for his own performance on the football field and at social events.

Sessions 15 and 16

To increase Patrick's motivation to address fears regarding change, a 'vampire' analogy was introduced: 'In Transylvania there lives a tribe who believe in vampires. For 300 years they have lived in fear of being bitten. In order to protect themselves, they have worn cloves of garlic around their necks at night. During that time, not one person has ever been bitten by a vampire, and so this ritual continues. How could they test out the garlic's protective power for certain?' After considering this, Patrick decided to take a risk by adopting satisfactory (but less than perfect) standards at work. He tested out his concerns about doing a 'good enough' job using a behavioural experiment. He agreed to send a report to his line manager without re-checking it for grammatical errors. He predicted that he would be severely reprimanded, but when he was called to see his boss this was to discuss the content of the report and several mistakes had gone apparently unnoticed. He also deliberately inserted three minor spelling mistakes into PowerPoint slides accompanying a talk he gave to surgical staff. In practice only one of the errors was noticed and his prediction that this would affect his feedback ratings and reputation did not materialize. Patrick therefore decided to drop checking of paperwork more than once until this felt more comfortable.

Session 17

Patrick explored his belief 'I must get everything right 100% of the time otherwise I am a failure and useless' using an 'assumptions flashcard' (Clark and Beck 1988). This allowed him to consider reasons why he felt this rule was unhelpful and the possible value of holding alternative, more adaptive beliefs (Figure 10.3). He concluded that his old ideals for achievement at work could be compared to the stars at night: good to look up to as a guide, but impossible to reach in practice.

Session 18

Patrick declared that adopting lower but still satisfactory standards was giving him the confidence to reduce his working hours to those he was paid for, and go home on time without taking a full briefcase with him. He found his

1. I hold the belief that . . .

I must get everything right 100% of the time otherwise I am a failure and useless

2. It is understandable that I hold this belief because . . .

My parents always wanted me to be an achiever

I want high standards for myself

I don't want people at work to think I'm incompetent

3. However the belief is unreasonable because . . .

I can't always be right

Getting something wrong doesn't mean I am useless

I don't expect others to be perfect, why one rule for me and another for them?

4. It is also unhelpful because . . .

It is making me short-sighted in my relationships

I feel depressed and dissatisfied with my career

I can learn from my mistakes

5. A more reasonable and helpful belief would be . . .

It is OK to be wrong, everyone makes mistakes

I can be happy with my achievements without always giving 100%

'Patrick Perfect' is an old name!

6. Given that I have held the belief for a long time, it will take time and work to change it. What I need to do is . . .

Remember my successes, not failures

Ask myself: 'How would I advise a friend?'

Get the right balance (work, family, relaxing)

Don't be so serious, have a sense of humour

Figure 10.3 Example of a flashcard.

efficiency at work did not suffer: in fact, he became less anxious about falling behind. He decided to adopt a new belief: 'Life is still worthy and meaningful even if I devote less time to my job.' This allowed him to schedule in at least one leisure activity each week involving his family and he also joined a local five-a-side football team. His marriage improved and his wife commented that he seemed more interested in the children.

OUTCOME

Patrick now re-rated his original problem definition. Depression due to a feeling of underachieving at work was now upsetting him only 'very slightly' (1 on a 0–8 scale) and interfering with normal activities 'not at all' (0). The first target (get rid of an existing responsibility before taking on any new task), and the third target (resume one hobby and one weekly family activity) were both rated as 'achieved almost all of the time' (1 or 0). He rated the second target (to leave work and his briefcase after an eight-hour shift) as being achieved 'most of the time' (3), admitting that he occasionally fell back into old habits of working until after 6pm.

His Beck Depression Inventory score fell from 28 to 13/63 (not clinically depressed) and his Beck Anxiety Inventory score from 19 to 4/63 (not anxious). His rating on the Dysfunctional Attitudes Scale had dropped from 187 to 155/256, including an important shift in the belief 'If I do not do well all the time, people will not respect me' from 7 ('totally agree') to 3 ('agree slightly').

RELAPSE PREVENTION

As homework, Patrick listed the most important ideas and coping techniques from therapy. In Session 19, he agreed to his therapist's suggestion to 'reverse role play' and they swapped roles and chairs. His therapist argued the case for spending longer hours at work to achieve results, while Patrick came up with positive reasons for changing this behaviour. As a result he was able to list the key learning points below as a relapse prevention after therapy ended:

Helpful actions

1   I will keep my targets going: leave work on time, take lunch breaks and do at least two social activities each week.
2   I won't take on responsibility for everything at work: then if things don't work out, I am not a failure.
3   If negative thoughts occur in my job I will either:

- distance the problem ('not me, a friend') to give myself advice or
- write down the thought and challenge it later or
- discuss with friends how I could react differently or
- review my notes and audio-recordings.

Helpful attitudes

1 Recognize my past successes: if I am good at something then I'm good at it!
2 If I am not good at something then people will still respect me.
3 If I do not perform at 100% that is fine: no need to be a perfectionist.
4 Take a long-term approach to work tasks – a realistic timescale instead of wanting to achieve everything immediately as in the past.

Session 20 (follow up and review) was held three months later, to check progress and discuss difficulties. Patrick stated that although the content of his job had not changed significantly, he was much more satisfied with work. He felt more in control and used more humour to deal with work stress. For example, he had put a cartoon image of a duck hitting a computer with a hammer onto his work computer as a screen saver. He had also created a credit card-sized copy of the relapse prevention plan to keep in his wallet ('coping card').

DISCUSSION

It is known that job strain (high demands and low job control) and effort–reward imbalance (high demands, low security and few career opportunities) promote work stress (Siegrist 1996). CBT does not claim that unhelpful thoughts and behaviours are the sole cause of job-related depression, but rather that they maintain and exacerbate it (Beck 1995). Patrick's low mood made him think negatively, while his perfectionism drove him to work harder. This led to increasing fatigue and job strain that tended to confirm his sense of failure. Therapy involved shifting this negative emotional cycle into a positive one. Session 15 and the resulting behavioural experiments represented a key point in treatment. He became confident enough to tolerate minor flaws in his work, worry less what others thought about him and achieve a 'good enough' standard. This in turn allowed him to redress the balance between his work and leisure time.

CBT protects against relapse into depression for at least four years after therapy, compared to standard care (Enright 1997). Patrick's depression became activated only after promotion to nurse manager. However, his underlying beliefs suggest that he was psychologically 'unwell' before this, despite outwardly appearing to cope with challenges at work. Activity scheduling using a diary was not used in this case. It would be useful for more severely depressed individuals who lack motivation to plan a structure to their day, as well as those who have difficulty concentrating on cognitive techniques.

Patrick did attend regularly and completed most homework tasks as planned. However, people who cite a lack of time due to their 'busy job' as a reason for not attending CBT or carrying out homework may be asked: 'Do you have anything in your weekly routine that you do regularly, such as have a bath or watch a favourite television programme?' Asking individuals to consider how they are able to make time for these other activities enables them to reconsider their priorities and motivation more clearly.

Patrick's perceived setbacks (not achieving targets or completing homework to the highest standard) were worsened by his belief that anything but rapid progress was a failure. The fact that his therapist agreed to further CBT after the 12th session to address this may have modelled a more realistic attitude to progress. On the other hand, Patrick harnessed his perfectionist characteristics (regular homework, testing out fears) in order to tackle situations where he risked not being very successful at first. Hence his perfectionism contributed both to the initial occupational difficulties and to his eventual success with using CBT to overcome depression.

Chapter 11

Colin: A case of health anxiety

Mark Latham

INTRODUCTION

Preoccupation with one's own health is not a recent phenomenon (Burton 1927: 272), with current estimates of the prevalence of hypochondriasis ranging from 1% to 5% (American Psychiatric Association 2000: 505). This chapter describes the case of Colin, a junior doctor in the National Health Service, whose long-standing health anxiety was successfully treated using short-term cognitive behavioural therapy (CBT).

DEFINITION OF THE DISORDER

Hypochondriasis is 'a preoccupation with fears of having, or the idea that one has, a serious disease based on the person's misinterpretation of bodily symptoms', and this preoccupation 'persists despite appropriate medical evaluation and reassurance' (American Psychiatric Association 2000: 507). In addition, the individual recognizes that their fears are exaggerated, the concern regarding their health is not just one of several domains causing anxiety (as is the case in generalized anxiety disorder), and it causes significant distress or impairment to their life. The focus of anxiety may be on one or many areas of the body, and on a single disease or a whole plethora of serious medical conditions. Many writers use the term 'health anxiety' instead of hypochondriasis because it has fewer negative connotations.

THE HEALTH SERVICE CONTEXT

It is widely recognized that a temporary phenomenon occurs in many medical students, whereby they become excessively preoccupied with their own health (Woods *et al.* 1966). The most obvious explanation is their exposure to knowledge about the signs and symptoms of a vast range of diseases, many of which have serious consequences. A cursory check of one's own body to reassure oneself of the lack of any of these symptoms can, however, reveal the presence of symptomatology, since many of us experience headaches, pain, pins and needles, tiredness, poor sleep, and so on, at one time or another. The discovery of these symptoms tends to lead to a further focus on them, which in turn increases the likelihood of finding more potential signs of illness. Coming to the conclusion that there is something seriously wrong is, therefore, more likely to happen with medical students because they are studying disease.

THE COGNITIVE MODEL

A CBT model of hypochondriasis that takes into account factors involved in both the development and maintenance of the disorder has been proposed (Salkovskis and Warwick 1986). Patients' histories are likely to include events that predispose them to anxiety about their own health; examples might include illness and death of a family member or friend, instances of medical mismanagement, or parents' over-concerned attitude towards illness. According to Beck's original cognitive model (Beck 1976; Beck et al. 1979), these early experiences lead to certain beliefs that then affect how an individual person perceives situations. Examples of these beliefs could be: 'I am vulnerable to illness,' 'The world is full of dangerous diseases,' 'Doctors' judgements cannot be relied upon,' or 'Symptoms always mean something bad.'

People with health anxiety see far more threats to their physical well-being from illness and disease than do other people, because they hold beliefs that cue them to notice, for example, physical symptoms that others might not (Warwick and Salkovskis 1990: 111). When they become aware of the symptoms, underlying beliefs lead to automatic thoughts regarding their meaning – often, that they are indicative of life-threatening illness. Thus, people with health anxiety are likely to both perceive and interpret bodily symptoms in a particularly threatening way, leading to anxiety.

Certain behaviours are common in those with health anxiety. Checking for symptoms may take the form of internal scanning of the body, visual inspection, or physical manipulation (e.g. poking or squeezing an area of concern). All these actions increase the likelihood of symptoms being noticed or, indeed, of them actually occurring. If one looks for something, one is more likely to find it, whether it is chest pain or skin blemishes. If a woman touches and squeezes a breast repeatedly to check for lumps, the area is likely to tingle or throb, and the skin may redden, thus providing two forms of physiological feedback that something is wrong.

Reassurance seeking is not unusual, either (Warwick and Salkovskis 1985). This may involve asking doctors to check that a disease has not been contracted, requesting specific medical tests, looking up information in books or on the Internet, or informing relatives about the symptoms experienced and then monitoring their responses for any signs of alarm. In the short term these actions usually produce a reduction in anxiety, but in the longer term this sense of relief gradually disappears and is replaced by an even stronger need to gain further reassurance that there is no health threat. An all-clear for health only applies at a single point in time and therefore needs constant renewal. All medical tests are fallible and can produce 'false negatives', thereby not giving the absolute guarantee of good health that is sought.

REFERRAL

Colin, a 28-year-old man, was referred by his GP to the Psychotherapy Department. The letter mentioned that he had a 'neurotic concern with his health' and that he had had several hospital tests that had proved negative. Colin had specifically requested referral for CBT.

ASSESSMENT

Symptom profile

His main concern was that he had cancer in some part of his body, the location varying according to his symptoms. He felt anxious about his health 80% of the time, though the intensity fluctuated. Physiological symptoms that particularly troubled him included general aches and pains, weakness, fatigue, variations in appetite, headaches, and nausea. His usual behavioural response to the fear was to seek reassurance from sources of medical information, especially textbooks, and from his uncle who was a semi-retired GP. He also ruminated a lot about what symptoms might mean, usually concluding that cancer was a distinct possibility.

History of the disorder

Onset was gradual during his second year as a medical student and it got steadily worse throughout his training as a doctor. He had always been very concerned about his health, even as a small child, but he did not regard it as a problem until it got worse during medical training. He had hoped that it would get better again when he qualified, since several of his fellow students had reported milder versions of his problem that had subsequently remitted. However, if anything, the problem had got worse in the 18 months since he had been a senior house officer (SHO), and was the worst it had ever been by the time he sought help from his GP, who twice carried out blood tests and sent him for a CT scan and an endoscopy, all of which were negative.

Personal background

Colin came from a family of doctors, his father, paternal uncle, and paternal grandfather all having been GPs. His mother still worked as a primary school teacher. He was the eldest of three children, with a brother training to be an architect and a sister at music college. Colin went to public school and did well academically but was not very keen on sports. He was an average student at medical school. He lived in a two-bedroom flat in a fashionable part of a major UK city and his leisure interests included reading, going to the theatre, and walking.

Presentation

At the initial interview Colin appeared somewhat ashamed and embarrassed about his problem. He asked lots of questions and wanted to know about the therapist's CBT training and his level of expertise. It is common for therapists to find it difficult to engage patients with health anxiety, since the latter are often suspicious about being referred for psychological help when they perceive their problems as physical in nature (Wells 1997: 139). Colin, however, recognized his difficulties as being anxiety-based and had requested CBT, but was sceptical about whether it would help him. He was smartly dressed, maintained fairly good eye contact, and was articulate regarding his problem.

Suitability for short-term CBT

Good prognostic indicators included his ability to focus, to identify readily his automatic thoughts, and to differentiate between emotions, and his compatibility with the cognitive model, alliance potential in and out of session, and the lack of what some have termed 'security operations' (Safran and Segal 1990: 262). However, the chronicity of his problem and his lack of optimism were less encouraging (Safran and Segal 1990: 262–3).

Psychometric measures

An individualized problem definition was constructed as follows: 'Thoughts about having cancer or other illnesses, leading me to feel anxious and to seek reassurance from doctors and textbooks.'

End-of-treatment targets were as follows:

- To have physiological symptoms and/or thoughts about cancer without getting excessively anxious
- To have physiological symptoms and/or thoughts about cancer without seeking reassurance from doctors

- To have physiological symptoms and/or thoughts about cancer without looking up symptoms in textbooks
- On getting thoughts about cancer, to think about alternative explanations for the symptoms.

Standardized measures were as follows:

- Beck Depression Inventory (BDI; Beck *et al.* 1961)
- Beck Anxiety Inventory (BAI; Beck *et al.* 1988)
- Health Anxiety Questionnaire (HAQ; Lucock and Morley 1996).

FORMULATION

The development and maintenance of Colin's problem were conceptualized using a combination of Beck's cognitive model (Beck 1976; Beck *et al.* 1979, 1985) and a model specific to health anxiety (Salkovskis and Warwick 1986; Warwick and Salkovskis 1989, 1990; Wells 1997), and was built up collaboratively over several sessions. The final version is shown in Figure 11.1.

The key events that seemed most likely to have predisposed him to health anxiety were his frequent childhood illnesses ('I am physically weak'), the many conversations he overheard between his father, grandfather, and uncle on medical matters ('Symptoms are dangerous if you ignore them'), and, more recently, his grandmother's prolonged death from cancer that he found very upsetting ('Cancer means death'). This last belief was surprising, given that his medical training had provided him with ample evidence to the contrary. However, this belief became far more credible to him when his other beliefs were activated, especially regarding his vulnerability.

He had been quite sensitive about his health as a child and adolescent, but it was not until he commenced training as a doctor that these beliefs seem to have been activated, since his studies necessitated that his attention was focused on the signs and symptoms of many diseases. Once activated, the beliefs made him hypersensitive to physiological changes in his body, many of which would then trigger his health anxiety problem.

In the example given in Figure 11.1, he not only noticed the back pain, but also interpreted it as meaning he had cancer, a conclusion he would be unlikely to draw if he did not hold these beliefs. Understandably, he became anxious and fearful at the thought that he might have cancer, and these emotions, in turn, led to some physiological responses (tiredness, feeling weak, loss of appetite, general aches) which he then interpreted as further evidence that he had cancer. Thus, a vicious cycle was evident between his thoughts, emotions, and physiological symptoms.

The thought that he had cancer also set off a couple of important cognitive processes that created two further maintenance cycles: first, it caused him to

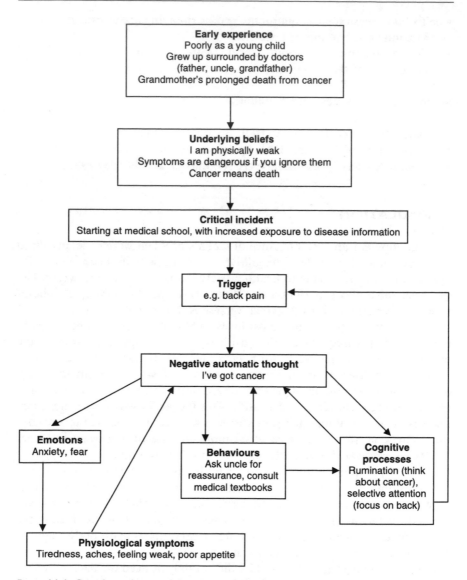

Figure 11.1 Case formulation of Colin's health anxiety.

focus on the pain in his back, thereby exacerbating his perception of its intensity; second, he tended to have further thoughts about cancer, which made it seem like a more realistic possibility.

Colin's behaviours also played a role in keeping the problem going. Unlike some people with health anxiety, he did not try to avoid contact with sources of information regarding illness and disease (Wells 1997: 137). On the contrary, he deliberately sought it out in order to provide himself with reassurance. The effects of consulting this information, though, were mixed. Sometimes it had the desired outcome of relieving his anxiety, by providing evidence that helped reduce his belief in the thought that he had cancer. At other times, however, it caused him further alarm because it confirmed his worst fears and/or triggered fresh concerns about his health.

Reassurance seeking was Colin's other major way of trying to cope with his anxiety. Although he used his GP for this from time to time, it was far more common for him to discuss his symptoms and his fears with his Uncle Roger, who was a semi-retired GP himself, and who was more patient and tolerant of Colin's difficulties than was his own father. Invariably this behaviour brought relief to him, convincing him that he did not have cancer. Although reassurance is often effective at reducing anxiety in the short term, the effect only lasts for a limited period of time before further reassurance is needed. In this respect an analogy can be drawn with drug addiction, with the patient needing another 'fix' after the effects of reassurance have worn off (Marks 1981: 41). The analogy can be extended further, as sometimes increasingly large amounts of reassurance are needed over time to produce the same sense of relief, the patient thus developing 'tolerance' for its effects.

TREATMENT PLAN

A treatment plan was devised, closely based on the work of Salkovskis and Warwick (Salkovskis 1989; Salkovskis and Warwick 1986; Warwick and Salkovskis 1989, 1990) and Wells (1997). It consisted of four stages to be followed sequentially but with considerable overlap, where appropriate.

Socialization to the model

The first step was to increase Colin's understanding of his difficulties and to socialize him to the CBT model, since he was more likely to engage in therapy if he understood the rationale behind interventions. Discussion of the formulation and behavioural experiments were the two proposed means of achieving this. The arm was to lay the foundations for an alternative, psychological explanation of his problem. This is sometimes referred to as 'Hypothesis A/ Hypothesis B' (Salkovskis and Bass 1997) or the 'dual model strategy' (Wells 1997: 157), where Hypothesis A is that his problem is that he has cancer and Hypothesis B is that his problem is that he mistakenly believes he has cancer. The patient can then examine and gather evidence to see how well each of these competing theories is supported.

Thought records

Thought records (Greenberger and Padesky 1995) help to develop alternative explanations for the symptoms experienced. This verbal reattribution of symptoms was used to encourage Colin to consider the range of possibilities other than his automatic conclusion that they signified cancer (i.e. to build up evidence for Hypothesis B).

Behavioural experiments

It was planned that he would refrain from reassuring himself through information gathering and consulting with his uncle, predict what would happen if he did this, and find out what actually occurred in both the short and long term and how these outcomes compared with his predictions.

In the case of selective attention, there are several experiments that manipulate the focus of attention and can demonstrate just how powerful this cognitive process is in giving only a partial picture (Wells 1997: 146). Similarly, contrasting this cognitive 'behaviour' with distraction can show the bias that results from rumination. These behavioural experiments may, because they are genuine tests, occasionally provide evidence that supports Hypothesis A rather than the alternative explanation offered in the formulation. However, provided the formulation is fairly accurate and the experiments are well designed, most behavioural experiments will have the effect of weakening the patient's original view of their problem and at the same time strengthening the alternative explanation (Bennett-Levy *et al.* 2004).

Belief modification

Although the early stages of the treatment plan were aimed at altering factors involved in the maintenance of Colin's problem, there was also a need to modify the underlying beliefs that had predisposed him to developing the problem in the first place; he would be vulnerable to relapse in the future if they remained largely intact (Fennell 1989: 202). Modification of the beliefs would occur through accumulation of evidence from experiments and an examination of how well this fitted with each belief.

PROGRESS OF THERAPY

After an initial contact to screen for suitability for short-term CBT, and a more detailed assessment, Colin had a total of 11 CBT treatment sessions.

Sessions 1 and 2

Colin could recognize that his thoughts about having an illness or disease were excessive and unreasonable, but he couldn't understand why he had these 'ridiculous' thoughts and why they made him so fearful. A detailed examination allowed him to see how his earlier experiences had 'primed' him to be anxious about his health, via development of several underlying beliefs, and that his thoughts, therefore, far from being ridiculous, were in fact largely understandable. When this explanation was combined with an appreciation of the role of both selective attention and rumination in keeping the problem going, he was able to see that his level of fear was appropriate to the perceived threat, but that it was this perception and the subsequent interpretation that were the problem. The 'distance' he had put between himself and the problem through his increased understanding not only enabled him to be more object-ive, but also helped him to start to come up with ideas for change strategies.

Two behavioural experiments helped reinforce some of the principles involved. The first focused on his ruminative thoughts about cancer, and involved manipulating the duration of the rumination and then noting the effects this had both on his belief that he had cancer and on his anxiety. As homework Colin spent one hour deliberately ruminating on the possibility that he had cancer, followed by another hour when he carried out an activity (reading a novel) that occupied his mind and largely stopped rumination from occurring. He did this experiment four times over the week, altering the sequence of the two activities so as to counteract any order effects (Robson 1977: 26–7). On all four days he found that rumination made the problem worse, thus supporting the vicious cycle proposed in the formulation.

The second behavioural experiment took place in Session 2 to demonstrate the effects of selective attention to bodily symptoms. Colin was asked to close his eyes and focus his mind on any sensations that he noticed in his left knee. As time went by, he experienced a growing number of symptoms in his knee, starting with tingling sensations and then mild pain. The ensuing dis-cussion, with reference to the diagrammatic formulation, focused on how this illustrated that if you look for trouble, you usually find it.

Sessions 3–4

Colin was introduced to the formula proposed by Salkovskis to explain which factors we take into account when assessing risk in any given situation (Salkovskis 1996):

$$\text{Anxiety} = \frac{\text{Perceived probability of threat} \times \text{perceived cost/awfulness of danger}}{\text{Perceived ability to cope with danger} + \text{perceived rescue factors}}$$

In anxiety disorders, one or more of the following processes are likely to be occurring: over-estimation of the likelihood of the feared consequence occurring, and/or the cost if it did, and under-estimation of one's own ability to cope if it did occur, and/or of the help available from external sources (people, places, etc.).

He discovered by doing this that he most often over-estimated the likelihood that he had a life-threatening illness. This was useful to Colin because it meant that he could ask himself the specific question, 'Am I over-estimating the likelihood that I have cancer?' As homework between Sessions 3 and 4, he completed several examples of health anxiety thought records (Wells 1997: 153) in order to evaluate and modify his assessment of the risk to his health. At the beginning of Session 4, he reported that consciously focusing on the likelihood of getting cancer, combined with searching for alternative, more innocuous explanations for the symptoms he was experiencing, was having a beneficial effect on reducing his anxiety.

However, what remained unchanged was how he perceived the cost of having cancer, exemplified by his belief 'Cancer means death.' To evaluate the validity of this idea, a behavioural experiment was set up as homework whereby Colin was to carry out research into survival rates for a variety of different cancers. This experiment carried the risk that he might attend to information in a highly selective manner, especially if he became anxious. The session focused on how he might deliberately note information that did not fit with his belief. He decided to note supporting evidence on one side of a piece of paper and non-supporting evidence on the other.

Session 5

The homework review revealed the behavioural experiment to have been a mixed blessing. On the one hand, he had carried out a lot of research and had found substantial evidence that did not support his belief that 'Cancer means death,' and this had had quite a dramatic impact on how much he believed it (reduction from 70% to 30%). On the other hand, he had become quite low in mood during the week. It transpired that he had had several thoughts about how stupid he was for having a health anxiety problem, and that these thoughts had lowered his mood. This is not uncommon, with depressed patients in particular often being depressed about being depressed (Moore and Garland 2003: 40), and this phenomenon can be exacerbated by the insight sometimes provided through change techniques used in CBT. Most of the rest of the session was spent completing a thought record with the thought 'I'm stupid and irrational worrying about my health like this,' in order to try to counteract this effect.

Sessions 6–7

The next couple of sessions targeted his reassurance seeking. This was particularly important, given that this behaviour was the main way in which he controlled his anxiety, and it was also preventing him from finding out whether or not his fears were accurate. The concept of habituation (Marks 1987: 256) was introduced, along with the technique of response prevention (Marks 1981: 99): by resisting the urge to ask for reassurance it would eventually reduce to very manageable levels. At Session 7 Colin reported that he had found the homework quite difficult and had requested reassurance several times from his Uncle Roger. It became apparent that it might be helpful to include his uncle in this aspect of the treatment, so Colin said he would invite him along to the next session.

Session 8

This was a key session for several reasons. At the beginning Colin was asked to explain the CBT formulation of the problem to his uncle, which achieved three important objectives; first, it ascertained that Colin had an accurate understanding of the formulation; second, rehearsal of the explanation enabled consolidation of his learning of the CBT model; and third, it helped his uncle to understand the approach. The ensuing discussion was about the role of reassurance in particular in maintaining his problem, and what would constitute helpful and unhelpful responses on the part of his uncle. It was agreed that Colin would continue to try to resist the urge to seek reassurance, but that when he found this too difficult to do and telephoned or spoke to his uncle, the latter would respond with a stock phrase along the lines of, 'Sorry Colin, you know your therapist has asked me not to give you any reassurance,' and would not otherwise engage in discussion of symptoms (Marks 1981: 84). This was rehearsed in session, with the therapist modelling the response initially and then Roger practising how he would say it to Colin.

Sessions 9–10

The homework review at the beginning of the next session a fortnight later was very upbeat, as Colin recounted how good it had been to be able to talk with his uncle in the car on the way home from the previous session. It was the first time that he had felt able to discuss the problem openly and honestly with a family member and his uncle had been very supportive towards him. A knock-on effect from this seems to have been that he found it easier to resist the urge to seek reassurance.

Nevertheless, he had phoned his uncle twice, each time on the pretext of talking about something else and then mentioning his concerns in passing as a way of obtaining reassurance. On both occasions his uncle was alert to what was happening and responded with the stock phrase, thus denying Colin reassurance.

The rest of Session 9 focused on his underlying beliefs. He had identified three beliefs very early on in therapy and had worked at modifying one of them ('Cancer means death'). He came up with the alternative belief 'More people survive cancer nowadays than die from it, depending on the type of cancer,' based on his earlier experiments involving researching the evidence.

To work with his belief 'I am physically weak,' he learned how to complete an 'assumptions flashcard' (Clark and Beck 1988). This is a structured format for constructing an alternative belief and then collecting evidence to support it:

1   I hold the belief that . . .
    I am physically weak.
2   It is understandable that I hold this belief because . . .
    I was quite poorly as a child and my mother treated me as if I was very vulnerable to diseases and illness.
3   However, it is an unreasonable belief because . . .
    There is very little evidence that, as an adult, I am anything but in fine health. I have had two bouts of flu in the past six years, the odd cold, and one stomach upset, but otherwise I've been free from illness. I eat a fairly healthy diet and I exercise a couple of times a week. My age and family history suggest that it will be many years before I need to worry about serious illness.
4   It is also an unhelpful belief because . . .
    I am preoccupied with my health and this stops me leading a normal life. My job as a doctor has become a nightmare at times, causing me great anxiety, and leading to hours spent checking out symptoms in books and on the Internet. Uncle Roger is getting increasingly fed up with me asking him for reassurance.
5   A more reasonable and helpful belief would be . . .
    I am physically strong and in robust health.
6   Given that I have held the original belief for a long time, it will take time and effort to believe the new one, so I need an action plan to help me. The plan is . . .

    •   Keep a diary logging all evidence that my health is good, completing it daily at first and then at least once a week.
    •   Continue to use thought records to come up with benign explanations for symptoms.
    •   Increase my levels of exercise, including taking up cycling again.

Session 11

Relapse prevention is considered vital in order to maintain the gains made in therapy (Moore and Garland 2003: 319–40). The 'Summary of CBT' sheet completed by Colin consisted of three sections: a succinct re-cap of what the problem was, how it may have developed, and the cognitive and behavioural factors maintaining it; a resume of the changes that had taken place since treatment began, and which specific interventions he found most helpful in therapy; and a plan for the future in terms of how to maintain the gains made, how to build on them, and how to deal with any setbacks that may occur.

OUTCOME

Colin's problem improved considerably. He had a better understanding of his health anxiety and a marked reduction in reassurance seeking. Consequently, he was a lot less preoccupied with his health and was able to deal with thoughts about cancer, etc., when they did occur by thinking of plausible alternative explanations that were far less threatening to him. The psychometric measures were repeated at Session 11 and are shown in Table 11.1.

DISCUSSION

Colin's case illustrates how short-term CBT can be effective in treating health anxiety. The single most powerful intervention seemed to be the collaboratively derived case formulation. It helped Colin to understand his problem so much better and it provided a rationale for all of the subsequent techniques used in the therapy.

Cognitively, the use of thought records to help reattribute symptoms provided structure and focus, and formalized the search for alternative explanations. Colin asking himself the question 'Am I over-estimating the

Table 11.1 Psychometric measures used to assess Colin's health anxiety

Measure	Pre	Post
Problem definition (upset) (0–8)	6	2
Problem definition (interference) (0–8)	4	1
Target 1 (0–8)	7	3
Target 2 (0–8)	5	1
Target 3 (0–8)	6	1
Target 4 (0–8)	7	0
Beck Depression Inventory (0–63)	14	6
Beck Anxiety Inventory (0–63)	27	12
Health Anxiety Questionnaire (0–63)	48	19

likelihood that I have cancer?' was aimed at getting him to evaluate his thinking style (catastrophizing). According to recent CBT models of anxiety disorders, more may be gained through re-evaluation of the appraisal of thoughts (e.g. Salkovskis 1999) or the meta beliefs (e.g. Wells 2000) than by evaluating the content of negative automatic thoughts.

With regard to reassurance seeking, it was primarily a behavioural intervention – response prevention – that helped break this habitual vicious cycle of negative reinforcement. Colin had to resist the urge to contact his uncle, in the knowledge that if he could manage this for long enough it would get easier.

The work on underlying beliefs helped reduce his vulnerability to relapse, although the earlier techniques that provided him with symptomatic relief also appeared to have had an impact on how strongly he held these beliefs.

Overall, Colin's cognitive behavioural therapy followed a fairly typical path in helping him overcome his health anxiety. The fact that he was a doctor made it easier in some respects but more difficult in others to engage him with the CBT approach. Ultimately, CBT proved worthwhile in ridding him of a handicapping problem and enabling him to lead a normal life.

Part III

A schema-focused approach to occupational stress

Chapter 12

A schema-focused model of occupational stress

Martin Bamber and Jason Price

INTRODUCTION

While the standard CBT interventions outlined in Part II of this book have been demonstrated to be effective in treating the symptoms of employees with occupational stress syndromes, they are not appropriate for that proportion of the employee population which presents with more vague, diffuse and complex presentations. This group makes up approximately a quarter of referrals to occupational health clinical psychology services (Bamber 1995). In 1984 Lazarus and Folkman reported that occupational health services did little to cater for the needs of such employees, who required more in-depth, individually tailored psychological treatment programmes and tended to oversimplify the issues involved. However, 22 years after they identified this gap in service provision, it has still not been addressed and very few (if any) occupational health services offer the sort of in-depth individually tailored treatment approaches that they were proposing (Lazarus and Folkman 1984).

Cognitive behavioural therapy is in a constant state of evolution (Blackburn and Twaddle 1996; Safran and Segal 1996). Since the 1980s there has been an increasing integration of therapeutic approaches, which has taken the 'best bits' of different therapeutic approaches and attempted to put them into a more coherent and comprehensive framework. For example, there has been a growing recognition of the importance of the therapeutic relationship, emotional experience and the use of experiential techniques in cognitive therapy (Safran and Segal 1996). There is a realization that many problems are identifiable as life-long themes, resulting from unhealthy early experiences and faulty attachment patterns, and that an individual's inner experience can provide important clues about their interpersonal and cognitive style (Safran and Segal 1996; Wachtel 1982).

Many individuals with very significant interpersonal problems do not benefit from the standard CBT approach, since their difficulties stem from unconscious, extreme and rigid core schemata, which are not amenable to superficial change or examination. The standard CBT approach does not sufficiently address the notion of 'interpersonal schemata' (Guidano and

Liotti 1983; Safran *et al.* 1986, 1990a, 1990b). It also has difficulties in explaining the principle of 'complementarity', which is the process whereby specific interpersonal behaviours tend to define a relationship. For example, the individual who acts dominantly in an interaction bids to define the relationship in a certain way. The other individual is thus pulled or coerced into behaving in a complementary way and fulfilling their role or 'script' as the submissive one within the context of that relationship (Safran and Segal 1996). Behaviours such as aggression, dependency, trust, over-compliance, avoidance, non-compliance, lack of commitment and resistance are no longer seen as 'technical problems' (Beck *et al.* 1979) but as important bits of information, which give us clues as to the underlying schemas driving an individual's behaviour. Similarly, while the standard CBT model de-emphasized 'transference' in the therapeutic relationship, transference issues are also now seen as important in providing clues about an individual's underlying schemata.

The integration of factors such as a greater focus on childhood experiences in the development of (unconscious) core interpersonal schemata, a greater emphasis on the therapeutic relationship, transference issues and trying to uncover the unconscious content of core schemata as the cause of pathology has led to a second generation of cognitive therapies, which are more powerful and robust forms of therapy (James 2001; Perris 2000; Vallis 1998; Young 1999; Young *et al.* 2003). It is, however, perhaps more than anything else, the focus on the deeper cognitive structures or 'core schemata' which separates first and second generation cognitive therapies. In particular, Young's schema-focused therapy (Young 1994a, 1999; Young *et al.* 2003) was developed for patients with a diffuse presentation and often ill-defined complaints that do not fit neatly into 'syndromes' or current illness classifications such as the *DSM-IV-TR* (American Psychiatric Association 2000), who are not able to identify specific triggers and yet display very significant disturbance in personal adjustment over time. While it was originally developed for working with individuals with personality disorders, it has recently been successfully applied to a wider range of clinical problems and disorders (Bamber 2004; Schmidt *et al.* 1995; Stopa *et al.* 2001; Young and Klosko 1993).

TOXIC EARLY CHILDHOOD EXPERIENCES AND THE DEVELOPMENT OF EARLY MALADAPTIVE SCHEMATA (EMS)

The first and second levels of the model outlined in Figure 12.1 refer to the development of EMS through exposure to toxic early environmental experiences. Young (1994a, 1999) and Young *et al.* (2003) have developed Beck's concept of underlying assumptions (Beck 1972, 1976; Beck *et al.* 1979) and call them 'early maladaptive schemas' (EMS). These are described by Young *et al.* (2003) as broad pervasive themes or patterns regarding oneself and

Toxic early childhood experiences

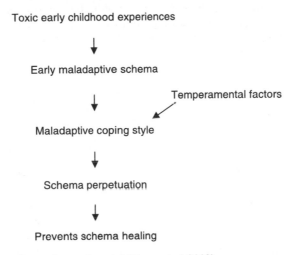

Figure 12.1 The schema-focused model (Young *et al.* 2003).

one's relationships that are dysfunctional to a significant degree, which are developed during childhood or adolescence and are elaborated throughout one's lifetime.

Young *et al.* (2003: 14–17) identify 18 early maladaptive schemata (EMS) in five schema domains. Briefly summarized, these are:

1   Disconnection and rejection – the individual has an expectation that their needs for security, safety, stability, nurturance, empathy, acceptance and respect will not be met in a consistent manner. The typical early family dynamics involve cold, rejecting, withholding, lonely, explosive, unpredictable or abusive behaviour from others. The EMS in this domain are abandonment/instability (perceived instability or unreliability of personal support), mistrust/abuse (expectation that others will hurt, abuse, humiliate, lie, manipulate, cheat, etc.), emotional deprivation (perception that one's needs for emotional support will not be met), defectiveness/ shame (the feeling that one is defective, bad, unwanted, inferior, flawed or invalid in some important respect) and social isolation/alienation (the feeling that one is different from others and isolated from any social group).

2   Impaired autonomy and performance – the individual does not perceive that they are able to function independently, or perform successfully in any way, leading to feelings of inadequacy. Typical family dynamics involve overprotective parenting, enmeshment and failure to support independent activity, all undermining the individual's self-confidence. The EMS in this domain are dependence/incompetence (unable to perform tasks competently without substantial help), vulnerability

to harm (exaggerated fear that there will be an imminent disaster), enmeshment (excessive emotional involvement which is at the expense of the individual's own development) and failure (belief that one is a failure or destined to fail).

3   Impaired limits – this domain essentially describes individuals who show a deficiency in being able to set internal boundaries, act responsibly or engage in long-term goal achievement. The typical early family dynamics of these individuals involves permissiveness, over-indulgence and lack of boundary setting. The EMS associated with this domain are entitlement/grandiosity (belief that one is superior to others and should have special rights) and insufficient self-control/self-discipline (difficulty with impulse control).

4   Other directedness – this domain highlights an excessive emphasis on meeting the needs of others rather than one's own needs, in order to gain love and approval, maintain emotional connection or avoid feared retaliation. The early family dynamics are based upon conditional acceptance. The EMS in this domain are subjugation (excessive surrendering to others to avoid feared anger, retaliation or rejection), approval seeking/recognition seeking (excessive emphasis on gaining recognition or approval from others) and self-sacrifice (excessive but voluntary focus on meeting the needs of others at the expense of one's own needs).

5   Over-vigilance and inhibition – this domain highlights an excessive emphasis on inhibiting or suppressing one's spontaneous feelings, impulses and choices, or on meeting rigid internalized rules and expectations about performance and ethical behaviour, often at the expense of happiness, relaxation, self-expression, close relationships or health. Typical early family dynamics include strict, demanding, punitive, puritanical parenting. The EMS associated with this domain are emotional inhibition (inhibition of emotional expression usually to avoid disapproval or loss of control), punitiveness (the belief that people should be harshly punished for making mistakes, leading to anger and intolerance), negativity/pessimism (pervasive pessimism in all aspects of life, minimizing the positive aspects) and unrelenting standards (belief that perfection should be achieved at all times, usually to avoid criticism).

Young et al. (2003) argue that these EMS are triggered when the individual encounters environments which are reminiscent of the toxic childhood environment that produced them. When this happens, an intense and often overwhelming negative affect is elicited. There is a growing body of evidence for the existence of EMS (Lee et al. 1999; Rittenmeyer 1997; Schmidt et al. 1995).

Factors such as the severity of early toxic experiences, frequency of exposure to the toxic stimuli, the duration of exposure, the developmental stage of the child and the amount of modifying experiences (e.g. healthy parenting from significant care-givers) are all important in the development of EMS. The more frequent and severe the toxic experiences, the more likely they are to be damaging to personality development (Terr 1991). There appears to be a dose effect, in that repeated experiences of an abusive nature are remembered in a different way to single episodes, as a summary 'generic' script (Bowlby 1969; Stern 1985). Toxic experiences at an early age are more likely to be damaging than similar experiences when a child is older, since flexible, adaptive and healthy core interpersonal schema are less likely to have had a chance to develop prior to the exposure to the toxic experience. Younger children are also more likely to follow a more distorted developmental trajectory than an older child, who may have consolidated healthy schemata before exposure to toxic experiences. An older child's experience is more likely to be one of disintegration of healthy schemata but in a younger child it is likely that healthy schemata have failed to develop in the first place. Reactions of care-givers, age at onset of exposure to a toxic environment, frequency, duration and severity of exposure to the toxic environment and the presence or absence of moderating healthy role models are all important in determining the eventual impact that these early toxic experiences will have on the individual (Pollock 2001).

It is important to recognize that experiencing toxic early experiences does not necessarily condemn an individual to developing later life problems and EMS can be modified at any point in the developmental trajectory by 'corrective' healthy experiences. If there is positive involvement of other significant care-givers in the child's life at the time of the toxic experiences, such as extended family, school peers or teachers, good friends or caring professional involvement, then some of the adverse effects can be compensated for. The new more positive experiences of care-giving can compensate to a degree but they cannot remove the EMS totally, since they have already been learned and internalized.

THE ROLE OF TEMPERAMENT

The next level in the model refers to temperamental factors. The temperament of the child is considered to be important to their developmental trajectory and explains why one individual will turn out less disturbed than another exposed to very similar toxic early experiences. For example, two children living in the same household will experience very similar adverse experiences but may show a very different developmental trajectory. One may end up having mental health problems and the other may have none. Young et al. (2003: 12) list a number of temperamental factors found in the literature. These include calm–anxious, passive–aggressive, shy–sociable and optimistic–pessimistic continua. It may also be the case that children have different core emotional needs at different stages in their development (as in Freudian theory's oral, anal and phallic stages) and it is possible that they will be more sensitive to different specific kinds of toxic experiences at different critical developmental stages.

MALADAPTIVE COPING STYLES AND THE ROLE OF TEMPERAMENTAL FACTORS

The fourth level identified in Figure 12.1 relates to the development of maladaptive coping styles. Young *et al.* (2003) assert that EMS are expressed through maladaptive coping styles. They describe three coping styles, which correspond to the three basic responses of fight, flight and freeze. These are surrender (freeze), avoidance (flight) and overcompensation (fight). In any given situation the individual will probably only utilize one coping style but can exhibit different coping styles in different situations or with different EMS. While they are 'needs led' and are aimed at getting one's core emotional needs met, the problem with them is that they serve to perpetuate the EMS and keep the individual cognitively trapped and imprisoned within their EMS. The more rigid, inflexible and extreme the EMS, the more rigid, inflexible and extreme are the coping responses.

1   Schema surrender – the individual yields to the schema and lets it win. They do not try to fight or avoid it. They accept the schema as true and act in ways which confirm it for them. They continue to relive as adults the childhood experiences that created the EMS.
2   Schema avoidance – the individual tries to arrange their life so that the schema is never activated and try to act as if it does not exist. They avoid situations that may trigger the schema and if the schema does start to surface, they may indulge in behaviours which allow them to avoid and escape the emotional distress associated with the schema. Examples of such behaviours include excessive drinking, taking drugs, becoming workaholics and burying themselves in their work, overeating or indulging in compulsive behaviours in order to avoid feeling the schema.
3   Schema overcompensation – the individual fights the schema by thinking, feeling and behaving as if the opposite of the schema were true, for example by adopting perfectionist attitudes to compensate for underlying feelings of worthlessness. If the individual was subjugated as a child then they become rebellious as an adult, if controlled as a child then they try to control others as an adult, or if abused as a child then they may abuse and bully others as an adult.

The style of coping adopted depends to a large extent upon temperamental factors. Passive individuals are more likely to adopt a surrender or avoidance coping style, whereas aggressive individuals are more likely to use an over-compensatory coping style. However, it also depends upon environmental factors, such as early learning from the coping behaviour modelled by significant care-givers. This is obviously problematic if maladaptive strategies were learned. Thus the strategies adopted are a result of an interaction between innate disposition and environmental influences. In the context of occupation, the adoption of maladaptive coping styles in the workplace can result in significant adjustment problems when facing traumatic experiences at work.

SCHEMA PERPETUATION

The final two levels in the model (Figure 12.1) relate to the concepts of schema perpetuation and schema healing. These are central to the model, and schema healing or weakening of an EMS is ultimately the aim of therapy. However, schema perpetuation prevents this from happening.

Schema perpetuation refers to everything that an individual does to keep the EMS going. The model postulates that people are unconsciously drawn to events that trigger their EMS and select situations and relationships that perpetuate them, while paradoxically avoiding those that are likely to lead to schema healing (Young et al. 2003: 30–1). Young and Klosko (1993: 5) report the irony of the repetition of these self-defeating patterns of behaviour and describe this tendency to be drawn to events that are potentially toxic as being related to the Freudian concept of 'repetition compulsion'. This refers to the motivation of individuals to put themselves in situations reminiscent of past traumas, in order to repeat them and work through them (Freud 1914, 1920). It is thought to be an attempt to remember, assimilate, integrate and heal the traumatic experience (Levy 1998).

These re-enactments are manifested particularly in the interpersonal domain, where the individual relates to others in the here and now as if they were actually back in the toxic relationship from the past which led to the development of the EMS. Individuals act out their EMS either with themselves in the child role and the other in the offending parent role (for example they may take on the abused, bullied, criticized, rejected victim role) or, alternatively, with themselves in the parent role and others in the child role (for example abusive, critical, bullying perpetrator role). Levy (1998) describes a number of examples of maladaptive re-enactments which result in re-traumatization, such as prostitution in adulthood, sexual abuse of others, bullying, physical attack of others, revenge through humiliation of others, self-destructive acts and staying in an abusive marriage.

Young et al. (2003: 30) argue that schema perpetuation does not allow the underlying EMS to reach the level of conscious awareness, since the maladaptive coping strategies adopted act to prevent the EMS from being activated. If the EMS remains unconscious, however, there can be no successful schema healing and the individual will go on experiencing and re-experiencing the hyper-activation of their EMS, which remains potent. It dominates their feelings and the maladaptive coping strategies described earlier remain strong in order to defend the individual. The individual will not be aware of it and not have any insight into or understanding of why they behave in a certain dysfunctional way. Others around the individual may also unwittingly get drawn into playing a role in the 'drama' through adopting the reciprocal role and allowing the individual with the EMS to re-enact their maladaptive script. The individual cannot take steps to change or heal it and it will go on perpetuating itself (Young *et al.* 2003: 30–2).

Schema healing, which is the ultimate goal of schema-focused therapy, can only take place if the underlying EMS and maladaptive coping styles are brought into the conscious awareness of the individual (Young *et al.* 2003: 30). Thus, schema healing is the process whereby EMS and maladaptive coping styles brought into the conscious awareness of the individual are weakened and eventually replaced with more healthy adaptive schemata, coping behaviours and ultimately emotional responses. The EMS has to be activated and the patient aware of its presence if it is to be altered and mastered (McGinn and Young 1996). This is more likely to occur when EMS are flexible, less rigid and less severe (Levy 1998). Even if the EMS is bought only partially to the individual's conscious awareness, it can assist in the process of schema healing by creating situations where success and mastery are more likely to be assured. Young *et al.* (2003: 32) state that while EMS can never be totally replaced or disappear altogether, they can through therapy become less activated and occur less frequently. The patient can also learn to respond to them in a healthier manner, through for example choosing more loving partners and friends and viewing him/herself in a more positive way.

SCHEMA PERPETUATION IN THE OCCUPATIONAL CONTEXT

While there is a considerable amount in the literature relating to the re-enactment of EMS in the interpersonal domain generally, there is very little reported about re-enactment of EMS in the work context. This is quite surprising, especially since we spend a significant proportion of our time at work and on average spend more time in the company of our work colleagues than with our marital partners! Also, issues such as power, control, influence and status are all an integral part of the work experience setting and provide the ideal stage upon which interpersonal re-enactments can take place. We are no doubt all familiar with the stress that is caused by working with people who behave in abrasive, interpersonally abusive, ineffectual or self-defeating ways and the problems that this can cause for the individual at work, for those who work with them and for the organization in which they work (Lowman 1997).

Such re-enactments in the workplace can also elicit strong reactions and emotions from those who work alongside, manage or are managed by such individuals, who they may for example experience as being aloof, insensitive, aggressive, bullying or arrogant. They can also result in considerable stress for the victim, inadequate work performance, repeated job losses, destructive relationships and problems with authority figures in the organization. This is most visible and damaging in occupations that require a significant amount of interpersonal interaction as an integral part of the job. This is of course very much the case in the caring professions, where there is a high degree of face-to-face interaction, and in the NHS where people are the organization's main asset and managing people and team working are of crucial import-ance, especially in intrinsically stressful environments which involve dealing with a range of emergency situations.

Price (2002) applied the concept of schema perpetuation to the work con-text. In his dynamic schema model, he argued that for some individuals with less rigid and extreme EMS and coping styles, re-enactment of EMS in the work context was a positive experience and resulted in successful adaptation and schema healing, for example through career success, caring for others or being 're-parented'. So for many it provides a corrective emotional experience and is adaptive, resulting in good occupational health, and it can be reward-ing for the majority of workers (Khaleelee 1994; Levy 2000; Price 2002). However, Price also argued that for some individuals, namely those with more rigid (unconscious) EMS, work-related stressors lead to an exacerbation of unconscious conflicts. This sub-group finds work aversive, and their EMS and coping styles predispose them to occupational stress. The re-enactment of their EMS and maladaptive coping styles exacerbate their problems and ultimately result in occupational ill health, which is manifested in the stress syndromes outlined in Chapter 6.

EMS, CAREER CHOICE AND RE-ENACTMENT IN THE WORKPLACE

There is a growing body of evidence that an individual's EMS play a signifi-cant role in determining career choice, and that people with certain types of EMS are attracted to particular types of career (unconsciously) for the pur-pose of re-enacting their EMS. The work environment readily lends itself to this, since the analogies between the early family environment and the work situation are numerous. For example, managers and supervisors are author-ity, parent-like figures and colleagues or peers can be seen to be analogous to one's siblings in the family system. This makes it in many ways an ideal scenario for the re-enactment of earlier familial dynamics.

A number of researchers have suggested that individuals select specific occupations (particularly vocational ones) to fulfil unconscious desires and to heal unconscious traumas (e.g. Bion 1961; Khaleelee 1994; Obholzer and Roberts 1994; Owen 1993; Peck 1987; Pines 2000; Sherman 1996). Khaleelee (1994) also argues that individuals entering the helping professions are motivated to do so by an unconscious desire to 'put something right within themselves', in order to 'work through' unresolved psychical conflicts from childhood. Pines (2000) asserts that our unconscious desires lead us to seek vocations which will enable us to 'replicate significant childhood experiences, gratify needs that were ungratified in . . . childhood and actualise occupational dreams and professional expectations passed on . . . [by] familial heritage' (Pines 2000: 634).

Individuals select their occupations based upon their traits, values and preferences – essentially their personality (Furnham 1997). Holland (1973) adds that because people choose vocational occupations which relate to their personality, then people in specific vocational occupations should share similar characteristics. McManus et al. (1996), in a study of 509 medical school applicants, found that personality variables were a highly significant predictor of speciality preference, being able to differentiate between 10 out of the 11 specialities. They concluded that individuals select their specialities based upon their own personality characteristics. Similarly, Borges and Osman (2001) investigated the personality differences between general surgeons, family practitioners and anaesthetists and found again that certain personality variables could differentiate the groups. Family practitioners were found to be warmer, more empathic and less dogmatic than those in the other two specialities. It is argued that doctors select specialities which are suited to their individual traits: individuals who exhibit dogmatic, controlling and detached traits select more technique-orientated specialities, whereas individuals who are more empathic select people-orientated specialities. Eron (1955) found that medical students reporting with higher levels of psychological distress were more likely to pursue careers in psychiatry.

Bartnick et al. (1985) found that medical students with lower self-assurance than average were more likely to pursue specialities with low patient contact such as pathology or pharmacology. Firth-Cozens (1999) found that characteristics such as high self-criticism in medical students were highly predictive of stress and depression in doctors 10 years later, and proposed that speciality choice may be involved in this pathway.

There is a considerable amount of evidence supporting the 'invisible hand' principle, which asserts that different personality types are attracted to different types of specialities, occupations and organizations (Holland 1985; Lowman 1991, 1993; Lowman and Schurman 1982; Schneider 1987; Smart et al. 1986).

Paris and Frank (1984) tested the hypothesis that amelioration of traumatic childhood experience is a major factor in the choice of a medical career. Their results exceeded expectations: evidence for the 'reparation hypothesis' was not confined to the medical speciality. Comparing a sample of 301 first-year medical students with 245 first-year law students, the authors found that male medical students were more likely to have experienced illness in the family during childhood than male law students, with both male and female law students more likely to have experienced legal problems within the family during childhood.

In an interview in *The Guardian* newspaper, celebrity psychotherapist Susie Orbach was quoted as saying: 'I don't know any analyst or therapist who didn't have personal issues that led them into the work' (Steiner 2002: 34). Research has highlighted how the personality of a psychotherapist is intrinsically linked to their theoretical orientation, and subsequently theoretical orientations can be differentiated on the basis of their practitioners' personalities (e.g. Arthur 2000; Scandell *et al.* 1997; Tremblay *et al.* 1986).

Owen (1993) argues that some therapists are attracted to the profession because of their own traumas, and so often come from a similar personality pool to their clients. This is echoed by Sherman (1996), who suggests that some individuals with problems may be attracted to psychotherapy as a profession, in order to resolve their own issues through their practice. Merodoulaki (1994) compared psychotherapists with computer scientists (control group), to test the hypothesis that psychotherapists are influenced in their occupational choice by early familial experiences. It was found that psychotherapists were significantly more affected by early experiences of separation and acting frequently as mediators in turbulent parental relationships.

Obholzer and Roberts (1994) assert that the (vocational) occupational choices we make, the client groups we wish to work with and the context, are all profoundly influenced by our need to come to terms with unresolved issues from our past. The authors offer several vignettes to illustrate their argument which are, in effect, re-enactments of childhood traumas. There is the lady who sacrifices her personal desires to look after disabled children (as a child she had to sacrifice her education to look after younger siblings while her mother worked); the family therapist who had difficulty controlling her rage at parents when she considered them to be behaving in harmful ways to their children (her father left home when she was four years old); and the man who was an unruly child and was made to feel guilty for burdening his single mother who became a strict disciplinarian headmaster at a boarding school for boys, where he envisaged his role as keeping the pupils under control and relieving the parents of a burden they found difficult to cope with.

Peck (1987) described a patient who was regularly beaten by his father as a child. As a result of his re-enactment, his chosen career was as a homicide detective, where he sought out the most violent crimes. Kets de Vries (1989), in a psychodynamic analysis of famous business leaders, suggests a frequent occurrence of absentee fathers (physical or emotional). The desire to be a leader/manager expresses the desire to become your own father and raise yourself again the 'right way', with total control over the events. It is hypothesized that this is why control is such an issue for these managers. This is supported by the findings of Holland (1985), who reported that managerial roles are filled by predominantly enterprising individuals who take pleasure in exercising authority and control over others (the parental role).

In conclusion, there is a considerable and growing body of evidence which provides support for the view that EMS play a significant role in career choice and that the work context provides a suitable setting in which individuals can re-enact their EMS.

The model presented in Figure 12.2 integrates the dynamic schema model developed by Price (2002) with the traditional Beckian model of stress (Beck 1987; Beck *et al.* 1985) outlined in Chapter 1 and Young's schema-focused model (Young *et al.* 2003) presented earlier in this chapter. The model places particular emphasis on the re-enactment of early maladaptive schemata (EMS) and behavioural coping strategies in the context of the workplace in the causation and maintenance of occupational stress.

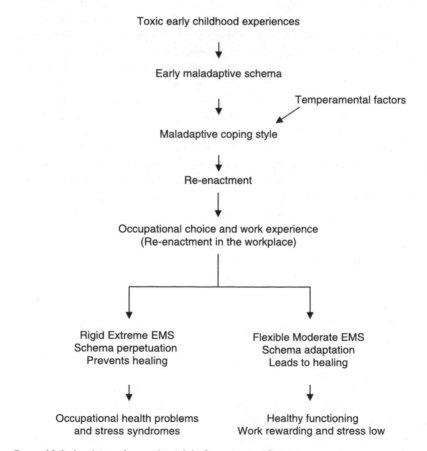

Figure 12.2 A schema-focused model of occupational stress.

CONCLUSIONS

Re-enactment of EMS in the workplace has both positive and negative mani-festations. For individuals with more flexible and less severe EMS and coping styles, it can be 'therapeutic'. Also, some EMS re-enactments have useful manifestations for health care organizations and are positively encouraged in the helping professions. However, if EMS are rigid and extreme, they can result in a build-up of stress and disillusionment in the individual who pos-sesses them. EMS constitute a psychological vulnerability, which makes the individual more prone to developing stress. If they are rigid and extreme, there is a greater likelihood that the individual who holds them will go on to develop a stress syndrome. It is also the case that if the EMS are rigid and extreme, then the individual is less likely to be consciously aware of them and that they will continue re-enacting their EMS 'ad infinitum'. In the work context, the impact on those they directly work with, or for the organiza-tion itself, can be great in terms of disruption of working relationships, underperformance and lost productivity.

It is important to recognize that within the schema-focused model pre-sented in this chapter, stress syndromes are not schema-specific and there is no direct one-to-one causal link between specific EMS and resulting stress syndromes. The same symptoms can result from a number of different under-lying schemata (Young *et al.* 2003: 65). For example, almost all EMS can result in anxiety or depressive symptoms. However, accurate identification of the specific underlying EMS is crucial since different EMS will require differ-ent treatment strategies. The model therefore emphasizes that one should be cautious not to jump to conclusions about underlying EMS solely on the basis of the presenting *DSM-IV* Axis 1 diagnosis

Also, in the model presented the correct identification of coping style is important. Like symptoms, coping styles are not considered to be schema-specific. For example, identifying that an individual is using an avoidant coping style tells us nothing about that individual's underlying EMS, since the avoidance could be in response to almost any EMS that causes the indi-vidual pain. The purpose of the coping style adopted is to block the EMS from awareness. However, in order to treat it the patient and therapist must be aware of the EMS. The purpose of schema-focused therapy is thus to bring the EMS to awareness and heal it.

Chapter 13

Work dysfunctions and their associated early maladaptive schemata and coping styles

Martin Bamber

INTRODUCTION

Due to the intense interpersonal nature of the work, health workers are frequently on the receiving end of the dysfunctional behaviour of others. For example, mental health workers are regularly exposed to patients with personality disorders, which manifest in a range of challenging behaviours. However, dysfunctional individuals are not just found in the patient population but also among the workforce – one's colleagues and managers. In fact, health care settings provide a fertile and attractive environment for such individuals to act out a broad range of dysfunctional behaviours. This can result in high levels of occupational stress, either for the dysfunctional individual or for those who are on the receiving end of their behaviours. The term 'work dysfunction' has been used to describe this maladaptive behavioural manifestation of occupational stress (Lowman 1997).

In this chapter it is proposed that a work dysfunction is the maladaptive behavioural re-enactment of an underlying EMS in the context of the work setting, and that each specific work dysfunction can be mapped onto its corresponding underlying EMS. It is also proposed that the severity of the work dysfunction is directly proportional to the severity of the underlying EMS driving it, and in the extreme the maladaptive behaviour displayed may fulfil the criteria for a personality disorder. The origins of work dysfunctions in the toxic environmental and family dynamics of the individual's early life are also hypothesized. However, no attempt is made to link EMS and maladaptive coping styles to specific occupational stress syndromes, since the model proposes that stress syndromes are not EMS-specific or coping style-specific. Three broad categories of work dysfunction are postulated, which correspond to the maladaptive coping styles of schema overcompensation, schema avoidance and schema surrender discussed in the last chapter. These are discussed in turn below.

OVER-COMPENSATORY PATTERNS OF WORK DYSFUNCTION

The workaholic employee

Workaholism is an 'addiction' to work, which results in a noticeable disturbance to the rest of the individual's life (Minirth *et al.* 1981; Morris and Charney 1983; Oates 1971). The workaholic employee typically presents with the Type A behavioural pattern discussed in Chapter 8, and is prone to burnout and lower self-esteem (Burke 2004; Burke and Matthiesen 2004; Machlowitz 1980; Minirth *et al.* 1981; Nagy and Davis 1985; Savickas 1990; Spruell 1987). Problems can also arise in the workaholic's personal life, since it is likely that their partner may eventually get fed up with their unavailability and inability to get the balance between work and home life right. This can result in marital disharmony and ultimately even divorce (Bartolome 1983; Klaft and Kleiner 1988; L'Abate and L'Abate 1981; Oates 1971; Spruell 1987).

The over-controlling employee

Over-controlling individuals allow little autonomy or independence in those they manage and find it difficult to delegate or allow decisions of any kind to be made without them being present. They do not trust others to get on with things and need to know everything that is going on in minute detail. Their behaviour can range from mild bossiness to autocratic behaviour and bullying at the extreme end of the continuum. In managerial positions they can cause a considerable amount of stress for those they manage and their behaviours can also be detrimental to the productivity of the organization.

In positions of unchecked authority, they can become 'control freaks'. Despite wielding their power, control freaks still feel insecure about their position and require constant and unrelenting reassurance of their power to control and dominate others. They can become envious or jealous of those who remind them of what they believe is missing in themselves, and perceive them to be a direct threat to their power. They perceive themselves to be in direct competition with these individuals, who they feel must be defeated. Consequently, they can engage in acts of harassment against these individuals, in an attempt to erode their confidence and psychologically defeat them. If this does not have the desired outcome for the control freak, he/she can resort to more extreme bullying tactics in an attempt to achieve power and control and may also encourage fellow workers to behave abusively towards their chosen victim (Einarsen 2000; Shengold 1989).

The rebellious employee

Work is a battleground for rebellious employees, since it allows them to re-enact their problems with authority figures. They are fighting against being subjugated or controlled by behaving in over-critical, angry, non-conformist, disobedient and antagonistic ways towards those who they perceive to be in authority. They make the most of every opportunity to try to catch their managers out, or show them up as inept and incapable of doing their job. They may also dress in 'anti-establishment' clothes to emphasize their rejection of the established order.

Another more subtle form of rebellion is passive-aggressive behaviour. These individuals present as superficially compliant but secretly get their 'revenge' by engaging in acts to undermine the organization or individuals within it. They demonstrate a pervasive pattern of negative attitudes and passive resistance to demands for adequate performance in occupational situations, and can elicit strong negative responses from their work colleagues as a result of their attitudes and behaviours. In the extreme, they may engage in acts of 'sabotage' aimed at getting their superiors into trouble and disrupting the smooth running of the organization (American Psychiatric Association [APA] 2000; Unterberg 2003).

The manipulative employee

Manipulation is defined as 'exploitation for one's own ends' (*Oxford English Dictionary*). In its milder form it can be adaptive in certain work settings, where it facilitates the employee's advancement and goal achievement. Consequently, manipulative individuals often get promoted to management positions where they can continue to manipulate others. However, as long as they do what is best for the organization's bottom line, they are unlikely to be discovered. The problem is that they can be extremely destructive for the organization and leave in their wake a trail of devastation and distress (Chitty and Maynard 1986; Davidhizer and Giger 1990; Jarczewski 1988; Lowman 1997; Shoestrom 1967; Vogal *et al.* 1987; Wiley 1968). In its extreme form it is known as 'Machiavellianism', after the 15th-century Italian politician Niccolo Machiavelli, whose name has become synonymous with deviousness, manipulation, deceit and opportunism in interpersonal relationships. This behaviour has been linked with antisocial and psychopathic personality disorders and such individuals are often described as 'con men' or, if in leadership positions, 'ruthless leaders' (APA 2000; Brune 2001; Christie 1970; Gupta 1987; Knecht 2004; Lowman 1997; McAlpine 2000; Smith 1999; Unterberg 2003).

The origins of over-compensatory work dysfunctions

When an individual over-compensates for an underlying EMS, they behave as if the opposite of the EMS were true in an attempt to distance themselves from it. Thus, it is proposed that workaholism is an attempting to 'undo' previous failures (Machlowitz 1980). In childhood, these individuals may have been made to feel fundamentally inadequate relative to their peers in areas of achievement such as academia or sports, and to feel that they were less successful than others. It is postulated that children who have been economically, socially or emotionally deprived, or who have experienced love as being conditional upon success, may be more prone to become workaholics in adulthood (Machlowitz 1980; Oates 1971; Thorne 1987).

Where the EMS underlying workaholism is one of defectiveness/shame, it is proposed that the over-compensatory behaviour is an attempt to distance oneself from feelings of inferiority. These individuals may have experienced adverse experiences such as rejection, criticism and blame from significant care-givers as a child, which have led to them feeling in some way unwanted, inferior, invalid and ashamed of themselves. However it is also proposed that, in some cases, workaholism can be a 'failure avoidance' coping strategy, in which work is used to provide a convenient distraction from other issues that are causing anxiety, such as avoiding closeness with others or other non-work roles (Bartolome 1983; Klaft and Kleiner 1988). For example, the individual may bury him/herself in work in order to avoid thinking about the breakdown or 'failure' of their marriage.

Thus, workaholics aim, through the process of over-compensation, to experience feelings of status, success and self-worth that they were unable to achieve in childhood and, as long as they are being successful in this respect, they are able to maintain a fragile sense of self-esteem. However, setbacks at work can be a shattering experience for such individuals and trigger the failure and/or defectiveness/shame EMS and elicit extreme stress reactions.

It is proposed that where over-controlling individuals possess the underlying EMS of mistrust and abuse, they may have experienced being abused or let down by significant care-givers as a child and want to make sure that this does not happen to them again in adulthood. The individual is hyper-vigilant to signals indicating that others might abuse them, and perceives others as untrustworthy, possessing malevolent motives and being out to hurt or harm them. More worrying is the possibility that these individuals may desire to abuse others, in order to make them feel as vulnerable and weak as they did in childhood (Freud 1961; Fromm 1974).

Where the subjugation EMS is the underlying schema, individuals may have experienced being controlled excessively by a dominating care-giver as a child and want to prevent the feelings of helplessness and hopelessness they felt then from happening again. Alternatively, as for the mistrust and abuse EMS, they may want to make others experience how they felt as a child by subjugating and controlling them. The individual is hyper-vigilant for signals which indicate that others are trying to control and dominate them, and their behaviour can be seen as a pre-emptive form of defence, aimed at stopping others from controlling or dominating them.

It is proposed that where the underlying EMS is one of defectiveness/shame, the individual was made to feel worthless as a child. The aim of the over-compensatory behaviour is thus forcefully to demand the recognition, respect and esteem that they believe they cannot win by other means, or by being simply who they are (i.e. not good enough, unloved, bad). It can also be an attempt to make others feel worthless, sidelined and unimportant, just as they did as a child.

In conclusion, autocratic individuals aim, through the process of re-enactment of their EMS in the workplace, to experience the feelings of power, control, esteem and recognition that they were not able to experience in childhood.

Rebellious individuals may have experienced being controlled excessively by a dominating care-giver as a child and want to prevent the feelings of helplessness and hopelessness they felt then from happening again. Where the EMS is one of subjugation, it is proposed that the individual fears that others will try to dominate, bully or control them, or try to curtail their autonomy, and they thus fight to prevent themselves from becoming subjugated in this way. It is proposed that where the EMS is one of failure, the over-compensatory rebellious behaviour may be a defensive strategy which the individual uses to distance themselves from their own feelings of failure and lack of achievement. The re-enactment is an attempt to 'undo' previous perceived failures, such as lack of academic success at school, in sports and in their career. It is misdirected at authority figures, and sometimes peers who they perceive as successful, or who are viewed positively by authority figures.

It is hypothesized that manipulative individuals may have experienced abuse or been let down by significant care-givers in childhood and have the expectation that others are untrustworthy, have malevolent motives and will abuse, lie to, manipulate, hurt or take advantage of them. The manipulative and devious behaviours are thus over-compensatory strategies for the underlying mistrust and abuse EMS, and the re-enactment is aimed at out-manoeuvring others before they get the chance to do it to them. They want to make absolutely sure that what happened to them in childhood does not happen to them again in adulthood.

AVOIDANT PATTERNS OF WORK DYSFUNCTION

The under-achieving employee

There are two main avoidant coping styles associated with under-achieving. These are failure avoidance and success avoidance. The failure-avoidant individual fears failure relative to their peers in areas of achievement such as career, status, income and educational attainment. They are thus unwilling to compete with others to improve themselves. Failure-avoidant individuals can be quite bright intellectually and may claim that they are wasted in their present job and are capable of better things. Yet they seem unable, or unwilling, to make the effort to improve themselves, for example by enrolling at college or doing further training. In contrast, success-avoidant individuals display a persistent tendency to avoid behaviours associated with achievement, such as decision-making, taking responsibility, using their initiative or going for promotion. They fear that they will not be able to cope with the responsibilities demanded of them if they are successful and may find face-saving ways of not taking on new responsibilities.

Both failure-avoidant and success-avoidant individuals may also engage in the maladaptive coping strategy of procrastination. This form of avoidance essentially involves 'putting off until tomorrow what one should do today'. Procrastinators repeatedly avoid the timely initiation and completion of assignments that need to be completed by a certain deadline. This often results in a surge of last-minute effort, considerable anxiety and a lower quality of work due to the task being rushed (Milgram *et al.* 1988).

The withdrawn employee

The withdrawn employee prefers not to associate with others and tries to isolate him/herself from work colleagues as far as possible. They are seen by others as unsociable, unfriendly and isolated. Their avoidant behaviour may have adverse effects on occupational functioning because they try to avoid the social situations that may be important for meeting the basic demands of the job or for career advancement. It is hypothesized that their restricted interpersonal contact may be the result of hypersensitivity to rejection, low self-esteem or fear of conflict or mistreatment by others. They avoid social groups at work because they feel 'different' from others and believe that they do not fit in to any group, and because they fear that they will be rejected if they try to fit in.

The mistrusting employee

Mistrusting employees range from those who are mildly suspicious of the motives of others to those who display paranoid personality traits (Reich *et al.* 1989; Unterberg 2003). They are highly sensitive to negative cues, readily blame others and are pre-occupied by doubts about the loyalty or trustworthiness of their work colleagues. They avoid confiding in or becoming close to others, since they fear that any information they give may be used against them at a later date. They have a strong need to be self-sufficient and autonomous and are often finely attuned to power and rank issues in the workplace. Interestingly they are often successful at work as 'leaders' in certain kinds of organizations, especially in highly competitive occupations, since they are able to channel their energies to counter perceived threats of abuse or control from enemies. In non-managerial positions, they may be attracted to trade union or shop steward activities as a means of re-enacting their EMS.

The timid employee

The timid employee perceives a wide range of situations as potentially dangerous and threatening. Whenever possible they avoid taking risks of any kind and emphasize 'playing safe' at all times. They seek consistency and predictability and become highly anxious when this is not the case. For example, organizational change, restructuring, having a new boss or being redeployed can lead to these individuals becoming paralysed with fear and insecurity. In such situations, they anticipate that things will go disastrously wrong, such as experiencing being made redundant, disciplinary action, being fired, financial ruin or accidents, and they anticipate that they will not be able to cope. They are particularly prone to panic attacks, chronic anxiety and worry and phobic avoidance.

Origins of avoidant patterns of work dysfunction

When an individual adopts an avoidant coping style, they are trying to prevent their underlying EMS from being activated by avoiding any situation that may trigger them. These individuals may have learned to believe as children that they were untalented and lack what it takes to succeed, and they fear being seen to be incompetent. Thus, failure-avoidant and success-avoidant individuals and procrastinators may have the failure or defectiveness/shame EMS and cope with it by avoiding situations where there is a risk of disapproval, criticism, rejection or failure. At the same time, they may experience strong feelings of resentment and frustration at their own inability to break out of their self-defeating patterns of behaviour (Brenner and Tomkiewicz 1982).

Withdrawn individuals experience anxiety and avoid social situations at work such as groups or meetings, where they perceive their competence to be 'on trial'. It is proposed that the underlying EMS for this avoidant coping style may be either social isolation/alienation or defectiveness/shame. Where the social isolation/alienation EMS is present, the individual is hyper-vigilant for signals that indicate that they are different from others. Where defectiveness/shame is the underlying EMS, the individual may be excessively self-conscious and feel inferior to others. The avoidance strategy stops these EMS from becoming activated.

The mistrusting employee with the mistrust and abuse EMS is hyper-vigilant for signals indicating that others might abuse them, and so avoids situations where they may be vulnerable or might have to trust others. Where there is an underlying subjugation EMS the individual is hyper-vigilant for signals which indicate that others are trying to control and dominate them, and so avoids situations where there is a possibility of this happening. Where the underlying EMS is a defectiveness/shame schema, the individual is hyper-vigilant for signals and will avoid situations that could expose their defectiveness.

Timid individuals avoid a whole range of situations that they perceive as dangerous and threatening. It is proposed that these individuals have the vulnerability to harm or illness EMS and the avoidant behaviour prevents this EMS from becoming activated.

SURRENDERING PATTERNS OF WORK DYSFUNCTION

The dependent employee

The dependent employee presents as childlike and helpless. They lack faith in their own judgements and decision-making and try to find a substitute parent in their boss or supervisor at work, who they look to for direction and structure. Their underperformance is due to a strongly held belief that they are incapable of taking on responsibility. They thus duck their responsibilities whenever possible, avoid decision-making and perceive that they are unable to take on new tasks on their own. They give up easily on tasks, repeatedly seek advice and, as one might expect, are unassertive at work. As a consequence of their beliefs about their own incompetence, they inevitably gravitate to lower level jobs where independent thinking and decision-making are not required, and they refuse promotion at work if it is ever offered. Because of their ineffectual behaviours, their colleagues often label them as 'shirkers'. They are usually resented by their peers, who feel that they are carrying them, and also by the boss, who gets fed up with constantly having to give them support, directions and advice, and who becomes frustrated that they cannot work autonomously when required. Their failure to achieve the expected level of performance or reach their potential is not due to lack of ability but is more about their reticent style of behaviour (Lowman 1997).

The submissive employee

The submissive employee relinquishes power and control to others who they perceive to have more power and control than them. They are unassertive, do not stand up for their rights and allow others who they perceive as more powerful or better than them to get their own way with little resistance. Some of the main reasons for surrendering to the control of others include a lack of self-confidence to confront others, fear of conflict, fear of disapproval and rejection, fear of others becoming angry and retaliating, fear of losing one's job and fear of failure (Alberti and Emmons 2001; Back and Back 1999; Bond 1988; Burnard 1992; Dickson 1986).

Another form of submissive behaviour is found in the self-sacrificing individual. These are slightly different from unassertive individuals: whereas unassertive individuals experience a strong sense of coercion to submit to others, self-sacrificing individuals perceive their submissiveness to be a voluntary act. The voluntary nature of their always putting the needs of others first allows them to avoid feelings of guilt or selfishness. Self-sacrificing individuals are of at least average and often above-average intelligence, but appear to underperform and never seem to achieve their potential. In situations where it seems that they may be about to be successful, they engage in acts of self-sacrifice, for example declining an interview, giving up a training course in the final year, refusing promotion when they are clearly able to do the job, flunking exams through not preparing properly and so on. They often rationalize these acts by saying that they were putting others first.

Submissive employees are more susceptible to becoming victims of abuse by unscrupulous colleagues and managers. The abusive individual may well be one of the over-compensating individuals described earlier, such as the bully, the control freak or the Machiavellian, who are usually good at recognizing these vulnerable individuals since they may share the same underlying EMS. Because they are excessively compliant, abusers can create many unofficial and often humiliating roles for them in the workplace. For example, they may be reduced to a 'gofer' who runs errands for them, or a 'lackey' who takes on the role of a servile follower. In the grasp of a particularly manipulative or bullying individual, a submissive employee may be reduced to the role of an unofficial 'spy' who acts as an informer on others, or the 'pet', 'joker' or 'sycophant' whose role is to massage the ego of the bully and keep them amused, entertained or flattered. Exposure to workplace bullying has been associated with anxiety, depression, aggression, insomnia, melancholy, apathy and cognitive effects such as concentration problems, insecurity and lack of initiative (Bjorkqvist et al. 1994; Einarsen et al. 1994; Koss 1990; Leymann 1992; Quine 1999; Richman et al. 1999).

The overly loyal employee

A certain degree of loyalty to the organization is seen as adaptive, a sign that the employee is experiencing job satisfaction; it can also have significant benefits for the organization. This is known as 'organizational citizenship', which is defined as 'individual behaviour that is discretionary, not directly or explicitly recognized by the formal reward system and that in the aggregate promotes the effective functioning of the organization' (Organ 1988: 4). However, overly loyal individuals persist in an area of work or relationships associated with it long after it is seen to be beneficial to either their own emotional welfare or their career prospects. They are often unable to set limits with respect to the job and consequently are often taken advantage of by unscrupulous managers and colleagues, for example by being paid less than the job is worth, working long hours without appropriate remuneration or doing unofficial errands for the boss. It is hypothesized that they are seeking a good parent figure, which they did not have as a child, and that their subservient behaviour can be seen as an attempt to maintain connectedness with the 'parental' figure. They can ultimately lose their own identity and take on their boss's problems as their own.

The demanding employee

Demanding individuals are often described as difficult employees, since they usually experience a lot of conflict at work and are continually expressing a sense of injustice about how unfairly they feel they are being treated. They are often the 'high maintenance' employees who take up a disproportionate amount of a supervisor's time and are continually taking from, rather than giving to, the organization. Two types of demanding employee are identified below. These are the entitled employees and the attention-seeking employees.

Entitled employees have an exaggerated sense of their own importance and worth. They feel that they are superior to others, do not need to live by the same rules and have difficulty tolerating frustration or respecting the rights of others. They tend to lack self-control, are easily bored, give up easily and are habitually unreliable. Yet, at the same time, they expect constant unearned high praise, no matter what their actual effort or result, and see authority figures at work, such as supervisors or managers, who do not give them this as being unfair and withholding.

In more senior and managerial positions these individuals may bend or break policies, procedures and rules to achieve their own ends, with little concern about the impact this may have on others. They are also prone to becoming abusive and aggressive when thwarted or frustrated in their goals. This can create a hostile environment and lead to complaints and grievances from work colleagues and patients. At the extreme end of the continuum, they may fulfil the criteria for a narcissistic personality disorder (Adams 1992; APA 2000; Berg 1990; Cramer 2000; Raskin and Shaw 1988; Ronningstam and Gunderson 1988; Unterberg 2003).

Attention-seeking employees place an excessive emphasis on being the centre of attention by behaving dramatically and dressing flamboyantly. They display overly emotional reactions to everyday situations. At first their superficial charm can be attractive and engaging but, over time, they can cause problems by constantly over-reacting and demanding attention. They also tend to show a lack of substantive achievement but react particularly strongly to criticism or disapproval. This can present problems for the manager or supervisor who is trying to give them constructive feedback. In the extreme they may fit the criteria for a histrionic personality disorder (APA 2000; Lowman 1997; Millon 1981; Pfohl 1991; Unterberg 2003).

The obsessive employee

Obsessive individuals compulsively insist on rigid adherence to rules and strict standards of performance for themselves and others, and are perceived as stubborn, obstinate, controlling and unyielding by their work colleagues. They tend to be perfectionists and spend an inordinate amount of time constantly striving to prevent feelings of failure. The characteristics of the perfectionist have already been described in detail in Chapter 8, so will not be duplicated here. They are hypersensitive to criticism, rejection, disapproval and blame and set excessively rigid, moralistic and overly punitive standards for themselves and others. This may be the source of counter-productive disruptions among fellow workers. In the extreme the behaviour of these individuals may fulfil the criteria for an obsessive-compulsive personality disorder (APA 2000; Naughton 1987; Pollak 1979; Schwartz 1982).

Another manifestation of the obsessive employee can be found in overly moralistic individuals, whose expectations regarding standards of conduct go way beyond those expected in professional codes of conduct. They are unable to tolerate even minor transgressions due to human frailties and rigidly adhere to 'principles'. In the extreme they may even see themselves as a sort of 'moral crusader' who puts the decision to inform over a breach of ethical principle above loyalty to the organization, and perhaps even their colleagues, and become what is known as a 'whistle blower'. While whistle blowers may be individuals of marked principle, their idealistic stance and willingness to inform on their colleagues or the organization makes others treat them with suspicion, and they are seen as a potential embarrassment to the organization. Additionally, a culture in which employees readily tell on their colleagues, and managers readily encourage them to, can lead to low morale (Faugier and Woolnough 2001; Francis 1999).

The 'disciplinarian' manifests another form of obsessive behaviour. These are overly punitive individuals who believe that people, including themselves, should be harshly punished for their mistakes. Like overly moralistic individuals, they are undiscriminating, lack mercy for any human imperfections or frailties and display a rigid, inflexible, dichotomous 'all or nothing' quality to their thinking. The main reaction of the disciplinarian is anger and for employees who are managed by such an individual it is anxiety.

The divisive employee

Divisive employees subtly influence their co-workers by creating rifts and engaging in child-like divisive conflicts, in which they over-idealize or devalue others.

They are characteristically impulsive, unpredictable and interpersonally intense. They experience rapid and intense mood changes and consequently can cause seriously disruptive effects in the workplace. Managers, supervisors and others in the workplace need to be constantly aware, when handling such employees, that the divisive employee tends to polarize his/her views of work colleagues into two categories, 'all good' and 'all bad', and react to them accordingly. Most work organizations will not tolerate this kind of behaviour for too long, since it is too disruptive. In the extreme, this pattern of behaviour may fulfil the criteria for borderline personality disorder (APA 2000; Kaplan 1986; Lowman 1997; Millon 1981; Salz 1983; Shapiro 1979; Snyder et al. 1986; Trimpy and Davidson 1994; Unterberg 2003).

The origins of surrendering patterns of work dysfunction

Individuals who adopt the surrender coping style yield to their EMS and let it control their behaviours. They do not try to fight (compensate) or avoid it but accept the schema as true, and act in ways which confirm it for them. They continue to re-enact the EMS in the same unadulterated form that they did in childhood, and relive as adults the childhood experiences that originally created it. For example, dependent employees are re-enacting their dependency/ incompetence EMS, and effectively behave in a way which is asking others to look after them and make their decisions for them.

Submissive employees may be re-enacting an underlying defectiveness/ shame EMS: the individual may be lack the self-confidence to stand up to others, who they feel inferior to. Where there is an underlying subjugation EMS, the individual surrenders by letting others, who they perceive as being stronger and more powerful than them, take control. Where there is an underlying self-sacrifice EMS, the voluntary act of putting others first stops the individual from experiencing feelings of guilt or selfishness. Where the EMS is one of emotional deprivation, submissiveness is a strategy for ensuring that they will not be abandoned or rejected by significant others. One example of this was a nurse who was at risk of outdoing her partner career-wise, who voluntarily turned down promotion to a managerial post since she believed it would jeopardize their relationship.

Alternatively, the submissive behaviour may be a strategy for getting approval, which is driven by an underlying approval-recognition-seeking EMS. These individuals believe that if they do not engage in these acts of subjugation or self-sacrifice, they will be disapproved of and ultimately rejected. One example of this was the hospital porter from a working class background who voluntarily turned down the offer of a place to do a nursing degree, for fear of being rejected and alienated from his working class roots. He feared that his family and friends would see him as 'becoming a "snob" and "too big for his boots". Submissive individuals are often more concerned about getting external approval by pleasing their family, friends, boss or work colleagues, than advancing their own career.

It is proposed that where the underlying EMS is one of mistrust/abuse, the individual's submissive behaviour is a strategy aimed at preventing the adverse consequences of standing up against others, who they believe may abuse and harm them. It is also hypothesized that linked to the mistrust and abuse EMS may be the dependency/incompetence and/or the emotional deprivation EMS. Where there is a linked dependency/incompetence EMS, the individual fears that they will be unable to function independently if the protection of a stronger individual is removed from them, and sees putting up with abuse as preferable to being on their own. Where the emotional deprivation EMS is present, the individual may accept the abuse as an inevitable part of their inferiority and un-lovability, and see this treatment as preferable to the alternative of rejection and abandonment. 'Better the devil you know' is their view.

Individuals who adopt the overly loyal type of surrendering coping style may have the underlying enmeshment/undeveloped self EMS. As for those with subjugation, dependency and mistrust and abuse EMS, they are easy targets for unscrupulous manipulative and bullying individuals.

It is hypothesized that demanding individuals with the entitlement/grandiosity EMS typically come from family backgrounds where the main care-givers were over-indulgent, excessively permissive and failed to set limits in terms of discipline, respect for others and frustration tolerance. They have consequently adopted the belief that it is acceptable to achieve one's own desires without empathy or concern for others' feelings or needs (Cannella and Monroe 1997; Lally 1997). On the other hand, it is proposed that attention-seeking employees experienced conditional love and acceptance from care-givers and had to suppress important aspects of their own individuality in order to gain love, acceptance and approval, and consequently developed the underlying approval-seeking/recognition-seeking EMS.

It is proposed that obsessive individuals with perfectionistic or moralistic coping styles are surrendering to their underlying unrelenting standards/hypercriticalness EMS. They are constantly striving to meet their own (or their parents') unrealistically high expectations or standards, and failure to excel is experienced every bit as strongly as genuine failure. One example of this was the student who got a place at university but felt a failure because she did not get into Oxford or Cambridge. Being average is interpreted as being a failure. The typical family origin of disciplinarians is hypothesized to be strict and punitive, emphasizing rigid adherence to rules and avoiding mistakes over enjoyment and relaxation, and underlying this type of behaviour is the punitiveness EMS.

Table 13.1 Summary of work dysfunctions and associated EMS and coping styles

Work dysfunction	Underlying early maladaptive schema	Coping style
The workaholic employee	Failure/defectiveness-shame	Over-compensation
The over-controlling employee	Mistrust-abuse/subjugation/ defectiveness-shame	Over-compensation
The rebellious employee	Subjugation/failure	Over-compensation
The manipulative employee	Mistrust-abuse	Over-compensation
The under-achieving employee	Failure/defectiveness-shame	Avoidance
The withdrawn employee	Social isolation-alienation/ defectiveness-shame	Avoidance
The mistrusting employee	Mistrust-abuse/subjugation/ defectiveness-shame	Avoidance
The timid employee	Vulnerability to harm-illness	Avoidance
The dependent employee	Dependency-incompetence	Surrender
The submissive employee	Subjugation/self-sacrifice/ approval-recognition-seeking/ emotional deprivation/mistrust-abuse/defectiveness-shame	Surrender
The overly loyal employee	Enmeshment-undeveloped self	Surrender
The demanding employee	Entitlement-grandiosity/ insufficient self-control or self-discipline/approval-recognition-seeking	Surrender
The obsessive employee	Unrelenting standards-hypercriticalness/punitiveness	Surrender
The divisive employee	Multiple EMS	Switches between over-compensation, avoidance and surrender

Divisive individuals may have experienced inconsistent, unpredictable and interpersonally intense parenting, and possibly early childhood trauma or abuse. Because of their multiple EMS and unstable coping styles, it is proposed that these individuals are more suitable candidates for schema mode therapy, rather than standard schema therapy (see Chapter 14 for the criteria for using mode therapy).

A schema-focused approach to treating work dysfunctions

Martin Bamber

INTRODUCTION

The schema concept is not a new one (Beck 1967, 1976; Beck *et al.* 1990; Piaget 1962). More recently, however, there has been a growing consensus about the validity of the schema concept (Lee *et al.* 1999; Schmidt *et al.* 1995; Shah and Waller 2000; Stopa *et al.* 2001; Waller *et al.* 2001; Young and Brown 2001; Young *et al.* 2003). Similarly, the evidence base for schema therapy has also been growing and the results are promising (Bamber 2004; McGinn *et al.* 1995; Young and Behary 1998; Young *et al.* 1993, 2003). However, while there has been some literature applying the schema concept to the work setting (e.g. Price 2002), there is none applying the schema concept or the schema-focused approach specifically to treating the occupational stress associated with work dysfunctions.

This chapter addresses the gap in the literature by applying the schema-focused approach to the treatment of work dysfunctions. It extrapolates from the application of schema therapy in other settings to the work place. Unfortunately, an in-depth discussion of the detailed schema treatment strategies for each specific work dysfunction identified in Chapter 13 is beyond the scope of this book. However, this chapter presents an overview of the assessment, formulation and some of the main schema treatment strategies which can be applied to treat work dysfunctions.

ASSESSMENT

The clinical interview

The aim of the interview is to identify dysfunctional work patterns and the associated underlying early maladaptive schemata (EMS). The therapist also aims to obtain a better understanding of the origins of these EMS and, using this information, attempts to understand the nature of the re-enactment taking place through the work dysfunction manifested. The information gathered is similar to that covered in the standard CBT interview in Chapter 3, with some differences. One difference is that the history is taken in reverse chronological order. It starts in the present and moves back through time; as it does so, the therapist looks for periods of schema activation in the past. In particular, the therapist looks for examples of 'repeating themes' and the triggers for them. Eventually the therapist and the patient end up exploring the early childhood origins of the EMS identified. The therapist also looks for clues about the patient's temperament and coping styles, by identifying their responses to adverse childhood experiences.

Questionnaires

There is a range of questionnaires to assist the therapist in identifying underlying EMS and maladaptive coping styles, such as the Young Schema Questionnaire long and short versions (Young 1998; Young and Brown 1994), the Young Parenting Inventory (Young 1994b), the Young-Rygh Avoidance Inventory (Young and Rygh 1994) and the Young Compensation Inventory (Young 1994c).

Techniques for eliciting underlying EMS

The use of 'Socratic questioning', together with the 'downward arrow' technique, allows the therapist to move down a chain of cognitions and access deeper-level meanings and cognitions and ultimately end up at the underlying EMS. The following example illustrates this technique in relation to the defectiveness/shame EMS. It is taken from a therapy session with an NHS unit manager who had particularly rigid and uncompromising standards for his own performance and who had made a relatively minor miscalculation in his budget for the unit in a report sent to his senior manager:

Therapist: OK so you made a miscalculation with the budget. What is so upsetting about this for you?
Patient: It means that I have failed.
Therapist: Supposing this is true and you have failed, what does this mean to you?
Patient: I am not up to the job.
Therapist: Suppose this is true. What would that mean to you?
Patient: My manager might spot the mistake and discipline or even sack me. I could lose my job.
Therapist: And if this happened, what would it say about you?
Patient: If I lost my job it would mean I was totally incompetent. People would think I was useless and not want to have anything to do with me any more. My wife would probably leave me and take the

children with her. I would not be able to pay the mortgage and could end up homeless.

Therapist: What would that mean to you?

Patient: It would mean that I had totally messed up my life.

Therapist: And if that were true. What would it mean to you?

Patient: It would mean that my life was not worth living.

Another useful technique for eliciting underlying EMS is known as the 'satellite technique'. The patient is asked to identify five important things about their past. The therapist and the patient then work together to identify one theme common to all five things identified. This can also be used as a homework exercise and if the patient doesn't come back with a central theme it can form the basis for the next therapy session. An example of this is illustrated in Figure 14.1.

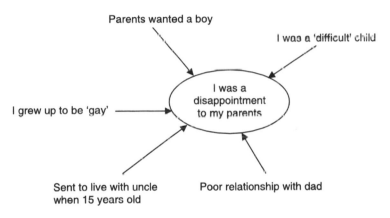

Figure 14.1 The satellite technique.

Assessing suitability for schema therapy

Patients who indulge in moderate to severe drug or alcohol abuse are not considered suitable, since the therapy aims to work with emotions, and these are numbed by the substance abuse. Those with acute and severe untreated DSM-IV axis one problems requiring more immediate attention, such as panic attacks, insomnia or an eating disorder, for example, are best treated using the standard CBT symptom relief approach as described in Part II of this book. Also, problems that are identified as situational and do not seem to be related to a maladaptive life pattern or underlying EMS (i.e. state rather than trait), and those where there is a major life crisis in some life area, are not considered suitable for schema therapy. For example, if the employee is on the verge of being sacked, then it is more appropriate to work on resolving the crisis first, before undertaking schema therapy. Psychotic patients are not considered suitable for this form of therapy either.

DEVELOPING A SCHEMA-FOCUSED FORMULATION OF WORK DYSFUNCTION

A schema-focused formulation involves identifying the toxic early experiences, the severity and rigidity of the underlying EMS, the maladaptive coping styles used and the temperament of the individual. A hypothesis is made about the link between these and what is being re-enacted in the workplace, through the work dysfunction identified. The patient is then encouraged to read books, or watch movies, which the therapist considers might trigger their EMS, and the patient's reactions to them can be used to confirm or disconfirm the hypotheses made. A typical developmental formulation is shown in Figure 14.2.

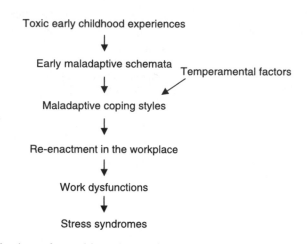

Toxic early childhood experiences

Early maladaptive schemata   Temperamental factors

Maladaptive coping styles

Re-enactment in the workplace

Work dysfunctions

Stress syndromes

Figure 14.2 A schema-focused formulation of work dysfunction.

Socializing to the model

Socializing the patient to the schema model of work dysfunction begins with helping them to understand the origins of their EMS in their childhood and adolescence. They are then taught to monitor their EMS and maladaptive coping styles through self-monitoring assignments using a schema diary. One good way of explaining EMS to patients is by using the 'weed' analogy. Positive functional thoughts are described as a bed of flowers and negative automatic thoughts, dysfunctional assumptions and EMS are the weeds in the flower bed. The three different levels of dysfunctional belief are seen as being analogous to different parts of the weeds. Surface-level negative automatic thoughts are the part of the weed that is above the ground, while dysfunctional assumptions and EMS are analogous to the roots beneath the surface. Cutting the weeds at ground level may solve the problem in the short term and make the garden look pretty again but sooner or later they will grow again. Schema-focused work is analogous to removing the weeds by the roots that penetrate most deeply in to the soil (Padesky 1994).

AN OVERVIEW OF SCHEMA TREATMENT STRATEGIES

Schema-focused treatment strategies consist of cognitive, experiential and behavioural techniques which aim to modify EMS and maladaptive coping styles. Young *et al.* (2003) recommended that the therapist starts with cognitive and experiential techniques, in order to prepare the individual for behavioural change, which is the ultimate aim of the therapy. The cognitive techniques aim to help the patient articulate a healthy voice with which to dispute and build a logical, rational argument against the EMS. Experiential techniques help the individual identify their unmet core emotional needs and find ways to heal these through 'partial re-parenting' in therapy. Schema therapy thus focuses on modifying dysfunctional EMS and breaking behavioural patterns. In the context of work dysfunctions the ultimate aim of the therapy is to replace dysfunctional work patterns with more adaptive functional patterns.

Cognitive strategies

Cognitive techniques help the patient develop a healthy adult voice to dispute their EMS. They allow the patient to step outside their EMS, build a logical case against it and fight it with an alternative truth. EMS take longer to change than surface-level automatic thoughts or intermediate-level dysfunctional assumptions, because the patient requires a lot more evidence over a prolonged period of time to convince them that these 'absolute' and usually long-held beliefs are not 100% true. Therefore, schema-focused work is done over a longer time span than standard CBT (20-plus sessions). The cognitive techniques described can be used for the whole range of EMS identified in the work dysfunctions in Chapter 13 (see Table 13.1).

Systematic challenging of EMS

The patient is encouraged to think about what it would be like if they did not have the EMS, and also about how they would like others to behave towards them. They are then asked to list the evidence that supports and does not support the EMS. The patient is encouraged to record any bit of evidence, however small or apparently insignificant, which suggests that the EMS is not 100% true. Noticing small positive experiences is particularly important to counteract the automatic tendency to remember the negative ones that support the EMS.

The next stage is to identify and strengthen a new alternative healthy schema. As the patient identifies and tests the validity of the EMS, they are encouraged to identify alternative beliefs that are less extreme, absolute and negative. For example, if the individual believes at first that they are totally unloveable, but then they shift a small amount to the belief 'there are one or two people that love me', the new alternative belief can be substituted for the original more absolute negative belief. Such a shift may appear to be small, but it can be very significant and powerful for the patient and is indicative of the EMS crumbling around the edges. The patient is then given homework assignments in which they are asked to record evidence in a schema diary that supports the new alternative schema.

Historical test of the evidence

An additional technique used to evaluate and strengthen new schema consists of reviewing the patient's past for experiences that support the new schema. The patient is asked to recall and write down past experiences that are consistent with the new schema. This often involves the patient having to think long and hard to remember schema-congruent experiences, or talking to other people who knew them at different stages in their life to gather this information. For example, if the original EMS was 'I am unloveable' and the new core belief is 'I am loveable', the therapist and patient explore events at each stage in the patient's life from birth onwards that support the belief that the patient is loveable. It is useful to break the patient's life up into 'age bands' such as from birth to two years, three to five, six to twelve and so on, in order to categorize their experiences.

Taking oneself to court

This technique is linked to the historical test of the evidence. The patient is asked to imagine that they are in a court of law. With them in the room are the judge, a jury of fair-minded and rational individuals, the lawyer for the prosecution and the lawyer for the defence. The job of the lawyer for the prosecution is to present evidence which can convince the judge and jury that the patient in the dock is guilty of the EMS as charged, for example by being a failure, flawed, inadequate, bad, worthless, unloveable and so on. The job of the defence lawyer is to convince the judge and jury that the patient is innocent of all the charges made against them. The only permissible evidence is factual evidence; subjective opinions and hearsay are not permitted. Evidence from any point in the patient's life can be presented and this is where the historical test of the evidence can be introduced. Once all the evidence has been presented, the judge and jury consider their verdict. Because the evidence presented against the patient is usually irrational, polarized and excessively negative, it is the experience of the author that the judge and jury invariably find the patient innocent of all charges against them.

Weighing up the advantages and disadvantages

The patient is asked to consider the advantages and disadvantages of continuing to hold the EMS, versus adopting the new schema. This can be done as a written exercise in which the patient draws two columns entitled 'advantages' and 'disadvantages' and makes lists accordingly. This technique can also be used to explore the advantages and disadvantages of continuing to use the particular maladaptive coping style identified at the assessment stage. The aim of this technique is to help the patient recognize the self-defeating nature of their EMS and coping styles. With respect to work dysfunctions, it is similarly helpful in getting the patient to recognize the self-defeating nature of the dysfunction.

The flashcard technique

Flashcards are used to help the patient identify healthy responses to specific schema triggers. The flashcard should contain the most powerful evidence and arguments against the EMS and outline more helpful rational responses to it. The patient carries the flashcard around with them in the form of a postcard and is able to refer to it at any point, when they feel they need to. An illustration of the flashcard technique was given in Chapter 10.

The continuum technique

The continuum technique is useful to keep track of how the patient's beliefs are changing. For example, if the patient believed at the beginning of schema therapy that they were unloveable (underlying defectiveness/shame EMS), this would form the basis of the continuum, which would have 0% loveable at one extreme and 100% loveable at the other extreme. The patient can then be asked to rate themselves and a number of other significant people in their lives at various points on this continuum.

0% ─────────────────────100%

Lovability

It is also useful to break down the continuum further by asking the patient to define the characteristics of someone who is loveable. Each one of these characteristics can then form the basis of a sub-continuum in itself. The therapist can end up with six, seven, eight or more sub-continua and the patient can rate themselves on each one.

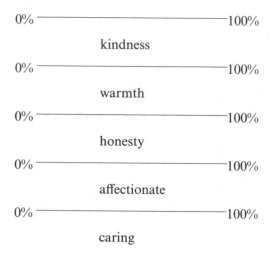

0% ——————————————————100%

kindness

0% ——————————————————100%

warmth

0% ——————————————————100%

honesty

0% ——————————————————100%

affectionate

0% ——————————————————100%

caring

Thus the patient can monitor any changes in their position on the continuum or sub-continua as therapy progresses. Changes that appear small to the therapist may nonetheless be extremely significant and encouraging to the patient. For example, if the patient has for the first time in their whole life begun to feel that they are at all loveable, this can result in a dramatic improvement in their mood state (see Greenberger and Padesky 1995 Chapter 9 for a more detailed description of this technique).

The internal dialogue technique

This technique teaches the patient to conduct a dialogue between the 'schema side' and the 'healthy side' of his/her cognitions. The 'empty chair' technique can be a powerful adjunct to this technique. The therapist instructs the patient to switch chairs as they switch to play each of the two sides. In one chair they play the schema side and in the other chair the healthy side. Because the patient usually has little or no experience of expressing the healthy side, this may have to be modelled initially by the therapist (Young et al. 2003). As the dialogue progresses, a case is built up against the schema side and can be used as ammunition against it. Through this technique the patient learns more rational healthy adult responses to their EMS. Later on in therapy, this technique can form part of an internal dialogue, in which the patient uses positive self-talk to challenge the unhealthy side.

Experiential strategies

Experiential strategies are used to help the individual make the transition from knowing intellectually that their schemata are false to believing it emotionally. Whereas cognitive and behavioural techniques draw their power from an accumulation of small changes achieved through repetition, experiential techniques are more dramatic. They draw their power from allowing the individual to 'feel' the schema and turn cold cognitions into hot affect-laden cognitions. They also help the patient to identify their core unmet emotional needs and how they relate to their current problems in the here and now. They aim to trigger the emotions connected to EMS and, through the process of limited re-parenting, heal these emotions and partially meet the unmet childhood needs (Young *et al.* 2003: 110). The primary technique used is 'imagery'.

Imagery exercises are conducted with the patient's eyes closed. The patient starts by practising safe imagery and is asked to think of a particular event or time in the past when they were happy and relaxed. This is subsequently known as the patient's 'safe place' and the patient can return to this safe imagery at any time in the therapy. The patient is then asked to recall some distressing imagery from childhood. These may, for example, be 'invalidating' experiences in childhood, which are then used in the imagery. As the patient describes the imagery, they begin to identify strong emotional reactions related to the early childhood images.

The imagery technique is then used as a change technique. A dialogue is developed; the patient is encouraged to conduct a conversation between the people who caused the EMS in childhood and those who reinforce it in their current life. The dialogue is usually between the vulnerable child, the dysfunctional parent and the healthy adult. The patient imagines they are in an upsetting situation with the dysfunctional parent figure, and then the patient is encouraged by the therapist to experience strong affect towards the parent. Thus the therapist can help the patient elicit which core emotional needs have been unmet. The patient is then encouraged to 'fight back' against the EMS and to distance from it emotionally. The schema becomes externalized as the parent's voice. An example of this technique is given in the case study in Chapter 15. The expression of anger is of significant importance in experiential work.

It can also be helpful to bring a healthy adult into the imagery, to help the vulnerable child defend themselves against the dysfunctional parent figure and also to assist the patient in getting their core unmet emotional needs met. The healthy adult can initially be modelled by the therapist, who asks the patient how they would have liked the dysfunctional parent figure to behave in the imagery. This is then practised in imagery, with the role of the healthy adult being modelled by the therapist. The healthy adult begins to 'do battle' with the dysfunctional parent figure. Standard CBT techniques can be used at this point in the imagery to expose the parent as the irrational, illogical and dysfunctional person they are. Later on in therapy, the patient is encouraged to develop their own healthy adult in the imagery and give him/her a name. The healthy adult they choose should be based upon a person that they really admire and respect, either from their childhood or more recently. The aim of this part of the therapy is to restructure the patient's experiences from a more adult perspective.

The imagery technique can also be used to prepare the patient for the next stage in therapy – behavioural pattern breaking. The patient is asked to rehearse changing their coping behaviours in imagery. Examples of this include confronting something that the patient has been avoiding, being more assertive, or behaving in a more confident and relaxed way. Often the patient reports that when they start doing the behavioural pattern-breaking exercises in imagery, they feel as though they are just acting, but as they continue to rehearse them, they begin to feel more real.

The patient is also encouraged to make links between the childhood images elicited and the upsetting images and situations they are currently experiencing. In the context of the workplace, the patient is encouraged to rehearse standing up to a bullying manager, for example, or to imagine themselves doing a presentation or a lecture courageously, behaving more assertively towards colleagues, answering someone back who they have been afraid to confront or confronting a particular work task that they have been avoiding.

Limited re-parenting

The therapeutic relationship is seen as an important part of the schema healing process in therapy. The patient internalizes the therapist as a healthy adult in imagery, who fights against the maladaptive schemas and pursues an emotionally fulfilling life. The therapist also displays two key skills which assist in this process. The first is empathic confrontation, where the therapist shows empathy towards the patient's schemata when they arise towards the therapist, while at the same time showing the patient that their reactions are distorted or dysfunctional in some way. The second is called 'limited re-parenting', which is supplying (within appropriate boundaries of the therapeutic relationship) what the patient needed but did not receive from their parent(s) in childhood, for example warmth, nurturing, encouragement, support, understanding and so on.

Behavioural pattern-breaking strategies

In many ways behavioural pattern breaking is the most important change strategy. Without behavioural change old habitual ways of thinking are likely to re-emerge and the individual will continue to re-experience problems. It involves making difficult choices, taking risks and making significant changes in lifestyle. Unlike standard CBT, schema-focused therapy starts with the most distressing and problematic behaviour rather than the easiest, and only if the patient is unable to do the task or finds it overwhelming does the patient shift to a less difficult problem. In the workplace, behavioural pattern breaking is particularly important. Work dysfunctions are usually picked up on through some failure to perform adequately in a particular work role; problems also manifest themselves in interpersonal conflicts in the workplace. Generally speaking, employers are concerned less with the intra-psychic world of the employee than with how their performance affects productivity, so demonstrating behavioural change is crucial.

The individual must be prepared to give up their dysfunctional behaviours or coping styles if therapy is to be successful. If the patient continues to surrender to the EMS, if the over-compensator remains too busy over-compensating or the avoider continues to escape the pain of their EMS, therapy will not be successful. The surrenderer has to learn to fight back, the over-compensator has to learn to modify over-compensatory behaviours and the avoider has to learn to confront those things which they have been avoiding. The standard behavioural techniques introduced in Chapter 3 can be helpful in behavioural pattern breaking. These include behavioural experiments in which the patient practises new ways of behaving in real-life situations and monitors the outcome. Similarly, they can be used to test out the consequences of 'disobeying the dysfunctional parent' discussed earlier in this chapter.

Other common behavioural techniques include activity scheduling, mastery and pleasure ratings and graded task assignments. When inactivity is identified as a problem, activity scheduling is used to get the patient to be more active. Where there is a lack of enjoyment in the activities conducted, mastery and pleasure rating techniques can be employed. Where avoidance is a problem, graded exposure to the feared situation can be helpful. Sometimes an individual may already be confronting their feared situation, in which case a graded exposure hierarchy is not necessary, but in order to help them cope with the situation, the patient is making use of safety behaviours which need to be dropped (all these behavioural strategies are discussed in more detail in the section on behavioural interventions in Chapter 3). The new behaviours adopted are practised as homework assignments. Role play can also be a useful technique when rehearsing new behavioural repertoires. It is important to acknowledge that behavioural change takes time and perseverance. It may involve confronting oneself over and over again. It is thus important to acknowledge small changes and gains. It is also important to recognize that unhealthy relationships may need to end, or the individual may have to get out of a hopeless situation, in order for schema healing to take place. Thus, sometimes very tough decisions have to be made.

Breaking patterns of over-compensation

Behavioural pattern breaking for the over-compensatory work dysfunctions identified in Chapter 13 essentially involves reducing the frequency and intensity of these behaviours. For example, the workaholic needs to practise modifying type A behaviours and fight their over-commitment to work. The behavioural techniques used to achieve this have already been discussed in the section on type A modification in Chapter 8 and so will not be duplicated here. However, to summarize, the aim of these interventions is to combat work addiction, achieve a better balance between work and non-work roles and find alternative ways of obtaining status and self-esteem other than through the work role. The over-controlling employee needs to practise being less bossy and controlling. Behavioural experiments in which they delegate more, allow greater autonomy, put their trust in others and relinquish control can assist with this. The rebellious employee needs to practise behaviours that involve being more co-operative and compliant, and less critical and obstructive. Rebellious employees may also benefit from engaging in more collaborative, team-based exercises where co-operation is required to achieve the task in hand, and from learning the anger management strategies outlined in the section on managing anger in Chapter 8. The manipulative employee can benefit from practising more open, transparent and honest ways of communicating their needs, developing their assertiveness skills (as discussed in Chapter 5) and self-disclosure skills, and behavioural experiments based around learning to trust others more.

Patterns of avoidance

Breaking the avoidant patterns of work dysfunction identified in Chapter 13 essentially involves getting the employee to confront the work situations they have been avoiding. For example, the failure-avoidant employee is encouraged to carry out behavioural experiments in which they come out of their comfort zone and put themselves more in situations where there is a risk of failure. This could, for example, be through enrolling at college, doing further training or going for promotion. Similarly, success-avoidant employees could be encouraged to confront situations where they could be successful. This may involve taking on greater responsibility, practising more autonomous decision-making or going for promotion. Procrastinators should be encouraged to stop putting things off and do them as soon as is practically possible, plan ahead, do tasks in manageable chunks and aim to meet deadlines. Withdrawn employees could, for example, be encouraged to be more involved in social contact, spend less time in isolated situations and engage in more team-based activities. The mistrusting employee could be encouraged to confide in others more, disclose more confidential information about themselves and carry out behavioural experiments based upon being more dependent on and trusting of their work colleagues. The timid employee could be encouraged to take risks more, seek change and unpredictability and take on new tasks where the outcome is uncertain or unknown. This is not an exhaustive list of behavioural interventions, but is indicative of the types of interventions that would assist pattern breaking in avoidant individuals.

Patterns of surrender

Breaking patterns of behaviour in the surrendering work dysfunctions identified in Chapter 13 essentially involves getting the employee to fight back against surrendering behaviours. For example, the dependent employee needs to practise more autonomous behaviour patterns, which aim to break their dependence. This could involve more independent decision-making rather than simply relying on others for support. The submissive employee needs to practise being more assertive in various situations, such as saying no to requests, confronting others more, learning to managing conflict and disagreeing with others. The self-sacrificing employee can benefit from learning to put their own needs and preferences first sometimes and not allowing themselves to be placed in the role of a victim. The overly loyal employee needs to learn to identify more of their own needs, preferences, likes and dislikes and practise ways of getting these met. He/she also needs to learn to be more assertive and set limits and boundaries on the work role, working only the contracted hours with corresponding financial remuneration. The entitled employee needs to practise sticking to the protocols and procedures of the organization more, listening to and respecting the rights of others, being more reliable and managing their anger appropriately. The attention-seeking employee needs to practise alternative ways of getting their emotional and self-esteem needs met other than through attention-seeking behaviours. The obsessive employee needs to practise being less rigid and more flexible with respect to the rules and regulations of the organization, accepting that imperfection is the norm. They need to practise doing tasks in a less perfectionistic way, being more tolerant of their own and others' mistakes, changing their routines, doing tasks in a different order, seeking out more situations of uncertainty and ambiguity and embracing change. Finally, the disciplinarian needs to learn to behave in a less intolerant and punitive manner, be more encouraging of others, make greater use of positive reinforcement techniques, show more compassion and greater forgiveness for human frailties and foibles and generally learn more positive ways of getting the best out of people.

SCHEMA MODE THERAPY

It is proposed that certain individuals have more complex problems and may benefit from a particular kind of schema therapy known as schema mode therapy, rather than standard schema therapy. Young *et al.* (2003) identified those individuals with rigidly avoidant or compensatory coping styles, those who are highly self-critical or self-punitive, those with internal conflicts which make them feel confused and those who display frequent and rapid changes in mood and/or coping style as being appropriate candidates for this form of therapy.

It was proposed in Chapter 13 that divisive employees are characterized by multiple underlying EMS and unstable coping styles. They shift between the over-compensatory, avoidant and surrendering coping styles, depending on the situation and their mood state at the time. Such individuals may have several underlying EMS and display unpredictable coping styles. Schema mode therapy blends a number of EMS into one mode, allowing therapy with such patients to become manageable. According to Young *et al.* (2003), most schema modes can be placed under four main headings:

- Child modes (e.g. angry child, vulnerable child)
- Maladaptive parent modes (punitive parent, demanding parent)
- Maladaptive coping modes (compliant surrender, detached protector, over-compensation modes)
- Healthy adult modes (nurturing, validating, affirmative).

The experiential techniques already described above, such as limited re-parenting, the extensive use of imagery and the use of dialogue between the healthy and schema sides, are also central to mode therapy. The current thinking (Young *et al.* 2003) is that schema therapy and schema mode therapy are not two separate therapies, but mode work is seen as an advanced component of schema work which can be used whenever the therapist feels blocked. The main difference between the two is that mode therapy involves working with clusters of EMS, whereas schema therapy involves working with a single EMS. The therapist works with both adaptive and maladaptive modes and aims to help the patient find ways of switching from a dysfunctional to a healthy mode as part of the healing process. Unfortunately a more detailed account of schema mode therapy is beyond the scope of this book, but it is described in detail in Young *et al.* (2003) (Chapters 8–10) and a case illustration of the schema mode approach can be found in Bamber (2004).

Chapter 15

Conceptualizing and treating a case of workaholism and burnout using the schema-focused approach

Martin Bamber

INTRODUCTION

In this chapter, a schema-based formulation of workaholism and burnout is proposed. It integrates the schema-based model of occupational stress (presented in Chapter 12) with the literature on workaholism (presented in Chapter 13) and burnout (presented in Chapter 8). In particular, it is noted that the workaholic employee typically presents with the 'type A' coping style and appears to be more prone to occupational stress, burnout, low self-esteem and work-related problems than non-type A workers (Burke 2004; Burke and Matthiesen 2004; Burke and Greenglass 1988; Cherniss 1980; Conte *et al.* 2002; Evans *et al.* 1987; Greenglass 1990; Idemudia *et al.* 2001; Jamal 1990; Kushnir and Melamed 1991; Lavanco 1997; Machlowitz 1980; Mazur and Lynch 1989; Minirth *et al.* 1981; Nagy and Davis 1985; Nowack 1988; Price 1982; Savickas 1990; Schwartz 1982; Spruell 1987).

The model also integrates some of the conceptualizations of burnout reviewed in Chapter 8 (Cherniss 1980; Golembiewski *et al.* 1986, 1988; Harrison 1983; Leiter and Maslach 1988; Maslach 1976; Maslach and Jackson 1984) with the concept of workaholism.

The mechanisms by which underlying EMS, temperamental factors and individual coping strategies predispose an individual to becoming a workaholic, and how these interact with job conditions to cause burnout, are identified in the model presented in Figure 15.1. It proposes that workaholics are more vulnerable to experiencing burnout as a consequence of their underlying EMS of defectiveness/shame or failure and also their predisposing temperament. Individuals with a more aggressive temperament are more likely to adopt the over-compensatory coping style of workaholism than individuals with a more timid and shy temperament, who are more likely to adopt a surrender or avoidance coping style. Workaholics thus over-compensate for their EMS by adopting a type A coping style. At work their whole sense of self-worth becomes equated with achievement and career success, and the type A behaviour is driven by the fear of being exposed as a failure or defective.

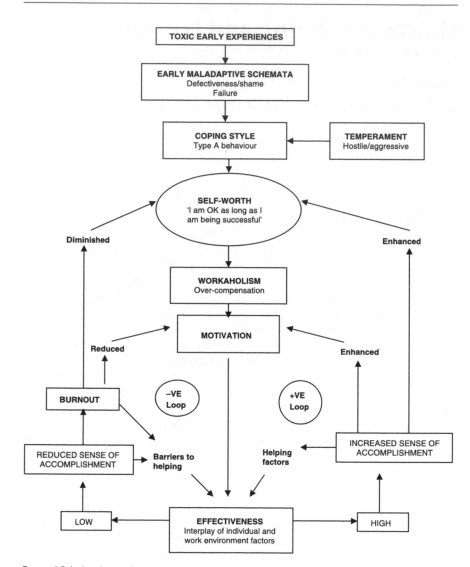

Figure 15.1 A schema-focused formulation of workaholism and burnout.

It is important to note that, according to the model, a workaholic with the necessary underlying EMS and coping style associated with the vulnerability to burnout does not automatically develop burnout. As long as the rewards of work keep coming the individual remains motivated in their work, the fragile sense of self-esteem is maintained and the individual does not experience burnout. It is also easy for the workaholic to rationalize maladaptive behaviour, since the work ethic is encouraged in our Western capitalist culture and workplace organizations. The associated striving and achievement-orientated behaviours are often well rewarded and can give the illusion of being adaptive. It is thus easy for the individual to become trapped in the positive reinforcement feedback loop identified in Figure 15.1.

However, problems can arise when the individual receives a 'knock' to their fragile sense of self-esteem. Feedback of ineffectiveness or failure can trigger extreme stress reactions, through hyper-activation of the failure and/or defectiveness/shame EMS. If the workaholic employee perceives that the situation can be rescued, he/she will initially increase efforts in an attempt to avoid the experience of failure. However, if feedback of ineffectiveness continues over a sustained period of time, the individual will eventually become physically and/or emotionally exhausted, and experience the reduced sense of accomplishment and loss of motivation associated with the burnout syndrome. With respect to health care professionals, the model proposes that prolonged feedback of ineffectiveness in helping or treating patients will result in vulnerable individuals developing burnout in the same way. The model bears some resemblance to Seligman's (1975) learned helplessness model, whereby the helper becomes a 'helpless helper'. Ultimately they may experience a loss of self-worth.

In keeping with their underlying EMS, workaholic individuals are more likely to blame themselves and attribute their lack of accomplishment almost exclusively to their own defectiveness or failures, rather than to external environmental factors in the workplace. However, the model presented in Figure 15.1 proposes that the experience of accomplishment through being successful in helping others is the result of an interaction between the individual vulnerability factors already described and factors in the work environment (as described in Chapter 2). If the helper is working in an environment with low staffing levels, excessive workload, inadequate resources, out-dated equipment and inadequate training opportunities, then this will very much contribute to the experience of failure, especially if it is accompanied by a blaming attitude from patients and their relatives, or an unsupportive manager.

AN ILLUSTRATION OF THE MODEL: THE CASE OF 'TREVOR'

'Trevor' was a 28-year-old charge nurse who worked on an elderly mentally ill inpatient unit. He was referred to the clinical psychology department for 'occupational stress due to a build-up of pressures at work'. He had already undergone a course of standard CBT and had also attended a stress management group, without success.

Assessment (Sessions 1–3)

At the initial assessment meeting Trevor was still on sick leave. He presented himself as a bright and articulate man, who was motivated to work on his problems. He described the build-up of pressures at work, which had led to him feeling increasingly resentful and de-motivated. These included working long hours on an understaffed unit, with colleagues who he believed did not really care about their work as much as he did. He reported putting 'everything' into making the unit a success but felt that his colleagues and senior managers did not appreciate his efforts. He reported that, prior to taking sick leave, he had experienced a number of physical symptoms including abdominal pains, headaches, muscular tension, frequent colds, sleep disturbance and chronic feelings of exhaustion. He had begun to drink more alcohol, was more irritable and angry and had experienced more interpersonal conflicts than usual.

Trevor reported that the key precipitating factor to his going off sick was a complaint made by one of his colleagues about his attitude towards the staff and patients on the unit. Although this did not result in any disciplinary action, he felt a great sense of anger and injustice about it. Shortly after this incident, he described waking up one morning and feeling that he had simply nothing left to give, and he no longer felt able to go to work. He had been off work for three weeks at the time of the initial assessment session.

Personal background

Trevor reported that he came from a family of high achievers. Both his parents were successful career people, who demanded the best from him. Trevor recalled being constantly compared negatively to his older brother, who was better both academically and in sports than he was. He described his father as a highly critical man, who was quick to spot and comment on his mistakes and failures. Trevor also felt different from his peers because he was taller, overweight, not sporty and not part of the 'in-crowd'. He developed bad acne as a teenager and did not have a girlfriend until he was 18 years old. However, Trevor was above average academically and did get some validation of his worth from his parents' attention and approval for doing well at school.

Consequently, Trevor buried himself in his academic work and did well in his exams. This further alienated him from his peers, who teased him for being a 'swot'. He tried to follow his brother into a medical career, since he felt this would get him the validation that he was craving from his parents, but was unsuccessful. He decided to modify his career ambitions a little and applied to train as a psychiatric nurse. He worked hard in his training and obtained a good honours degree. He did feel some sense of pride when his parents attended the degree ceremony but felt undermined by his father's comments about why a male should want to become a nurse.

History of problem

After qualifying Trevor took up a post on an elderly inpatient psychiatric unit and he recalled being enthusiastic and having high expectations about making a positive difference to the lives of the patients in his care. He worked long hours and well beyond the call of duty to meet these expectations. However, over time his initial high expectations began to evaporate and he found that, because of the resistance of staff to his ideas and low staffing levels, much of the day was spent doing 'mundane' (but essential) tasks such as toileting, bathing and feeding the patients. He began to realize that there was no time to put any of his original ideas into action, no-one acknowledged his efforts and none of the patients seemed to get better or respond to his interventions in the way he had been led to expect they would during his training. He became increasingly de-motivated, emotionally exhausted and increasingly cynical towards his colleagues and patients alike. It was this attitude that had led to Trevor being reported to his manager and being cautioned. Over time Trevor had gone from being enthusiastic and highly motivated to cynical and disillusioned. He began to experience many of the features associated with burnout.

At the time of referral, Trevor also reported being unhappy in his personal life. He was not in a stable or long-term relationship. He stated that he did have a serious relationship with a girl a few years previously, which lasted several months, but she ended it because she felt he was not paying her enough attention. Since then, he reported that he had not found the time to meet new people or develop a social life because his work took up most of his time. He was living in rented accommodation and had no specific hobbies or non-work-related interests or activities.

Pre-therapy psychometric measures

- The Beck Depression Inventory (BDI): the patient's score was 25, indicating that he was suffering from a moderate level of clinical depression (Beck *et al.* 1961)
- The Beck Anxiety Scale (BAI): the patient's score was 9, indicating that he was not clinically anxious (Beck *et al.* 1988).
- Young's Schema Questionnaire long version (YSQ-L2): the patient's profile on the YSQ-L2 identified a raised score on the defectiveness/shame and failure EMS, indicating that this was of clinical significance (Young and Brown 1994).
- The Maslach Burnout Inventory (MBI): the patient's scores on all three subscales indicated that he was suffering from a high level of burnout compared to the normative data on health workers (Maslach and Jackson 1981).
- The Jenkins Activity Schedule (JAS): Trevor scored at the 80th percentile

on the overall type A measure, indicating that he was high on the type A behavioural pattern (Jenkins *et al.* 1979).

Formulation (Sessions 4–6)

From the information gathered and the psychometric measures used in the assessment, it was hypothesized that Trevor's toxic early experiences had led to the development of the underlying EMS of defectiveness/shame and failure. This was supported by the information provided in response to Young's Schema Questionnaire. It was hypothesized that this EMS had developed as a result of constant negative comparison with his brother, and criticism for not being as good as his brother. His main coping strategy was overcompensation through the adoption of a type A behavioural pattern (as supported by the Jenkins Activity Schedule) and his main source of validation and sense of self-worth had become integrally linked to his accomplishments at work.

While Trevor was doing well in his school and degree studies, he was able to get regular validation of his self-worth through good marks in his academic assignments and placements. His motivation and sense of accomplishment was high and his coping strategy of type A behaviour appeared to be adaptive and rewarding. His EMS of defectiveness/shame and failure were dormant and inactive, and he stayed in the positive feedback loop described in the model of burnout in Figure 15.1.

However, Trevor's experience of working life was not nearly as validating as his academic studies and his lack of success in the work setting had a very negative impact on him. His EMS of defectiveness/shame and failure was activated and his coping strategy of type A behaviour, which appeared to have served him so well up to that point, began to work against him. He moved from the positive feedback loop to the negative feedback loop described in Figure 15.1. He began to experience symptoms of burnout such as feeling less motivated, with a reduced desire to help others, more negativity towards his patients and work colleagues and a diminished sense of self worth.

In line with his underlying EMS, Trevor blamed himself. He ignored the fact that there were a number of factors in his working environment which contributed to his lack achievement including limited resources, low staffing levels, lack of supervision in which to discuss his frustrations, lack of adequate feedback regarding his performance through regular appraisals, lack of any clear guidelines on what constituted a reasonable workload and lack of any clear continuing professional development training. The ongoing toxic work situation became personalized and a direct threat to his fragile sense of self-worth, which eventually shattered when he was cautioned by his line manager. In conclusion, Trevor had all the underlying psychological vulnerability factors predisposing him to burnout identified in the model (Figure 15.1). He was also exposed to a toxic work environment and it was the interplay of his individual psychological vulnerability factors with the work environment that resulted in him experiencing burnout.

Treatment plan (Session 7)

The goals of therapy were agreed with Trevor. Schema-focused treatment strategies for treating his workaholism consisted of a range of detailed cognitive, experiential and behavioural techniques, which aimed to modify the underlying EMS and dysfunctional assumptions and break the associated dysfunctional patterns of behaviour.

Schema-focused interventions used (Sessions 8–28)

Cognitive strategies

The cognitive goals of therapy were to modify Trevor's EMS of defectiveness/shame and failure, and to challenge the dysfunctional assumptions underlying his maladaptive coping strategy of workaholism. It was decided to begin with modifying Trevor's underlying EMS of defectiveness/shame and failure and then move on to challenging the dysfunctional assumptions or general 'rules for living' relating to his workaholic behaviour.

Modifying the defectiveness/shame and failure EMS

When activated, Trevor's underlying EMS led him to believe that he was inferior and a failure, and that he should be ashamed of himself. He was taught a combination of cognitive techniques aimed at helping him challenge his view of himself. These included a combination of some of the traditional cognitive techniques outlined in Chapter 5 and a number of the schema-focused techniques outlined in Chapter 14 of this book. He was encouraged to highlight his strengths and good qualities and to minimize the significance that he attached to his perceived flaws. He was also encouraged to see his problems not as inherited characteristics but rather as attitudes learned during childhood that were amenable to change, and which could be more aptly described as a form of over self-criticism. Trevor found the flashcard technique, listing his good qualities in a succinct way and in a convenient format, very helpful. He was also encouraged to keep a 'positive data' diary, in which he identified and recorded his successes on a daily basis. This helped him to practice focusing more on the positive than the negative aspects of his experiences.

Trevor's EMS were conceptualized as a form of 'self-prejudice' and he was taught to challenge them using techniques such as the historical test of the evidence and 'taking oneself to court', which were described in the last chapter. These techniques helped highlight the successes in his life. The continuum technique was used to challenge Trevor's beliefs that he was a failure and defective. This helped him see more of the middle ground, rather than simply rating his achievements in a dichotomous way such as win/lose, good/bad or success/failure. The use of the internal dialogue technique, between the schema and healthy side of his cognitions, as described in Chapter 14, helped him articulate a more healthy voice with which to challenge his EMS. He was also aided in setting more realistic and less ambitious longer-term expectations for himself, others and his career, which did not result in him labelling himself as a failure.

Challenging the assumptions underlying workaholism

Trevor's over-identification with his work meant that a major part of his sense of significance and self-worth had become bound up in his job. He dedicated very little time to activities outside work and saw his personal and social status in terms of his job label. Clearly, he needed to develop other roles outside work and a sense of worth and identity in tasks totally unrelated to work. Trevor's self-defeating beliefs were that his self-worth was proportional to his achievements at work, that he only earned the right to be happy through hard work and that success at work was his only route to self-esteem. He had, as a result of these beliefs, become a slave to his work in order to feed his self-esteem, which had also had a negative impact on his relationships, social life and personal happiness.

Trevor's relationship with his work needed to be changed – from one of continual striving to achieve at an unrelenting pace to a more relaxed one. In order to do this, he had first of all to challenge the link between work and self-worth, and his belief that he was only as good as his last success. Second, he was encouraged to weigh up the pros and cons of changing his behaviours and prepare himself to take the risk of trying new ways of relating to his work and life outside work. Trevor's biggest fear was that his world might fall apart if he took his foot off the accelerator pedal. He was helped to get out of the achievement trap by considering the possibility that one can be happy without all the trappings of success such as wealth, possessions and high job status, and that success and happiness not the same thing. Routes to self-esteem other than work were considered (see Burns 1980: 327–51). He was also encouraged to consider more what he liked, enjoyed, was good at and found rewarding, fun and satisfying, rather than simply focusing on the concept of being a slave to his work. His dysfunctional beliefs were challenged using standard CBT techniques (see Chapter 3).

Challenging assumptions about type A behaviour

Up to the time of therapy Trevor had seen his type A behaviour as a positive attribute, rather than something which was being driven by a chronic fear of his defectiveness being exposed. In addition, he was not aware of the recent research findings relating to the harmful health consequences of maintaining the pace associated with type A behaviours (as outlined in Chapter 8). Through education Trevor began to accept that type A behaviour could be physically and psychologically damaging to him, and he also began to recognize that it was an unhealthy coping strategy. He was then able to consider the pros and cons of modifying his type A behaviour pattern in a more informed way, and concluded that it had to change.

Experiential strategies

The main experiential techniques used in schema-focused therapy are outlined in Chapter 14. Trevor started by practising safe imagery. He was asked to think of a particular event or time in his past when he felt happy and relaxed. He used the example of being on a summer holiday with a few of his ex-school friends shortly after having received his A level exam results. He described lying on a sun-bed on a beach in Greece and described the imagery associated with all his sensory modalities. This subsequently became his 'safe place' and he was able to return to this safe imagery at any time in the therapy.

Trevor then moved on to distressing imagery from his childhood. He was able to identify a number of invalidating experiences in his childhood and used these in the imagery. One example was an incident which for him was typical and summed up his childhood. His father had come to watch him play in goal for the school football team. His father rarely paid him such close attention, so it was a big event for him. He unfortunately let in six goals and he recalled running up to his father after the match and seeing what he interpreted as a loathing expression on his father's face. His father would not even acknowledge him and when he got home called him 'useless'. As he described this imagery, he initially identified strong emotional reactions of worthlessness and shame, followed by feelings of anger.

The imagery technique was then used as a change technique. A dialogue was started in imagery between the young Trevor and his critical and rejecting father. Trevor was encouraged to confront his father's behaviour and attitudes and fight back against the schema. He asked his father to acknowledge that this was an unreasonable way to treat a child and to recognize how it made him feel. He also stated that all children deserve respect whatever their talents. Trevor found this very difficult since, in the imagery, his father continued to denigrate him. Consequently, a healthy adult was brought into the imagery to help defend him against his dysfunctional parent, and also to assist him in getting his core unmet emotional needs met. The healthy adult was initially modelled by the therapist, who asked the young Trevor in the imagery what he would have liked to happen after the football match. Trevor stated that he simply wanted his father to put an arm round him and console him, to say 'never mind' and just accept him for what he was. This was then practised in imagery with the role of the healthy adult being modelled by the therapist.

The healthy adult then began to 'do battle' with the critical parent and traditional CBT techniques were used to expose him as the irrational, illogical and dysfunctional person he was. Later on Trevor developed his own healthy adult called 'Mr Metcalfe', who was modelled on an old school teacher that he really admired and respected. The aim of this part of this therapy was to restructure his experiences from a more adult perspective – essentially to come out of hiding, stop criticizing and blaming himself and to learn to accept himself 'warts and all'. Eventually, Trevor was able to challenge successfully his own EMS of defectiveness/shame and failure. As a result of using these experiential techniques Trevor reported feeling stronger emotionally and more able to fight his EMS.

The imagery technique was also used to prepare Trevor for the next stage in therapy – behavioural pattern breaking. He was asked to rehearse changing his behaviours in imagery. Examples of this included acting as if he were a more relaxed and easygoing person, going home from work on time, engaging in hobbies and interests outside of work, spending more time with his family and friends, going on holiday and engaging in other behaviours associated with more of a type B person, such as doing something imperfectly, behaving in a more vulnerable way and disclosing something 'shameful' about himself to someone. Trevor reported that when he started doing these imagery exercises he felt he was just acting, but as he continued to rehearse them he felt that they were becoming more real to him.

Behavioural pattern-breaking strategies

A list was made of Trevor's self-defeating problematic behaviours and they were prioritized into a hierarchy. New alternative behaviours were then identified and practised as homework assignments. He was encouraged to carry out a number of behavioural experiments related to developing a more relaxed and easygoing approach to life. This included practising in real life the scenarios he had rehearsed in imagery, such as acting as if he were a more relaxed and easygoing person, going home from work on time, engaging in hobbies and interests outside of work, spending more time with his family and friends and arranging to take a holiday. He was encouraged to modify his type A behaviours by being less competitive, being more sociable to others, giving more compliments, allowing others to have their own way more and scheduling breaks in a busy day. He was also encouraged to experiment with behaving in a more vulnerable way by disclosing something 'shameful' about himself to someone, rather than trying to hide his failures and flaws, and observing their reactions.

He developed other roles outside work and a sense of worth and identity in tasks totally unrelated to work. He was also encouraged to focus more on doing activities that he enjoyed doing and found satisfying, even if he was not particularly good at them. He was taught to strive less, accomplish less and accomplish it less perfectly, deliberately slow down and waste more time. At first Trevor felt that he was merely acting and being 'false'. However, over time he reported that these new more healthy ways of behaving had become more habitual and comfortable to him. He also gained confidence through observing the outcome of these behavioural experiments: the catastrophic consequences of dropping these over-compensatory coping strategies did not materialize.

Review, relapse prevention and self-help plan (Sessions 29 and 30)

In the final session of therapy a relapse prevention exercise was introduced (see Chapter 3). This aimed to ensure that the gains made in therapy by Trevor were consolidated. He was asked to consider what gains he felt had been made in therapy, what had changed as a result of therapy, what he had learned in therapy and how he would continue to practise it in his everyday life. A self-help plan was devised in which he was asked to consider how he might deal with set-backs, what the likely high-risk situations for relapse might be and what contingency plans he would have in place to deal with such a lapse. At the final therapy session the 'pre' and 'post' measures were compared to identify the success of the outcome of the interventions employed.

Outcome measures

- The Beck Depression Inventory (BDI): the patient's score was 9, indicating that he was no longer suffering from clinical depression (Beck *et al.* 1961).
- Young's Schema Questionnaire long version (YSQ-L2): the patient's profile on the YSQ-L2 indicated a clinically significant reduction in his score on the items relating to the defectiveness/shame schema and failure (Young and Brown 1994).
- The Maslach Burnout Inventory (MBI): the patient's scores on the MBI were within the normal range for health workers, indicating that he was no longer suffering from burnout (Maslach and Jackson 1981).
- The Jenkins Activity Schedule (JAS): the patient scored at the 70th percentile on the overall type A measure, indicating that there was a clinically significant reduction to within the normal range on the type A behavioural pattern (Jenkins *et al.* 1979).

The outcome measures above indicate that the clinical outcome of therapy was successful for Trevor. Over the course of 30 sessions of therapy, his clinical levels of distress were reduced to normal non-clinical levels for depression (BDI) and burnout (MBI). There were also clinically significant reductions in his EMS (YSQ) and type A behaviour (JAS). During the course of therapy, Trevor returned to his job as a charge nurse and reported that he felt more confident in his capacity to cope without having to use the dysfunctional over-compensatory strategies associated with workaholism. Through discussions with his line manager and the human resources department, a number of changes to his working environment were also made to assist Trevor to be more effective in his work. At the time of being discharged, Trevor was coping well with work, and felt that he had achieved a better balance between his work and non-work roles and had developed more realistic expectations of himself, his colleagues and his work.

Chapter 16

Occupation as re-enactment: Adaptive or maladaptive?

Jason Price

Introduction

This chapter provides data to support the theoretical model presented in Chapter 12. Briefly summarized, the model proposes that an individual's underlying EMS and maladaptive coping styles constitute a psychological vulnerability, which makes an individual more prone to developing the stress syndromes identified in Chapter 6. In this study, two main hypotheses relating to the model are tested:

1 Individuals within the helping professions choose their respective occupations partly in order re-enact their EMS. They place themselves in work situations reminiscent of some earlier trauma, in the hope that they will work through their (unconscious) conflicts, modify their early maladaptive schemata and achieve mastery. In this context work is therapeutic and adaptive for the majority of individuals.
2 For some individuals re-enactment is not an adaptive and healing process and work serves to re-traumatize them. These individuals are more likely to have rigid and severe EMS and maladaptive coping styles, experience negative affect from their working environment and consequently will be more prone to developing stress syndromes and PTSD.

BACKGROUND TO THE STUDY

It is argued in this study that if work re-enactments were maladaptive, then one would expect greater mental health problems in the helping professions with longevity of service. Conversely, if the re-enactment were adaptive, then one would expect to see greater personal growth correlated with length of service. Alexander and Klein (2001) cite several studies which found emergency services workers reporting high levels of personal gratification from their work, as did their own study. However, in ambulance personnel, psychopathology (somatic, depressive, anxiety, social dysfunction, depersonalization and emotional exhaustion) was found to be unrelated to years of experience (Alexander and Klein 2001). Alexander and Klein (2001) found that 49% of their ambulance personnel participants reported that frequent exposure to critical incidents helped them cope better, while only 2% reported coping less well under this condition (although 10% reported initially feeling better, but then finding it more difficult to cope). Patterson (2001) discovered that police officers with more years of experience reported lower levels of perceived work stress.

Farber (1985), in a study of 315 clinical psychologists, reported that only 2–6% perceived themselves as being greatly affected by work stress, and that clinical psychologists generally enjoy and respect their work. Radeke and Mahoney (2000) researched the personal lives of 275 psychotherapists and research psychologists, in response to previous research which suggested that therapists experience personal change as a result of their work. They found that although therapists reported higher levels of psychological dysfunction (anxiety, depression, emotional exhaustion), they also reported higher levels of personal and professional satisfaction, and that their work had influenced them in a positive direction and had enriched their personal lives. Psychiatric caseness on the General Health Questionnaire (GHQ; Goldberg 1978) – that is, a score above cut-off on the GHQ 28 which indicates a minor (yet clinically relevant) psychological/psychiatric disturbance (Goldberg and Williams 1988) – was found to be lower for qualified than for training clinical psychologists, and for senior than junior males (Cushway and Tyler 1994). Kuyken *et al.* (1998) investigated the psychological adaptation of 183 British trainee clinical psychologists. They found that this occupational group, despite reporting higher levels of stress (compared with a stratified sample), did not report higher levels of psychological distress. Their psychological and social functioning at work, and at home, fell within normal ranges. Kuyken *et al.* (2000) followed up this group of participants to see whether the training process had affected their functioning. It was found that many of the trainees who had experienced significant difficulties initially continued to do so, but, as a population, adaptation was within the normal range. However, as discussed in Chapter 2, occupational stress is a significant problem for the helping professions. It appears that working in the helping professions is more interpersonally intense than in other occupations, and while some individuals find this to be a positive experience, others find it aversive.

This study also proposes that post-traumatic stress disorder (PTSD) can be seen as a symptom of a maladaptive re-enactment experience when working in the helping professions. The cognitive theories of PTSD described in Chapter 7 and the schema-focused model presented in Chapter 12 are consistent with this view. Central to psychopathology in the model is the presence of extreme and rigid schemata, which are not able to adapt to new experiences in a positive way. It is argued here that those individuals who are most likely to find their work in the helping professions a re-traumatizing experience are the same individuals who are more likely to suffer from PTSD if they are exposed to a significant index event, as they lack schema adaptability to learn (cognitively and emotionally) from repeated traumatic experiences.

Research indicates that those individuals who suffer extreme and chronic noxious interpersonal experiences in childhood (and who are therefore more likely to develop more extreme and rigid maladaptive core schemas) are more likely to experience PTSD as the result of a traumatic work event (e.g. Brewin *et al.* 2000; Davidson *et al.* 1991; Follette *et al.* 1996; Paris 2000; Stallard and Law 1993).

THE STUDY: HYPOTHESES AND AIMS

The study hypothesized that if occupational choice in the helping professions is driven by the unconscious desire to activate and ameliorate early maladaptive schemas (EMS; e.g. Young 1999; Young *et al.* 2003), then the EMS salient for each profession should change over time, and there should be a significant difference on specific EMS and on a measure of psychological health between 'starting' and 'finishing' groups in the target occupational samples. Also, given the cognitive theories implicating maladaptive schemas in PTSD susceptibility, the study aimed to identify the EMS involved by generating a regression model of predictive core schemas in PTSD symptomatology.

METHOD

Participants

Two occupational groups were selected to represent the emergency services (paramedic trainees and police probationers) and two to represent mental health professions (student mental health nurses and clinical psychology trainees). Trainees/students in each occupational group (rather than qualified workers) were chosen as the target population for several reasons. First, individuals within the student samples are all at the same stage of career development, both in terms of professional rank and experience. Second, and most importantly, students represent the point of entry into the professions and so psychological changes in response to the working environment should be more evident within this population (as found by Kuyken *et al.*, 2000).

Participants were individuals either starting their professional training (within the first four weeks) or finishing it (finishing mental health nurse students and clinical psychology trainees were selected from individuals starting their third and final year of training, to be consistent with the two-year paramedic and police training courses).

The clinical psychology group was recruited from 16 UK clinical psychology training programmes. The police starting group was recruited from a national police training centre, with the finishing group recruited from five police forces. Mental health nursing samples were recruited from three university nurse training courses, and junior paramedics were recruited from seven training courses nationwide. The total number of participants involved in the study was 544. The participants were asked to complete a pack of standardized questionnaires, which will be outlined in the following section. Table 16.1 shows the numbers of male and female participants in each group.

Materials

The Young Schema Questionnaire: Short Form (YSQ-S1)

The YSQ-S1 (Young 1998) is a 75-item self-report measure of the 18 EMS outlined in Chapter 12, which are hypothesized to underlie psychopathology. Each EMS is measured by five items (the highest loading items from a factor analysis of the 205-item version of the form by Schmidt et al. 1995). (See Chapter 12 for a more detailed description of each schema described by Young.)

The 28-item General Health Questionnaire (GHQ-28)

The GHQ (Goldberg 1978) is suitable for measuring minor psychiatric disorder or psychological disturbance in community samples, allowing both ordinal scaling and categorical affiliation with regard to caseness. Four sub-scales can be generated; somatic, depressive, anxiety and social dysfunction. The 28-item version is recommended for research purposes. There are several ways of scoring the questionnaire, each for different uses of the measure. Likert scoring can be used for generation of means and standard deviations. GHQ scoring can be used to detect caseness. A cut-off score of 5 on the total scale score was used to indicate caseness for the groups in this study (i.e. a score of 5 or more), as indicated by Alexander and Klein (2001), Blenkin et al. (1995), Clohessy and Ehlers (1999), Cushway (1992) and Goldberg (1978).

Table 16.1 Numbers of male/female participants (percentages in parentheses)

	Paramedics		Nurses		Police		Clinical psychologists	
	Starting	Finishing	Starting	Finishing	Starting	Finishing	Starting	Finishing
Male	13 (43)	9 (50)	15 (31)	18 (32)	52 (65)	51 (67)	19 (16)	22 (19)
Female	17 (57)	9 (50)	34 (69)	39 (68)	28 (35)	25 (33)	100 (84)	93 (81)
Total	30 (100)	18 (100)	49 (100)	57 (100)	80 (100)	76 (100)	119 (100)	115 (100)

Impact of Event Scale (IES)

The IES (Horowitz *et al.* 1979) is a 15-item scale which measures two PTSD symptoms: avoidance and intrusion of traumatic material related to a target event. Each sub-scale (avoidance, intrusion) can be used as an independent measure, or a total scale score can be used.

RESULTS

Paramedic groups

The only measure to emerge as significantly different between the groups was the EMS of dependency, with the finishing cohort having the higher mean score ($t = -3.141$, $df = 46$, $p < 0.005$).

Clinical psychology groups

The only EMS to emerge as significantly different between the groups was self-sacrifice, with the finishing cohort having the higher mean score ($t = -2.562$, $df = 232$, $p = 0.01$). There were significant differences on two of the GHQ sub-scales, with the finishing group having the higher means on both measures (somatic complaints: $t = -2.242$, $df = 230$, $p < 0.050$; anxiety: $t = -3.898$, $df = 232$, $p < 0.001$).

Mental health nursing groups

There were no significant differences on any of the EMS. There was a significant difference on the GHQ sub-scale for social dysfunction, with the finishing cohort having the higher mean score ($t = -2.211$, $df = 104$, $p < 0.050$).

Police groups

The only EMS to emerge as significant between the groups was mistrust/abuse, with the finishing cohort having the higher mean rank ($z = -2.03$, $p < 0.05$). There was a significant difference on the GHQ sub-scale for somatic complaints, with the finishing cohort having the highest mean rank.

DISCUSSION

Three of the groups (paramedics, clinical psychology and police) showed significant differences on one EMS each, with the finishing groups scoring higher, although there were no significant changes between nursing cohorts on any EMS. The significant EMS emerging appear particularly relevant for each occupational group (as will be discussed later), and can therefore be seen to be theoretically valid in terms of the re-enactment theory. Therefore, the hypothesis that there would be a significant difference on specific EMS (e.g. Young 1999; Young *et al.* 2003), and on a measure of psychological health between starting and finishing groups in the target occupational samples can be seen to be generally supported.

Paramedic groups

The finishing cohort of the paramedic sample scored higher than the starting cohort on the EMS of dependence. Young defines the dependence EMS as the 'belief that one is unable to handle everyday responsibilities in a competent manner, without considerable help from others . . . and often presents as helplessness' (1999: 13).

When comparing all starting groups, it was found that the paramedic sample scored significantly lower than all the other starting groups on the EMS of dependence ($p < 0.01$ on all comparisons). This suggests that this EMS is particularly salient for paramedics, given that there appears to have been a suppression of this EMS prior to training, and it was activated during the working experience.

The salience of this particular EMS for paramedics is apparent if we consider the nature of their working experiences. Paramedics are essentially the emergency service at the 'front line' responsible for the physical well-being (or even survival) of patients. If the patient's problems cannot be resolved *in situ*, paramedics have responsibility for stabilizing the patient for hospitalization. In major incidents (e.g. serious road traffic accidents, violent assaults), the paramedics may rely heavily upon police and fire service personnel for access to the patient and for the overall safety of the situation. If the patient needs hospitalization, then the paramedics are relying heavily upon their hospital colleagues to effect a 'good ending' for the patient (and, vicariously, the paramedics themselves). Obviously there are times when the patient is dead before the paramedics arrive, or dies at the scene, en route to the hospital or after hospitalization.

Given that the paramedics, out of all our helping profession samples, arguably have the most direct responsibility for human life and survival, it appears contradictory that they should have the singular salient EMS of dependence, which indicates a perceived inability to deal autonomously with responsibility. One explanation may be that their reliance on other professionals at different stages of the treatment process alienates the paramedics from the 'whole' of the case, and in particular the ending in cases where the patient is hospitalized. Not knowing what eventually becomes of a patient may mean that a vital positive feedback channel about one's performance is not available ('stroking' in cognitive terms; e.g. Burns and Auerbach 1996).

When providing feedback regarding the results of this research to a senior paramedic training officer, the lack of vicarious positive feedback from paramedics work was noted. The officer stated that, in general, the only information they receive about patients' later progress was 'through the obituary columns'. To put this statement in context, it is obviously not what becomes of all paramedics' patients, but paramedics are not generally given feedback about the good outcomes of their patients; negative feedback channels are thus the most obvious. The lack of positive feedback channels may be compounded by being more exposed to potentially negative feedback scenarios, such as severe patient distress or patient death. Clohessy and Ehlers (1999) found that child deaths were particularly difficult for ambulance workers to deal with. Then there is the frequency of exposure to incidents which may inhibit adaptive processing of salient EMS. Alexander and Klein (2001) found in their paramedic sample that distress following a disturbing incident lasted from a few days to a few weeks in the majority of participants. Given that James and Wright (1991) reported that ambulance personnel attend more call-outs than the police and fire services combined, it appears likely that there is insufficient latency time between major incidents for paramedics to be able to deal with their activated maladaptive schemas. The paramedics may come to feel helpless (the dependency EMS) after being continually exposed to such traumatic events: they cannot always effect a good ending for the patient, do not know what becomes of them in the longer term and have insufficient time to contend with activated maladaptive schemas.

Clinical psychology groups

The EMS of self-sacrifice was significant, with the finishing group scoring higher. This EMS has been described as:

> excessive focus on *voluntarily* meeting the needs of others in daily situations. . . . [The] most common reasons are to prevent causing pain to others, to avoid guilt from feeling selfish, or to maintain the connection with others perceived as needy. This often results from an acute sensitivity to the pain of others . . . [and can lead to] resentment of those who are taken care of.
>
> (Young *et al.* 2003: 16)

In the seminal work *The Art of Psychotherapy* (1990), Dr Anthony Storr, an eminent psychotherapist, states that therapists have:

> to be affected without acting upon his own feelings: to feel, but to use his own feelings in the service of the patient. . . . The therapist spends the bulk of his professional life in situations in which his own self expression is forbidden, or at least severely restricted. . . . [His] own personality

is never fully expressed, but always orientated towards the need of the other.

(Storr 1990: 170–1)

Thus the activation of the EMS of self-sacrifice is consistent with the model in relation to clinical psychologists. As with the paramedic group, the starting group of clinical psychologists scored significantly lower on their salient EMS than the other starting groups ($p < 0.01$ on all comparisons), again alluding to this EMS being suppressed prior to training and then being activated during working experience.

The clinical psychology finishing cohort also scored significantly higher on the GHQ anxiety and somatic complaints sub-scales. It is difficult to ascertain why specific symptomatic changes occur, although it may be that anxiety is related to objective work pressures (such as starting specialist placements in the final year, thesis work, etc.). Somatic complaints (*in absentia* of organic disease) are commonly associated with maladaptive cognitive processes (e.g. Salkovskis 1994) which have a physiological affect.

Mental Health Nurses

There were no significant differences on any of the EMS between starting and finishing groups. The finishing cohort scored significantly higher on the GHQ sub-scale of social dysfunction. It is not clear why this occupational group did not show any changes on the YSQ-S1. It may be that mental health nurses as an occupational group have a more heterogenous personality profile than the other groups, and so changes may be more diverse across schemata. However, the finishing cohort did score significantly higher on the GHQ sub-scale of social dysfunction, highlighting that although no EMS were salient, mental health nurses appear to develop significant interpersonal difficulties as a consequence of the effects of their working experiences during training.

Police groups

Given the nature of police work, it is perhaps unsurprising that the finishing cohort scored significantly higher on the EMS of mistrust/abuse. Young *et al.* (2003) define the EMS of mistrust/abuse as 'the expectation that others will hurt, abuse, humiliate, cheat, lie, or take advantage. . . . [Harm] is intentional or the result of unjustified and extreme negligence. May include the sense that one always ends up being cheated relative to others' (14).

While such an activated schema may prove to be beneficial in police work, cognitive theory asserts that such extreme negative schemas will pervade all aspects of one's life. Therefore, police officers may find themselves becoming suspicious of others' motives, inappropriately and irrationally. This may include family, friends, colleagues, political systems, the general public and the police service itself.

Such mistrust in police officers has been found in previous research. Ellis (1992) found that the training period for police recruits was a crucial time in the development of cognitions of alienation and mistrust between the police, the public and the media. Van Maanen (1975) discovered that the police service had an effect on levels of cynicism in officers, which is echoed by Waddington's (1999) observations that the police service's organization promotes attitudes of cynicism and pessimism as normative attitudinal orientations.

Finally, Fielding and Fielding (1987) found, in a longitudinal study, that out of the 28% of police recruits who resigned within 42 months of service, a significant sub-group were individuals who harboured embittered attitudes towards crime and punishment. It may be suggested that these individuals had a severely rigid and extreme form of the mistrust/abuse EMS, and they unconsciously wanted to negate it (or compensate for it) by removing all the deceitful individuals from society (i.e. criminals). This being an impossible task would inevitably lead to feelings of disillusionment (unconscious needs not being met), resulting in resignation. Again, this is consistent with the proposed re-enactment theory of occupational choice.

The finishing cohort scored significantly higher on the somatic complaints GHQ sub-scale. It has been found in previous research that the male-dominated emergency services (police, paramedics, fire service) inculcate a 'macho' self-perception, whereby seeking psychological support or express-ing emotional distress is not viewed positively (e.g. Miller 1995; Pieper and Maercker 1999; Pogrebin and Poole 1991). Therefore, somatic complaints can provide a means of expressing emotional discomfort (somatization), which may be more acceptable within a 'macho' work culture.

EMS INVOLVED IN PTSD

As mentioned in the Introduction, this study also aimed to identify the EMS involved in PTSD by generating a regression model of predictive core schemata in PTSD symptomatology.

The responses on the IES were checked to ensure that the index incidents were consistent with DSM-IV or ICD-10 conceptualizations of incidents which may lead to PTSD, and they had to be work-related. As a result, an IES group was created in which the index incidents were consistent with the noted diagnostic systems ($n = 99$). Index incidents which were consistent included: attending major transport accidents, dealing with dead bodies/ serious injury, being physically attacked and having patients commit suicide. Incidents which were not consistent included: general situational factors (e.g. 'bad week at work'), verbal incidents (e.g. 'a client verbally threatened me', 'my supervisor shouted at me') or personal incidents which were unrelated to

Table 16.2 Regression models on the IES

Predictor variables	Dependent variable	Predictors in final model	Significance of model	R^2
All 15 EMS from YSQ-S1	Impact of event scale	Failure, mistrust, isolate, defect, enmesh, selfcont	$F_{6,92} = 9.78$, $p < 0.001$	0.389 (38.9%)

the workplace. The index event also had to have occurred more than one month prior to questionnaire completion, again for consistency with diagnostic criteria. Table 16.2 shows the regression model.

Six EMS (failure, mistrust/abuse, isolation, defectiveness/shame, enmeshment and insufficient self-control) explained 38.9% of the variance in the regression model on the IES. This is a rather high percentage of variance explained, considering the multitude of other possible contributing variables identified in previous PTSD research, such as subjective event experience, trauma severity, type of trauma, frequency of exposure, psychosocial support, organizational support and personal coping abilities (e.g. reviews by Alexander and Klein 2001; Clohessy and Ehlers 1999). These EMS are theoretically valid in relation to the diagnostic features of PTSD. Such features include withdrawn behaviour (isolation), helplessness (failure, defectiveness/shame, enmeshment), behavioural disturbances and neurotic states (insufficient self-control) and hyper-arousal (mistrust/abuse).

Cognitive theories of PTSD have merely described how certain cognitions may be affected by a traumatic experience, or have generally reported on the role of rigid or extreme core schemas in predisposition to developing PTSD. The above appears to be one of the first analyses of specific core maladaptive schemas implicated in PTSD.

Only the police group had a salient EMS emerging in the regression model (mistrust/abuse). This may indicate that the same EMS involved in directing an individual to seek a career in the police service may also predispose an individual to developing PTSD when confronted with a traumatic situation. The logical extension of this argument is that police officers may be more at risk of developing PTSD than the other helping professions represented in this study, because of the salient EMS of mistrust/abuse for the police group.

CONCLUSIONS

This study asked whether occupation as re-enactment is adaptive or maladaptive.

Three of the occupational samples showed an increase in EMS activation in their finish groups over their starting groups (paramedics, clinical psychologists and police). Therefore, the question is whether the EMS activation is part of a maladaptive process, or merely represents the first stage of the 'working through' process. McGinn and Young (1996) state that EMS have to be activated before they can be worked through, which would be expected to be accompanied by disturbances in one's mental health, initially. Research was presented earlier which showed that increased (post-qualification) work experience had an adaptive effect on employees' mental health in clinical psychology, police and paramedic groups, despite reports of high (symptomatic) stress levels. Job satisfaction and personal gratification were reported for experienced paramedics and clinical psychologists, and lower levels of stress were reported in more experienced police officers than in their less experienced colleagues. Thus it appears that EMS activation during the training period in the helping professions may actually represent the initial stages of amelioration and 'mastery', rather than psychopathology for professions as a whole. The research presented in this chapter highlights the need for a new approach to tackling occupational stress in the helping professions, based upon schema focused work and individual psychotherapy. Interventions specifically aimed at each occupational group in this study, based upon their EMS profiles, are considered in the discussion in Chapter 17.

The present research utilized a particular measure of EMS (YSQ-S1) which measures the specific schemata identified by Young (as outlined in Chapter 12). There may be many more EMS which need to be identified, and which may be more specific to particular occupations. The apparent lack of EMS activation in the nursing sample may simply reflect the fact that the YSQ-S1 did not tap the EMS which may be more salient for this occupational group. Future research could involve generating occupation-specific EMS (e.g. through focus groups), which could then be measured for change over time, to see whether they are activated and either exacerbated or ameliorated by the working experience.

Finally, there is another question: if the 'repetition compulsion' is resolved through re-enactment of the EMS at work, why would the individual continue working in that profession once the unconscious drive has abated? Unfortunately, only conjecture can be offered, as there is no literature directly addressing this question. It may be that the individual no longer needs to be involved in 'hands-on' work after resolving their re-enactments. Is it organizational coincidence that career structures in the helping professions move further away from hands-on work the higher up the ladder one gets, or does this reflect the unconscious life of the organization 'recognizing' that some individuals no longer have the drive for hands-on work? Is the focus moved, from serving one's own desires to helping colleagues achieve their own resolutions through being an effective manager, service developer, researcher etc.? These questions do have to be addressed if we are fully to understand unconscious occupational and organizational life, and the symbiotic relationship that exists between this and the individual's pathology or progression.

Chapter 17

Discussion and conclusions

Martin Bamber

While there is a large body of literature on defining, conceptualizing and assessing stress and occupational stress, there is relatively little on treating it. This book fills this gap in the literature, by translating standard CBT and schema therapy interventions developed in other settings to the treatment of occupational stress syndromes and work dysfunctions. Standard CBT is now generally considered to be the treatment of choice for relieving the symptoms of many DSM IV (American Psychiatric Association 2000) Axis 1 disorders (Department of Health 2001; National Institute for Clinical Excellence 2004b; Roth and Fonagy 1996) and is thus ideally suited to treat occupational stress syndromes. Schema therapy complements standard CBT by offering a more in-depth individually tailored approach to working with some of the more complex problems encountered in the workplace, especially those of an interpersonal nature. Although it does not currently have an evidence base as strong as standard CBT, it is growing rapidly (Bamber 2004; Lee *et al.* 1999; McGinn *et al.* 1995; Schmidt *et al.* 1995; Shah and Waller 2000; Stopa *et al.* 2001; Waller *et al.* 2001; Young and Behary 1998; Young and Brown 2001; Young *et al.* 1993, 2003).

There is also a growing body of evidence supporting the schema-based model of occupational stress presented in Chapter 12 and the proposal that people with certain types of EMS are attracted towards particular types of career (unconsciously), with the purpose of working through unresolved psychological conflicts from childhood to achieve 'schema healing' (e.g. Arthur 2000; Bartnick *et al.* 1985; Bion 1961; Borges and Osman 2001; Eron 1955; Firth-Cozens 1999b; Furnham 1997; Holland 1973, 1985; Kets de Vries 1989; Khaleelee 1994; Lowman 1991, 1993; Lowman and Schurman 1982; McManus *et al.* 1996; Merodoulaki 1994; Obholzer and Roberts 1994; Owen 1993; Paris and Frank 1984; Peck 1987; Pines 2000; Scandell *et al.* 1997; Schneider 1987; Sherman 1996; Smart *et al.* 1986; Tremblay *et al.* 1986). This is supported by the data presented in Chapter 16 of this book. The preliminary findings of research currently being carried out by the author are similarly very encouraging. Unfortunately this research will not be complete in time for publication in this book, but preliminary results indicate highly statistically significant positive correlations between EMS measured by the YSQ-S1 (Young 1998), measures of psychological distress on the GHQ-28 (Goldberg and Williams 1988) and burnout on the MBI (Maslach and Jackson 1981) in a population of health workers ($n = 240$). These data provide further support for the model and it is intended that this work will be published in the near future.

The health care setting provides an ideal arena for many employees to work through their dysfunctional EMS and coping styles successfully and ultimately achieve schema healing. In this context work is therapeutic and adaptive for the majority of employees, so one should be cautious not to overemphasize only the negative aspects of re-enactments. They are partly what motivate individuals to choose a career in the helping professions in the first place, and also the driving force behind many highly valued and socially reinforced behaviours within health care settings. For example, nurses are often stereotyped as 'angels' because of their selfless devotion to duty and their willingness to work long and unsocial hours for low pay. Caring for the elderly and dependents in our society can be seen as a re-enactment of the dependency EMS. Similarly the desire to rescue, save or fix people, and acts of selfless heroism, are all seen as admirable forms of behaviour which can lead to considerable rewards and gains for the health worker, the patient and the organization. Indeed society positively sanctions such altruistic demonstrations of the self sacrifice schema as being for the public good. However, for a minority of individuals it is not an adaptive and healing process – particularly those with more rigid and severe EMS and maladaptive coping styles. It is for these individuals that the therapeutic interventions outlined in this book are intended.

To date, much of the literature suggests that either personality issues have not been seen as important in the work context, or that they have been seen as existing differently in the work setting and outside work. This is a serious omission, since it is estimated that up to 8% of the workforce may have a personality disorder and it only takes one 'rotten apple' in the barrel to wreak havoc. In fact, far from negating the importance of the work context it has been argued that, with proper management, the workplace itself may ultimately prove more effective than traditional therapy in 'treating' many personality disorders (Frederick 2001; Lowman 1997). Given the prevalence of personality issues in the workplace and the potential disruption these can cause, it is argued that those involved in recruitment should be trained to recognize them at the selection stage – training programmes for those involved in selection should include 'schema awareness' training.

Schema awareness training would include learning to recognize maladaptive coping styles, such as manipulative, exploitative, callous, un-empathic, aggressive, blaming, boastful, rigid and/or entitled behaviours, or indeed any of the dysfunctional behaviours described in Chapter 13 of this book, which are indicative of underlying EMS and personality issues. These are hard to detect in the standard interview format of one hour or so, since the individual can often maintain a superficial charm and say and do all the right things over this time span. The introduction into the interview of difficult 'inter-personal dilemma' scenarios, which do not allow the individual to prepare in advance, can be useful in detecting such reactions. Also, team interviews over a whole morning or day may be more successful in exposing these traits.

However, one is urged to proceed with caution in this respect. There is an inherent problem in indiscriminately selecting out individuals on the basis of their maladaptive personality traits: we may be 'throwing the baby out with the bathwater'. As has already been pointed out, it is the associated under-lying EMS which largely attract people to helping profession roles (via re-enactment) in the hope of 'mastery'. This imbues these individuals with high ego investment in their working roles, which manifests in an extraordinary commitment to their work and many of the positive manifestations of the re-enactment of EMS described earlier in this chapter. Thus, if individuals are 'selected out' on the basis of such traits, there is a very real risk of creating a less motivated and committed workforce. Also, given the central role that EMS seem to play in occupational choice (at least in the helping professions), 'selecting out' based upon these traits may run the risk of not leaving enough eligible individuals to sustain the workforce (Price 2002).

It should also be remembered that for most of these individuals, these traits appear to be part of an adaptive re-enactment process in which schema heal-ing takes place. It is only in the minority of individuals that the re-enactment is a maladaptive process resulting in schema perpetuation. Utilizing personal-ity variables in selection can be detrimental if it is not properly and fully considered (Alexander and Klein 2001; Firth-Cozens 1987). Price (2002) argues that a possible conundrum may be selecting individuals who are more emotionally detached at the expense of compassionate characteristics and concludes, as Alexander and Klein (2001) did, that the challenge for a selec-tion system based at least partly on personality features is to determine what strength of trait serves to protect individual workers and yet enables them to fulfil their health care role sensitively and compassionately (Price 2002: 80). This essentially means that those involved in selection and recruitment should be looking to employ individuals with mild to moderate and flexible EMS and coping styles and to exclude those with more rigid and extreme EMS and coping styles.

Another major challenge for the workplace organization is to 'normalize' psychological support as an everyday part of organizational culture, rather than something to be stigmatized. Khaleelee (1994) advocates 'leading by example', whereby senior staff/management provide strong role models for junior employees by advocating psychological awareness, leading to a more positive and less stigmatized view of such interventions. Price (2002) suggests that the 'Balint' group (Balint 1957; Balint and Balint 1961) is an effective group intervention for medical and mental health professionals (Brock and

Stock 1990; Rabinowitz *et al* 1996). It operates through a peer supervisory approach, facilitated by two group leaders. Work experiences are discussed in relation to how they personally impact upon members of the group. Such occupation-based psychotherapy also appears to be effective in bringing EMS into awareness and hence allowing schema healing to take place more readily.

It appears that one of the main responsibilities of the employer in reducing occupational stress is to create the right working conditions, which maximize the chances of the employee being effective in achieving their work-related goals. Where employees are identified by their work organization as being psychologically more vulnerable, there is also an obligation on the part of the organization to assist them in developing the necessary coping strategies to work more effectively in the job they do. This is not merely a moral or ethical argument but, as argued in the introduction to this book, it makes sound economic sense to do so.

A comprehensive package of interventions at the primary, secondary and tertiary levels needs to be provided by the workplace organization and its occupational health services, aimed at reducing occupational stress. It is envisaged that the provision of these interventions would have a 'pyramidal' structure, as illustrated in Figure 17.1, with the interventions nearer the apex of the pyramid requiring more specialist therapeutic input for relatively fewer employees.

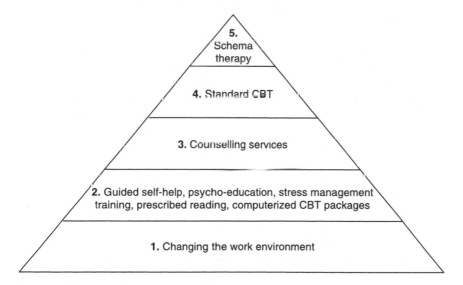

Figure 17.1 A stepped approach to treating occupational stress.

A comprehensive stress management package includes:

1   Organizational interventions aimed at providing a healthy working environment, such as creating the right organizational culture and climate,

and providing the necessary resources, equipment, training, supervision and support to do the job effectively (as outlined in Chapters 2 and 4 of this book).

2   Psycho-educational programmes, guided self-help materials, prescribed bibliotherapy and computerized CBT packages should be made readily available to staff, through occupational health departments and health service libraries. Stress management training aimed at alleviating normative levels of stress should also be made readily accessible to staff (as outlined in Chapter 5 of this book), as should Balint-type support groups (discussed earlier in this chapter).

3   Short-term individual and/or group counselling up to a maximum of eight sessions, aimed at employees who are displaying mild non-clinical levels of distress.

4   Standard CBT up to a maximum of 20 sessions, aimed at alleviating occupational stress syndromes (as outlined in Chapters 6–8 of this book).

5   In-depth individually tailored treatment programmes of schema-focused therapy for more complex problems and work dysfunctions (as outlined in Chapter 14 of this book).

Cooper (1986) proposed that in order to fulfil such a role, a new type of psychologist was needed. He advocated that a 'hybrid' between a clinical and an occupational psychologist, known as an 'occupational clinical psychologist', should be created. This would require someone with considerable expertise in both the organizational and the clinical fields. However, it is the opinion of the author that it is unrealistic to expect one individual to have expertise in all the areas required – it would probably result in them becoming a 'jack of all trades' and master of none. A more realistic model of service delivery would be one in which there is a coming together of experts from a range of different fields including clinical psychology, counselling, occupational psychology, human resources, management, organizational consultancy, therapy, counselling, training, health promotion and other areas as required. This coming together of experts would ultimately lead to a cross-fertilization of ideas and research findings, which could be incorporated into the practice of all involved.

It is proposed that the role of the occupational health psychologist should be one of a 'gate-keeper' to the more specialist counselling and therapy services (levels 3–5 in Figure 17.1) and also the 'link person' between these specialist services and the workplace, rather than directly providing these services. The main role for the occupational health psychologist would be to provide interventions at levels 1 and 2 in Figure 17.1. To be effective in this role, the occupational health psychologist would need to have a legitimate advisory-consultancy role at the highest levels in the strategic decision-making process, including senior management forums, and direct access to the chief executive level, with the remit of advising on occupational stress issues.

The traditional wisdom is that comprehensive clinical therapy services should be provided for all health care employees 'in-house'. However, there is a significant overlap in the types of problem seen by occupational health clinical psychology services and mainstream NHS services (Bamber 1995; McPherson 2004), and there appears to be no reason why mainstream psychological therapy and counselling services should not be better utilized. Although at the present time mainstream services are not geared up to working with those suffering from occupational stress, they could be relatively easily trained to work with occupational mental health problems, in the way described in this book.

In conclusion, there are many challenges ahead for occupational health services in health care settings, if they are to provide the more integrated and comprehensive occupational stress management services for staff that are required. To be fair, in recognition of these challenges, the Department of Health has in recent years come up with a number of initiatives to address the problem, including *Human Resources in the National Health Service* (Department of Health 2002) and *Improving Working Lives* (Department of Health 2000a), both of which have at their core a number of standards which require that good staff support mechanisms are available. Another Department of Health document entitled *The Provision of Counselling Services for NHS Staff* (2000b) also recognized the gap in service provision and the need for more specialist psychological interventions where the normal counselling provision is insufficient to deal adequately with the issues being presented.

The *Human Resources Performance Framework* (Department of Health 2000c) set as one of its main targets that NHS employers should achieve a 30% reduction in sickness absence against a pre-determined baseline figure. If these national targets are to be met, a more integrated and comprehensive occupational stress management policy needs to be developed. In addition to the standard primary, secondary and tertiary interventions identified in the literature, this book demonstrates the need for more specialist clinical services. Clinical psychology services, offering more in-depth individualized evidence-based CBT for stress syndromes and also schema-focused therapies for work dysfunctions, need to be developed if a comprehensive and integrated stress management policy is to be achieved. There is also a need to integrate the findings of the literature on the schema-based approach to occupational stress and work dysfunctions into existing staff selection, recruitment, induction, training and support programmes for health service staff at all levels. In addition, there needs to be a culture shift in health care organizations so that psychological support is seen as part of the normal culture of the organization and senior members of the organization lead by example, rather than it being something which is stigmatized. These are some of the major challenges which occupational health service providers need to address if they are to achieve successfully the targets they have set themselves for the future.

References

Achterberg, J. and Lawlis, G. F. (1980). *Bridges of the Bodymind*. Champaign, IL: Institute for Personality and Ability Testing.

Ackerley, G. D. *et al.* (1988). Burnout among licensed psychologists. *Professional Psychology Research and Practice* 19: 624–31.

Adams, A. (1992). *Bullying at Work*. London: Virago Press.

Adams, J. S. (1965). Inequity in social exchange. In L. Berkowitz (ed) *Advances in Experimental Social Psychology*. New York: Aademic Press.

Ader, R. (1981). *Psychoneuroimmunology*. New York: Academic Press.

Ader, R. (1987). Clinical implications of psychoneuroimmunology. *Journal of Development and Behavioural Paediatrics* 8: 357–8.

Adkins, B. (1989). Time management: Getting more for less. *Physician Executive* 15(4): 20–1.

Alberti, R. and Emmons, M. (2001). *Your Perfect Right: Assertiveness and Equality in Your Life and Relationships* (8th edn). Atascadero, CA: Impact Publishers Inc.

Albrecht, J. *et al.* (1985). A controlled study of cellular immune function in affective disorders before and during somatic therapy. *Psychiatry Research* 15: 185–93.

Alexander, D. A. and Klein, S. (2001). Ambulance personnel and critical incidents. *British Journal of Psychiatry* 178: 76–81.

Alexander, P. C. (1992). Application of attachment theory to the study of sexual abuse. *Journal of Consulting and Clinical Psychology* 60: 185–95.

American Psychiatric Association (APA) (2000). *Diagnostic and Statistical Manual of Mental Disorders (DSM-IV-TR)* (4th edn, text revision). Washington, DC: American Psychiatric Association.

Amicus (2004). CHI survey reinforces need for ombudsmen to tackle bullying. Press release emarked 16 March through *Reps Direct* 254.

Amkraut, A. and Solomon, G. F. (1975). From symbolic stimulus to the pathophysiologic response: Immune mechanisms. *International Journal of Psychiatry in Medicine* 5: 541–63.

Andrews, G. and Crino, R. (1991). Behavioural psychotherapy of anxiety disorders. *Psychiatric Annals* 21: 358–60.

Antonovsky, A. (1979). *Health, Stress and Coping*. San Francisco: Jossey-Bass.

Appelberg, K. (1996). Alcohol consumption and smoking: Associations with interpersonal conflicts at work and with spouse among 13,869 Finnish employees. *Addiction Research* 1: 257–67.

Arnetz, B. B. *et al.* (1987). Immune function in unemployed women. *Psychosomatic Medicine* 49: 3–12.

Arthur, A. R. (2000). The personality and epistemological traits of cognitive behavioural and psychoanalytic psychotherapists. *British Journal of Medical Psychology* 73: 243–57.

Asterita, M. F. (1985). *The Physiology of Stress*. New York: Human Sciences Press.

Back, K. and Back, K. (1999). *Assertiveness at Work* (3rd edn). London: McGraw-Hill.

Bair, J. P. and Greenspan, B. K. (1986). Teams: Team work training for interns, residents and nurses. *Hospital and Community Psychiatry* 37: 633–5.

Balint, M. (1957). *The Doctor, His Patient and the Illness*. London: Pitman.

Balint, M. and Balint, E. (1961). *Psychotherapeutic Techniques in Medicine: Mind and Medicine*. London: Tavistock.

Balloch, S. *et al.* (1998). Working in the social services: Job satisfaction, stress and violence. *British Journal of Social Work* 28: 329–50.

Bamber, M. R. (1995). *Annual Reports (1991–1995) of the Occupational Health Psychology Service to South Tees NHS Trust*. Unpublished report for South Cleveland Hospital, UK.

Bamber, M. R. (1996). *An Exploration of the Relationship between Psychosocial Stressors and the Immune Response in Humans*. Unpublished doctoral thesis, University of Edinburgh.

Bamber, M. R. (2004). The good, the bad and defenceless Jimmy: A single case study of schema mode therapy. *Clinical Psychology and Psychotherapy* 11: 425–38.

Banks, C. (2003). Careers: How to manage your time effectively. *Nursing Times* 99: 60–1.

Barefoot, J. C. *et al.* (1983). Hostility, coronary heart disease and total mortality: A 25 year follow-up study of 255 physicians. *Psychosomatic Medicine* 45: 59–63.

Barling, J. *et al.* (1993). Homemaker role experiences affect toddler behaviours via maternal well-being and parenting behaviour. *Journal of Abnormal Child Psychology* 21: 213–29.

Barrell, J. J. *et al.* (1985). The causes and treatment of performance anxiety: An experiential approach. *Journal of Humanistic Psychology* 25: 106–22.

Bartnick, L. W. *et al.* (1985). The value of the California Psychology Inventory in predicting medical students' career choice. *Medical Education* 19: 143–7.

Bartolome, F. (1983). The work alibi: When it's harder to go home. *Harvard Business Review* 61: 66–74.

Bass, B. M. and Avolio, B. J. (1990). The implications of transactional and transformational leadership for individual, team and organizational development. *Research and Organizational Change and Development* 4: 321–72.

Bates, A. and Clark, D. M. (1998). A new cognitive treatment for social phobia: A single-case study. *Journal of Cognitive Psychotherapy* 12: 289–302.

Battle, J. (1980). *Culture-Free Self-Esteem Inventories for Children and Adults*. Windsor, UK: NFER-Nelson.

Beck, A. T. (1967). *Depression: Causes and Treatment*. Philadelphia, PA: University of Pennsylvania Press.

Beck, A. T. (1972). *Depression: Causes and Treatment*. Philadelphia, PA: University of Pennsylvania Press.

Beck, A. T. (1976). *Cognitive Therapy and the Emotional Disorders*. New York: International Universities Press.

Beck, A. T. (1984). Cognitive approaches to stress. In R. Woolfolk and P. Lehrer (eds) *Principles and Practice of Stress Management*. New York: Guildford.

Beck, A. T. (1996). Beyond belief: A theory of modes, personality and psychopathology. In P. Salkovskis (ed) *Frontiers of Cognitive Therapy*. New York: Guilford Press.

Beck, A. T. and Emery, G. (1977). *Cognitive Therapy of Substance Abuse*. Philadelphia, PA: Centre for Cognitive Therapy.

Beck, A. T. and Steer, R. A. (1987). *Manual for the Beck Depression Inventory*. San Antonio, TX: Psychological Corporation.

Beck, A. T. *et al.* (1961). An inventory for measuring depression. *Archives of General Psychiatry* 4: 561–71.

Beck, A. T. *et al.* (1979). *Cognitive Therapy of Depression*. New York: Guilford Press.

Beck, A. T. *et al.* (1985). *Anxiety Disorders and Phobias: A Cognitive Perspective*. New York: Basic Books.

Beck, A. T. *et al.* (1988). An inventory for measuring clinical anxiety: Psychometric properties. *Journal of Consulting and Clinical Psychology* 56: 893–7.

Beck, A. T. *et al.* (1990). *Cognitive Therapy for Personality Disorders*. New York: Guilford Press.

Beck, J. S. (1995). *Cognitive Therapy: Basics and Beyond*. New York: Guilford Press.

Becker, M. *et al.* (1997). Intractability is relative: Behaviour therapy in the elimination of violence in psychotic forensic patients. *Legal and Criminological Psychiatry* 2: 89–101.

Beehr, T. A. and Bhagat, R. S. (1985). *Human Stress and Cognitions in Organizations*. New York: Wiley.

Beehr, T. A. and O'Hara, K. (1987). Methodological designs for the evaluation of occupational stress interventions. *Journal of Occupational Psychology* 53: 187–94.

Bennett-Levy, J. *et al.* (2004). *Oxford Guide to Behavioural Experiments in Cognitive Therapy*. Oxford, UK: Oxford University Press.

Benson, H. (1975). *The Relaxation Response*. New York: William Morrow.

Berg, J. L. (1990). Differentiating ego functions of borderline and narcissistic personalities. *Journal of Personality Assessment* 55: 537–48.

Bieliauskas, L. A. and Garron, D. C. (1982). Psychological depression and cancer. *General Hospital Psychiatry* 4: 187–95.

Bion, W. (1961). *Experiences in Groups*. New York: Basic Books.

Bjorkqvist, K. *et al.* (1994). Aggression among university employees. *Aggressive Behaviour* 20: 173–84.

Blackburn, I. M. and Davidson, K. (1990). *Cognitive Therapy for Depression and Anxiety*. Edinburgh, UK: Blackwell.

Blackburn, I. M. and Twaddle, V. (1996). *Cognitive Therapy in Action*. London: Souvenir Press.

Blenkin, H. *et al.* (1995). Stress in NHS consultants. *British Medical Journal* 310: 534.

Blenkiron, P. (2000). Cognitive behaviour therapy. *Family Medicine* 4: 6–9.

Blenkiron, P. *et al.* (1999). Associations between perfectionism, mood and fatigue in chronic fatigue syndrome. *Journal of Nervous and Mental Disease* 187: 566–70.

Bond, M. (1988). Assertiveness training: Part One. *Nursing Times* 84(9): 61–4.

Bootham Park Hospital (2002). *Annual Staff Survey of York Health Services NHS Trust*. York, UK: Occupational Health Department, Bootham Park Hospital.

Borg, M. G. (1990). Occupational stress in British educational settings: A review. *Educational Psychology* 10: 103–26.

Borges, N. J. and Osman, W. R. (2001). Personality and medical speciality choice: Technique orientation versus people orientation. *Journal of Vocational Behavior* 58: 22–35.

Borill, C. S. *et al.* (1996). *Mental Health of the Workforce in NHS Trusts: Phase 1; Final Report.* Sheffield, UK: Institute of Work Psychology, University of Sheffield; Leeds, UK: Department of Psychology, University of Leeds.

Borill, C. S. *et al.* (1998). *Stress Among Staff in NHS Trusts.* Sheffield, UK: Institute of Work Psychology, University of Sheffield.

Borkovec, T. D. and Costello, E. (1993). Efficacy of applied relaxation and cognitive-behavioural therapy in the treatment of generalized anxiety disorder. *Journal of Consulting and Clinical Psychology* 51: 611–19.

Borkovec, T. D. *et al.* (1983). Preliminary exploration of worry: Some characteristics and processes. *Behaviour Research and Therapy* 21: 9–16.

Borman, W. C. and Motowidlo, S. J. (1993). Expanding the criterion domain to include elements of contextual performance. In N. Schmidt and W. C. Borman (eds) *Personnel Selection in Organizations.* San Francisco, CA: Jossey Bass.

Bosch, G. (1999). Working time: Tendencies and emerging issues. *International Labour Review* 138: 131–50.

Bowlby, J. (1969). *Attachment and Loss Vol. 1: Attachment.* New York: Basic Books.

Bowling, A. (1997). *Measuring Health* (2nd edn). Buckingham, UK: Open University Press.

Brady, C. (1999). Surviving the incident. In P. Leather *et al.* (eds) *Work-Related Violence: Assessment and Intervention.* London: Routledge.

Brenner, O. C. and Tomkiewicz, J. (1982). Sex differences among business graduates in fear of success and fear of appearing incompetent as measured by objective instruments. *Psychological Reports* 51: 179–82.

Breslau, H. and Davis, G. C. (1986). Chronic stress and major depression. *Archives of General Psychiatry* 43: 309–14

Brewin, C. R. *et al.* (2000). Meta-analysis of risk factors of posttraumatic stress disorder in trauma-exposed adults. *Journal of Consulting and Clinical Psychology* 68: 748–66.

Briner, R. (1997). Improving stress assessment: Toward an evidence-based approach to organizational stress interventions. *Journal of Psychosomatic Research* 43: 61–71.

Broadbent, D. E. *et al.* (1982). The cognitive failures questionnaire and its correlates. *British Journal of Clinical Psychology* 21: 1–16.

Brock, C. V. and Stock, D. (1990). A survey of Balint group activities in US family practice residency programs. *Family Medicine* 22: 33–7.

Brook, P. P. *et al.* (1988). Discriminant validation of measures of job satisfaction, job involvement and organizational commitment. *Journal of Applied Psychology* 73: 139–45.

Brune, M. (2001). Social cognition and psychopathy in an evolutionary perspective. *Psychopathology* 34: 85–94.

Buchanan, D. and Huczynski, A. (2004). *Organizational Behaviour* (5th edn). London: Prentice Hall/Financial Times.

Budd, J. W. *et al.* (1996). Correlates and consequences of workplace violence. *Journal of Occupational Health Psychology* 1: 197–210.

Burke, R. J. (2004). Workaholism, self-esteem and motives for money. *Psychological Reports* 94: 457–63.

Burke, R. J. and Greenglass, E. R. (1988). Career orientations and psychological burnout in teachers. *Psychological Reports* 63: 107–16.

Burke, R. J. and Matthiesen, S. (2004). Workaholism among Norwegian journalists: Antecedants and consequences. *Stress and Health* 20: 301–8.

Burnard, P. (1992). Developing confidence. *Nursing* 4: 9–10.

Burns, D. (1999). *Feeling Good: The New Mood Therapy*. New York: Avon.

Burns, D. D. (1990). *The Feeling Good Handbook*. New York: Plume Penguin.

Burns, D. D. and Auerbach, A. (1996). Therapeutic empathy in cognitive-behavioural therapy: Does it really make a difference? In P. Salkovskis (ed) *Frontiers of Cognitive Therapy*. New York: Guilford Press.

Burton, R. (1927). *The Anatomy of Melancholy* (ed F. Dell and P. J. Smith). New York: Farrar and Reinhart.

Butler, G. and Hackmann, A. (2004). Social anxiety. In J. Bennett-Levy *et al.* (eds) *Oxford Guide to Behavioural Experiments in Cognitive Therapy*. Oxford, UK: Oxford University Press.

Butler, G. and Hope, T. (1995). *Manage Your Mind: The Mental Fitness Guide*. Oxford, UK: Oxford University Press.

Butler, G. *et al.* (1987). Anxiety management for persistent generalized anxiety. *British Journal of Psychiatry* 151: 535–42.

Butler, G. *et al.* (1991). Comparison of behaviour therapy and cognitive behaviour therapy in the treatment of generalized anxiety disorder. *Journal of Consulting and Clinical Psychology* 59: 167–72.

Cannella, A. and Monroe, M. (1997). Contrasting perspectives on strategic leadership. *Journal of Management* 23: 213.

Cannon, W. B. (1929). *Bodily Changes in Pain, Hunger, Fear and Rage* (2nd edn). New York: Appleton.

Cannon, W. B. (1932). *The Wisdom of the Body*. New York: Norton.

Cannon, W. B. (1935). Stresses and strains of homeostasis (Mary Scott Newbold Lecture). *American Journal of Medical Sciences* 189: 1–14.

Cannon, W. B. and de la Paz, D. (1911). Emotional stimulation of adrenal secretion. *American Journal of Physiology* 28: 64–70.

Caplan, G. (1981). Mastery of stress: Psychosocial aspects. *American Journal of Psychiatry* 138: 413–20.

Caplan, R. P. (1994). Stress, anxiety and depression in hospital consultants, general practitioners and senior health service managers. *British Medical Journal* 309: 1261–3.

Carson, J. and Kuipers, E. (1998). Stress management interventions. In S. Hardy *et al.* (eds) *Occupational Stress*. Cheltenham, UK: Stanley Thomas.

Cartwright, S. and Cooper, C. L. (1996). *Managing Mergers, Acquisitions and Joint Ventures*. Oxford, UK: Butterworth Heinemann.

Carver, C. S. *et al.* (1989). Assessing coping strategies: A theoretically based approach. *Journal of Personality and Social Psychology* 56: 267–83.

Chant, S. *et al.* (2002). Communication skills training in healthcare: A review of the literature. *Nurse Education Today* 22: 189–202.

Chartered Institute of Personnel and Development (2002, September). The guide to work–life balance. *People Management Guide*.

Chen, P. Y. and Spector, P. E. (1991). Negative affectivity as the underlying cause of correlations between stressors and strains. *Journal of Applied Psychology* 76: 398–407.

Cherniss, C. (1980). *Staff Burnout. Job Stress in Human Services*. Beverly Hills, CA: Sage.

Cherns, A. B. (1976). The principles of socio-technical design. *Human Relations* 29: 783–92.

Chitty, K. and Maynard, C. (1986). Managing manipulation. *Journal of Psychosocial Nursing* 24: 9–13.

Christie, B. (1984). Office systems. In C. L. Cooper and P. Makin (eds) *Psychology for Managers*. Leicester, UK: BPS Books.

Christie, R. (1970). *Studies in Machievellianism*. New York: Academic Press.

Clack, G. B. (1999). A retrospective study of medical speciality choice and job satisfaction in a sample of King's graduates who qualified between 1985/86 and 1989/90. *Medical Teacher* 21: 71–82.

Clark, D. M. (1986). A cognitive model of panic. *Behaviour Research and Therapy* 24: 461–70.

Clark, D. M. (1988). A cognitive model of panic. In S. Rachman and J. D. Maser (eds) *Panic: Psychological Perspectives*. Hillsdale, NJ: Erlbaum.

Clark, D. M. (2000). Panic and generalized anxiety In K. Hawton *et al* (eds) *Cognitive Behavioural Therapy for Psychiatric Problems*. Oxford, UK: Oxford University Press.

Clark, D. M. and Beck, A. T. (1988). Cognitive approaches. In C. Last and M. Hersen (eds) *Handbook of Anxiety Disorders*. New York: Pergamon.

Clark, D. M. and Wells, A. (1995). A cognitive model of social phobia. In R. G. Heimberg *et al.* (eds) *Social Phobia: Diagnosis, Assessment, and Treatment*. New York: Guilford Press.

Clark, D. M. *et al.* (1991) An experimental investigation of thought suppression. *Behavioural Research and Therapy* 29: 253–7.

Clegg, F. (1988). Bereavement. In S. Fisher and T. Reason (eds) *Handbook of Life Stress, Cognition and Health*. Chichester, UK: Wiley.

Clohessy, S. and Ehlers, A. (1999). PTSD symptoms, response to intrusive memories and coping in ambulance service workers. *British Journal of Clinical Psychology* 38: 251–65.

Clore, G. L. *et al.* (1993) Where does anger dwell? In R. Wyer and T. K. Shrull (eds) *Perspectives on Anger and Emotion*. Hillsdale, NJ: Lawrence Erlbaum.

Clutterbuck, D. (2001). *Everyone Needs a Mentor* (3rd edn). London: Chartered Institute of Personnel and Development.

Cobb, S. (1976). Social support as a moderator of life stress. *Psychosomatic Medicine* 38: 300–14.

Cohen, S. and Wills, T. A. (1985). Stress, social support and the buffering hypothesis. *Psychological Bulletin* 88: 82–108.

Collins, W. E. *et al.* (1991). Relationships of anxiety scores to screening and training of air traffic controllers. *Aviation, Space and Environmental Medicine* 62: 236–40.

Confederation of British Industry (2000). *Focus on Absence and Labour Turnover Survey*. London.

Connelly, J. (1976). Life events before myocardial infarction. *Journal of Human Stress* 2: 3–17.

Conte, J. M. *et al.* (2001). Criterion validity evidence for time urgency: Associations with burnout, organizational commitment and job involvement in travel agents. *Applied H. M. Research* 6: 129–34.

Cook, M. (1998). *Personnel Selection: Adding Value Through People* (3rd edn). Chichester, UK: John Wiley and Sons.

Cooper, C. and Marshall, J. (1976). Occupational sources of stress: A review of the literature relating to coronary heart disease and mental ill-health. *Journal of Occupational Psychology* 49: 11–28.

Cooper, C. L. (1986). Job distress: Recent research and the emerging role of the occupational clinical psychologist. *Bulletin of the British Psychological Society* 39: 325–31.

Cooper, C. L. and Mitchell, S. (1990). Nurses under stress: A reliability and validity study of the NSI. *Stress Medicine* 6: 21–4.

Cooper, C. L. and Payne, R. (1988). *Causes, Coping and Consequences of Stress at Work*. New York: John Wiley and Sons.

Cooper, C. L. *et al.* (1988). *Occupational Stress Indicator: Management Guide*. Windsor, UK: Hodder and Stoughton.

Cooper, C. L. *et al.* (1996). *Stress Prevention in the Workplace: Assessing the Costs and Benefits for Organizations*. Dublin: European Foundation for the Improvement of Living and Working Conditions.

Cooper, D. and Robertson, I. T. (1995). *The Psychology of Personnel Selection*. London: Routledge.

Cooper, J. (1999). Managing workplace stress in outpatient nursing. *Professional Nurse* 14: 540–3.

Cox, T. (1978). *Stress*. London: Macmillan.

Cox, T. (1993). *Stress Research and Management: Putting Theory to Work* (HSE contract research report 61). London: HMSO.

Cox, T. and Cox, S. (1993). *Psychosocial and Organizational Hazards: Monitoring and Control*. Occasional Series in Occupational Health, 5. Copenhagen: World Health Organization (Europe).

Cox, T. *et al.* (2000). *Research on Work-Related Stress*. Luxembourg: European Agency for Health and Safety at Work.

Cramer, P. (2000). Defence mechanisms in psychology today: Further processes for adaptation. *American Psychologist* 55: 637–46.

Crosley, J. M. (1980). Preventing nurse burnout: Assertiveness training can be cost effective. *Cost Containment* 2.

Crown, S. and Crisp, A. H. (1979). *Manual of the Crown–Crisp Experiential Index*. London: Hodder and Stoughton.

Cushway, D. (1992). Stress in clinical psychology trainees. *British Journal of Clinical Psychology* 31: 169–79.

Cushway, D. and Tyler, P. A. (1994). Stress and coping in clinical psychologists. *Stress Medicine* 10: 35–42.

Dalgleish, T. (1999). Cognitive theories of post-traumatic stress disorder. In W. Yule (ed) *Post-Traumatic Stress Disorders: Concepts and Therapy*. Chichester, UK: Wiley.

Davidhizar, R. and Eshleman, J. (2002). Starter's kit: Time management and you. *The Magazine for Healthcare Travel Professionals* 9: 40–1.

Davidhizer, R. and Giger, J. (1990). When subordinates go over your head: The manipulative employee. *Journal of Nursing Administration* 20: 29–34.

Davidson, J. R. *et al.* (1991). Post-traumatic stress disorder in the community: An epidemiological study. *Psychological Medicine* 21: 713–21.

Davis, M. *et al.* (1988). *The Relaxation and Stress Reduction Workbook* (3rd edn). Oakland, CA: New Harbinger Publications.

Davis, M. *et al.* (2000). *The Stress and Relaxation Reduction Workbook* (5th edn). Oakland, CA: New Harbinger Publications.

Dawkins, J. *et al.* (1985). Stress and the psychiatric nurse. *Journal of Psychosocial Nursing* 23(11): 8–15.

Dawson, P. (1994). *Organizational Change: A Processual Approach*. London: Routledge.

De Leo, D. *et al.* (1982). Anxiety and depression in general and psychiatric nurses: A comparison. *International Journal of Nursing Studies* 19: 173–5.

Dembroski, T. M. *et al.* (1978). Components of the type A coronary prone behaviour pattern and cardiovascular responses to psychomotor performance challenge. *Journal of Behavioural Medicine* 1: 159–76.

Dembroski, T. M. *et al.* (1979). Effects of level of challenge on pressor and heart responses in Type A and B subjects. *Journal of Applied Social Psychology* 9: 209–28.

De Moliner, A. F. and Hunsberger, R. W. (1962). Organization of the subcortical system governing defence and flight reactions in the cat. *Journal of Physiology* 160: 200–13.

Department of Health (2000a). *Improving Working Lives*. London.

Department of Health (2000b). *The Provision of Counselling Services for NHS Staff*. London.

Department of Health (2000c). *Human Resources Performance Framework*. London.

Department of Health (2001). *Treatment Choice in Psychological Therapies and Counselling*. London.

Department of Health (2002). *Human Resources in the National Health Service*. London.

Department of Trade and Industry (2003). *Flexible Working: The Business Case*. London: HMSO Books.

Dickson, A. (1986). *A Woman in Your Own Right: Assertiveness and You* (2nd edn). London: Quartet Books.

Dickson, R. *et al.* (1994). Intervention strategies to manage workplace violence. *Occupational Health Review* 50: 15–8.

Di Martino, V. (1992). Occupational stress: A preventative approach. *ILO Conditions of Work Digest* 11: 3–21.

Dunn, M. and Sommer, N. (1997). Managing difficult staff interactions: Effectiveness of assertiveness training for SCI nursing staff. *Rehabilitation Nursing* 22: 82–7.

Durham, R. C. *et al.* (1994). Cognitive therapy, analytic psychotherapy and anxiety management training for anxiety disorder. *British Journal of Psychiatry* 165: 315–23.

Earnshaw, J. and Davidson, M. J. (1994). Remedying sexual harassment via industrial tribunal claims. *Personnel Review* 23: 3–18.

Easton, S. (1990). Learn to relax and counter stress. *Occupational Health* 42: 172–4.

Economic and Social Research Council (1998). *British Household Panel Survey*. Swindon, UK.

Edelmann, R. J. (1993). *Interpersonal Conflicts at Work*. Leicester, UK: BPS Books.

Edwards, J. R. and Van Harrison, R. (1993). Job demands and worker health:

Three-dimensional re-examination of the relationship between person–environment fit and strain *Journal of Applied Psychology* 78: 628–48.

Egan, G. (1990). *The Skilled Helper*. Monterey, CA: Brooks Cole.

Einarsen, S. (2000). Harassment and bullying at work: A review of the Scandinavian approach. *Aggression and Violent Behaviour* 5: 379–401.

Einarsen, S. *et al.* (1994). Mobbing og harde personkonflikter. Heslefarlig samspill pa arbeidsplassen. In H. Hoel *et al.* (eds) *The Cost of Violence/Stress at Work and the Benefits of a Violence/Stress Free Working Environment*. Geneva: International Labour Organization.

Einarsen, S. *et al.* (1999). Tiden leger alle sar: Senvirkninger av mobbing I arbeidslivet. In H. Hoel *et al.* (eds) *The Cost of Violence/Stress at Work and the Benefits of a Violence/Stress Free Working Environment*. Geneva: International Labour Organization.

Einsiedel, A. A. and Tully, H. A. (1981). Methodological considerations in studying the burnout phenomenon. In J. W. Jones (ed) *The Burnout Syndrome*. Park Ridge, IL: London House Press.

Ellis, R. T. (1992). Perceptions, attitudes and beliefs of police recruits. *Canadian Police College Journal* 15: 95–117.

Endler, N. S. and Parker, D. A. (1990). Multi-dimensional assessment of coping: A critical evaluation. *Journal of Personality and Social Psychology* 58: 844–54.

Enright, S. J. (1997). Cognitive-behaviour therapy: Clinical applications. *British Medical Journal* 314: 1811–6.

Erikson, E. H. (1968). *Identity: Youth and Crisis*. New York: Norton.

Eron, L. D. (1955). Effect of medical education on medical students' attitudes. *Journal of Medical Education* 30: 559–66.

Evans, G. W. *et al.* (1987). Type A behaviour and occupational stress: A cross-cultural study of blue collar workers. *Journal of Personality and Social Psychology* 52: 1002–7.

Eysenck, H. J. and Eysenck, M. J. (1985). *Personality and Individual Differences: A Natural Science Approach*. New York: Plenum Press.

Farber, B. A. (1985). Clinical psychologists' perceptions of psychotherapeutic work. *Clinical Psychologist* 38: 10–3.

Farber, B. A. and Heifetz, L. J. (1982). The process and dimensions of burnout in psychotherapists. *Professional Psychology* 13: 293–301.

Faugier, J. and Woolnough, H. (2001). Whistleblowing and the implications for developing leadership. *Mental Health Practice* 5: 10–4.

Feindler, E. L. and Ecton, R. B. (1986). *Adolescent Anger Control Cognitive Behavioural Techniques*. New York: Pergamon.

Fennell, M. J. V. (1989). Depression. In K. Hawton *et al.* (eds) *Cognitive Behaviour Therapy for Psychiatric Problems: A Practical Guide*. Oxford, UK: Oxford Medical Publications.

Fennell, M. J. (2000). Depression. In K. Hawton *et al.* (eds) *Cognitive Behaviour Therapy for Psychiatric Problems*. Oxford, UK: Oxford University Press.

Fennell, M. J. V. and Teasdale, J. D. (1987). Cognitive therapy for depression: Individual differences and the process of change. *Cognitive Therapy and Research* 11: 253–71.

Fielding, N. G. and Fielding, J. L. (1987). A study of resignation during British police training. *Journal of Police Science and Administration* 15: 24–36.

Firth, H. (1986). Levels and sources of stress in medical students. *British Medical Journal* 292: 533–6.

Firth, H. and Britton, P. (1989). Burnout, absence and turnover amongst British nursing staff. *Journal of Occupational Psychology* 62: 55–9.

Firth, H. and Hardy, G. E. (1992). Occupational stress, clinical treatment and changes in job perceptions. *Journal of Occupational and Organizational Psychology* 65: 81–8.

Firth, H. *et al.* (1987). Professional depression, burnout and personality in long stay nursing. *International Journal of Nursing Studies* 24: 227–37.

Firth-Cozens, J. (1987). Emotional distress in junior house officers. *British Medical Journal* 295: 533–6.

Firth-Cozens, J. (1993). Stress, psychological problems and clinical performance. In C. A. Vincent *et al.* (eds) *Medical Accidents*. Oxford, UK: Oxford University Press.

Firth-Cozens, J. (1999). *The Psychological Problems of Doctors*. Chichester, UK: Wiley.

Fisher, S. (1986). *Stress and Strategy*. London: Lawrence Erlbaum Associates.

Flannery, R. B. (1996). Violence in the workplace 1970–1995: A review of the literature. *Aggression and Violent Behaviour* 1: 57–68.

Fletcher, B. C. (1988). The epidemiology of occupational stress. In C. L. Cooper and R. L. Payne (eds) *Causes, Coping and Consequences of Stress at Work*. Chichester, UK: Wiley.

Fletcher, B. C. (1991). *Work, Stress, Disease and Life Expectancy*. Chichester, UK: Wiley.

Foa, E. B. *et al.* (1991). The impact of fear activation and anger on the efficacy of exposure treatment for post-traumatic stress disorder. *Behaviour Therapy* 26: 487–99.

Folkard, S. and Hill, J. (2002). Shiftwork: Body rhythm and social factors. In I. P. Warr (ed) *Psychology at Work* (5th edn). Harmondsworth, UK: Penguin Books.

Folkman, S. and Lazarus, R. S. (1988). *Manual for the Ways of Coping Questionnaire*. Palo Alto, CA: Consulting Psychologists Press.

Follette, V. M. *et al.* (1996). Cumulative trauma: The impact of child sexual abuse, adult sexual abuse and spouse abuse. *Journal of Traumatic Stress* 9: 25–35.

Follete, V. M. *et al.* (1999). *Cognitive Behavioural Therapy for Trauma*. New York: Guilford Press.

Fontana, D. (1993). *Managing Time*. Leicester, UK: The British Psychological Society.

Fontana, D. (1994). *Social Skills at Work*. Leicester, UK: BPS Books.

Fontana, D. (1997). *Managing Stress* (5th edn). Leicester, UK: BPS Books.

Forsythe, C. J. and Compass, B. E. (1987). Interaction of cognitive appraisals of stressful events and coping: Testing the goodness of fit hypothesis. *Cognitive Therapy and Research* 11: 473–85.

Francis, R. (1999). *Ethics for Psychologists*. Leicester, UK: BPS Books.

Frankenhaeuser, M. (1983). The sympathetic-adrenal and pituitary-adrenal response to challenge: Comparison between the sexes. In E. M. Dembroski, *et al.* (eds) *Biobehavioural Bases of Coronary Heart Disease*. New York: Karger.

Frankenhaeuser, M. *et al.* (1980). Dissociation between sympathetic-adrenal and pituitary-adrenal responses to an achievement situation characterized by high controllability: Comparing type A and type B males and females. *Biological Psychology* 10: 79–91.

Frederick (2001). A vacancy is still better than a disruptive employee. *Patient Care Management* 16: 6–8.

Freud, S. (1914). Remembering, repeating and working through (further recommendations on the technique of psychoanalysis). In *The Standard Edition of the Complete Works of Sigmond Freud*, Vol. 12. London: Hogarth Press.

Freud, S. (1920). Beyond the pleasure principle. In *The Standard Edition of the Complete Works of Sigmund Freud*, Vol. 18. London: Hogarth Press.

Freud, S. (1930). Civilization and its discontents. In *The Standard Edition of the Complete Psychological Works of Sigmund Freud*, Vol. 21. London: Hogarth Press.

Freud, S. (1961). The future of an illusion. In *The Complete Psychological Works of Sigmund Freud*, Vol. 21. London: Hogarth Press.

Friedman, M. and Rosenman, R. H. (1974). *Type A Behaviour and Your Heart*. New York: Alfred Knopf.

Fromm, E. (1974). *The Anatomy of Human Destructiveness*. London: Jonathan Cape.

Fryer, D. and Payne, R. (1986). Being unemployed: A review of the literature. In C. L. Cooper and I. Robertson (eds) *International Review of Industrial and Organizational Psychology*. New York: Wiley.

Furnham, A. (1997). *The Psychology of Behaviour at Work: The Individual in the Organization*. Hove, UK: Psychology Press.

Furnham, A. and Schaeffer, R. (1984). Person–environment fit, job satisfaction and mental health. *Journal of Occupational Psychology* 57: 295–307.

Gambrill, E. (1995). Social skills deficits. In J. C. Thomas and M. Hersen (eds) *Psychopathology in the Workplace*. New York: Routledge.

Ganster, D. C. and Fusilier, M. R. (1989). Control in the workplace. In C. L. Cooper and I. T. Robertson (eds) *International Review of Industrial and Organizational Psychology*. New York: Wiley.

Geen, R. G. (1990). *Human Aggression*. Milton Keynes, UK: Open University Press.

Gibbons, J. C. (1964). Cortisol secretion rate in depressive illness. *Archives of General Psychiatry* 10: 572–5.

Gilbert, P. (1989). *Human Nature and Suffering*. Hove, UK: Erlbaum.

Gilbert, P. (1997). *Overcoming Depression: A Self-Help Guide Using Cognitive Behavioural Techniques*. London: Robinson.

Gitlin, M. J. and Gerner, R. H. (1986). The dexamethazone suppression test and response to somatic treatment: A review. *Clinical Psychiatry* 47: 16–8.

Glaser, R. *et al.* (1985). Stress, loneliness and changes in herpes virus latency. *Journal of Behavioural Medicine* 8: 249–60.

Glaser, R. *et al.* (1987). Stress-related immune suppression: Health implications. *Brain, Behaviour and Immunity* 1: 7–20.

Glass, D. (1977). *Behaviour Patterns, Stress and Coronary Heart Disease*. Hillsdale, NJ: Erlbaum.

Glass, D. C. and Singer, J. E. (1972). *Urban Stress: Experiments on Noise and Stressors*. New York: Academic Press.

Goldberg, D. (1978). *Manual of the General Health Questionnaire*. Windsor, UK: NFER-Nelson.

Goldberg, D. and Williams, P. (1988). *A User's Guide to the General Health Questionnaire*. Windsor, UK: NFER-Nelson.

Golding, J. M. (1989). Role occupancy and role specific stress and social support as predictors of depression. *Basic and Applied Social Psychology* 10: 173–95.

Golembiewski, R. T. and Kim, B. (1989). Self esteem and phases of burnout. *Organization Development Journal* 7: 51–8.

Golembiewski, R. T. and Munzenrider, R. F. (1988). *Phases of Burnout: Developments in Concepts and Applications*. New York: Praeger.

Golembiewski, R. T. *et al.* (1986). *Stress in Organizations*. New York: Praeger.

Goodhart, D. E. (1985). Some psychological effects associated with positive and negative thinking about stressful outcomes: Was Polyanna right? *Journal of Personality and Social Psychology* 48: 216–32.

Goodkin, K. (1988). Psychiatric aspects of HIV infection. *Texas Medicine* 84: 55–61.

Gordon, F. and Risley, D. (1999). *The Cost to Britain of Workplace Accidents and Work Related Ill-Health in 1995/96* (2nd edn). London: HSE Books.

Gorter, R. C. and Eijkman, M. A. (1997). Communication skills training courses in dental education. *European Journal of Dental Education* 1: 143–7.

Graham, N. M. H. *et al.* (1986). Stress and acute respiratory infection. *American Journal of Epidemiology* 124: 389–401.

Greco, M. *et al.* (1998). Real patient evaluation of communication skills teaching for GP registrars. *Family Practice* 15: 51–7.

Greenberger, D. and Padesky, C. A. (1995). *Mind Over Mood: Change How You Feel by Changing the Way You Think*. New York: Guilford Press.

Greenglass, E. R. (1990). Type A behaviour, career aspirations and role conflict in professional women. *Journal of Social Behaviour and Personality* 5: 307–22.

Grevin, F. (1996). Posttraumatic stress disorder, ego defence mechanisms and empathy among urban paramedics. *Psychological Reports* 79: 483–95.

Grosser, G. H. *et al.* (1964). *The Threat of Impending Disaster*. Cambridge, MA: M.I.T. Press.

Guidano, V. F. and Liotti, G. (1983). *Cognitive Processes and Emotional Disorders*. New York: Guilford Press.

Gupta, M. D. (1987). Machievellianism of different occupational groups. *Indian Journal of Psychometry and Education* 18: 61–6.

Hackman, J. R. and Oldham, G. (1976). Motivation through the design of work: Test of a theory. *Organizational Behaviour and Human Performance* 16: 250–79.

Hackmann, A. *et al.* (1998). Seeing yourself through others' eyes: A study of spontaneously occurring images in social phobia. *Behavioural and Cognitive Psychotherapy* 26: 3–12.

Halberg, F. (1960). The 24 hour scale. A time dimension of adaptive functional organization. *Perspectives in Biology and Medicine* 3: 491–8.

Hamacheck, D. E. (1978). Psychodynamics of normal and neurotic perfectionism. *Psychology* 15: 27–33.

Hamilton, S. *et al.* (1986). Sex, bias, diagnosis and DSM-III. *Sex Roles* 15: 269–74.

Hammer, M. and Champy, J. (1993). *Re-engineering the Corporation: A Manifesto for Business Revolution*. London: Nicholas Brearley.

Handy, J. (1988). Theoretical and methodological problems with occupational stress and burnout research. *Human Relations* 41: 351–69.

Harris, P. E. (1989). The nurse stress index. *Work and Stress* 3: 335–46.

Harris, R. B. (1988). Reviewing nursing stress according to a proposed coping-adaption framework. *Advances in Nursing Science* 11: 12–28.

Harrison, D. (1983). A social competence model of burnout. In B. A. Farber (ed) *Stress and Burnout in the Human Service Professions*. New York: Pergamon Press.

Hartman, L. M. (1983). A meta-cognitive model of social anxiety: Implications for treatment. *Clinical Psychology Review* 3: 435–56.

Hartman, L. M. (1984). Cognitive components of social anxiety. *Journal of Clinical Psychology* 40: 137–9.

Hartman, L. M. (1986). Social anxiety, problem drinking and self awareness. In L. M. Hartman and K. R. Blankstein (eds) *Perceptions of Self in Emotional Disorder and Psychotherapy*. New York: Plenum Press.

Harvard Business Review (2003). *Harvard Business Review on Building Personal and Organizational Resilience*. Boston, MA: Harvard Business School Press.

Hawton, K. *et al.* (2000). *Cognitive Behavioural Therapy for Psychiatric Problems*. Oxford, UK: Oxford University Press.

Health and Safety Executive (1995a). Labour force survey. In F. Gordon and D. Risley (eds) *The Costs to Britain of Workplace Accidents and Work Related Ill-Health in 1995/1996*. London: HSE Books.

Health and Safety Executive (1995b). *Stress at Work. A Guide for Employers* (HS(G)116). London: HSE Books.

Hecker, M. L. H. *et al.* (1988). Coronary prone behaviours in the Western collaborative study. *Psychosomatic Medicine* 50: 153–64.

Heim, E. (1991). Job stressors and coping in health professionals. *Psychotherapy and Psychosomatics* 55: 90–9.

Helzer, J. E. *et al.* (1987). Post-traumatic stress disorder in the general population: Findings of the epidemiologic catchment area survey. *New England Journal of Medicine* 317: 1630–4.

Henry, J. P. and Stephens, P. M. (1977). *Stress, Health and the Social Environment: A Sociobiological Approach to Medicine*. New York: Springer.

Herd, J. A. (1978). *Physiological Correlates of Coronary-Prone Behaviour*. New York: Springer Verlag.

Herzberg, F. *et al.* (1959). *The Motivation to Work*. New York: Wiley.

Higgins, N. C. (1986). Occupational stress and working women: The effectiveness of two stress reduction programs. *Journal of Vocational Behavior* 29: 66–78.

Hochschild, A. (1983). *The Managed Heart: Commercialization of Human Feeling*. Berkeley, CA: University of California Press.

Hockey, R. (2002). Human performance in the working environment. In P. Wall (ed) *Psychology at Work* (5th edn). Harmondsworth, UK: Penguin Books.

Hoel, H. and Cooper, C. (2000). Working with victims of workplace bullying. In H. Kemshall and J. Pritchard (eds) *Good Practice in Working with Victims of Violence*. London: Jessica Kingsley Publishers.

Hoel, H. *et al.* (2001). *The Cost of Violence/Stress at Work and the Benefits of a Violence/Stress Free Working Environment* (Report commissioned for the International Labour Organization). University of Manchester Institute of Science and Technology.

Holland, J. L. (1973). *Making Vocational Choice: A Theory of Careers*. New Jersey: Prentice-Hall.

Holland, J. L. (1985). *Making Vocational Choices* (2nd edn). Englewood Cliffs, NJ: Prentice Hall.

Hollin, C. R. and Trower, P. (1988). Development and applications of social skills training: A review and critique. In M. Hersen *et al.* (eds) *Progress in Behaviour Modification*. New York: Academic Press.

Holmes, T. H. and Rahe, R. H. (1967). The social readjustment rating scale. *Journal of Psychosomatic Research* 11: 213–8.

Holt, R. R. (1982). Occupational stress. In L. Goldberg and S. Breznitz (eds) *Handbook of Stress: Theoretical Aspects*. New York: Free Press.

Horowitz, M. J. (1986). *Stress Response Syndromes* (2nd edn). Northvale, NJ: Aronson.

Horowitz, M. J. *et al.* (1979). Impact of Event Scale: A measure of subjective stress. *Psychosomatic Medicine* 41: 209–18.

Hosaka, T. *et al.* (1995). Application of relaxation techniques in general hospital psychiatry. *Psychiatry and Clinical Neuroscience* 49: 259–62.

House, J. S. (1981). *Work, Stress and Social Support*. Reading, MA: Addison Wesley.

Houston, D. and Allt, S. K. (1997). Psychological distress and error making among junior house officers. *British Journal of Health Psychology* 2: 141–51.

Howard, A. (1995). A framework for work change. In A. Howard (ed) *The Changing Nature of Work*. San Francisco, CA: Jossey-Bass.

Howells, K. (1988). The management of angry aggression: A cognitive behavioural approach. In W. Dryden and P. Trower (eds) *Developments in Cognitive Psychotherapy*. London: Sage.

Howells, K. (1989). Anger management methods in relation to the prevention of violent behaviour. In J. Archer and E. Browne (eds) *Human Aggression: Naturalistic Approaches*. London: Routledge.

Howells, K. (1999). Cognitive behavioural interventions for anger and aggression. In N. Tarrier and G. Haddock (eds) *Treating Complex Cases: The Cognitive Behavioural Therapy Approach*. Chichester, UK: John Wiley and Sons.

Hulsman, R. L. *et al.* (1999). Teaching clinically experienced physicians communication skills: A review of evaluation studies. *Medical Education* 33: 655–68.

Huselid, M. A. (1995). The impact of human resource management practices on turnover, productivity and corporate financial performance. *Academy of Management Journal* 38: 635–72.

Idemudia, S. E. *et al.* (2001). Type A behaviour and burnout among bank managers in Nigeria. *Journal of Psychology in Africa* 10: 189–96.

Income Data Services (2002). Negligence: Employer's liability for psychiatric illness. In *IDS Brief 704: Employment Law and Practice*. London.

Industrial Relations Law Reports (1991). *Johnstone v Bloomsbury Health Area Authority*. London: Industrial Relations Society.

Irish, L. E. *et al.* (1994). Basic dental-anxiety management. *West Virginia Dental Journal* 68: 19–21.

Irwin, M. *et al.* (1987). Impaired natural killer cell activity during bereavement. *Brain, Behaviour and Immunity* 1: 98–104.

Irwin, M. *et al.* (1990). Reduction of immune function in life stress and depression. *Biological Psychiatry* 27: 22–30.

Iverson, L. *et al.* (1987). Unemployment and mortality in Denmark. *British Medical Journal* 295: 879–84.

Jackson, P. R. and Warr, P. (1987). Mental health of unemployed men in different parts of England and Wales. *British Medical Journal* 295: 525.

Jackson, S. (1983). Participation in decision-making as a strategy for reducing job-related strain. *Journal of Applied Psychology* 68: 3–19.

Jackson, S. E. *et al.* (1987). Correlates of burnout among public service lawyers. *Journal of Occupational Behaviour* 8: 339–49.

Jacobsen, E. (1938). *Progressive Relaxation*. Chicago, IL: University of Chicago Press.

Jamal, M. (1990). Relationship of job stress and type A behaviour to employee's job satisfaction, organizational committment, psychosomatic health problems and turnover motivation. *Human Relations* 43: 727–38.

James, A. and Wright, I. (1991). Occupational stress in the ambulance services. *Health Manpower Management* 17: 4–11.

James, I. (2001). Schema therapy: The next generation, but should it carry a health warning? *Behavioural and Cognitive Psychotherapy* 29: 401–7.

James, L. A. and James, L. R. (1989). Integrating work environment perceptions: Explorations into the measurement of meaning. *Journal of Applied Psychology* 74: 739–51.

Janoff-Bulman, R. (1989). Assumptive worlds and the stress of traumatic events: Applications of the schema construct. *Social Cognition* 7: 113–36.

Jarczewski, P. H. (1988). Managing the manipulative employee. *Nursing Management* 19: 58–62.

Jenkins, C. D. *et al.* (1979). *Jenkins Activity Survey Manual*. New York: Psychological Corporation.

Jex, S. M. (1998). *Stress and Job Performance: Theory, Research and Implications for Managerial Practice*. Thousand Oaks, CA: Sage.

Jex, S. M. and Spector, P. E. (1996). The impact of negative affectivity on stressor-strain relations. *Work and Stress* 10: 36–45.

Jones, D. L. *et al.* (2003). Stress management and workplace disability in the US, Europe and Japan. *Journal of Occupational Health* 45: 1–7.

Jones, J. (1980a). *The Staff Burnout Scale for Health Professionals*. Park Ridge, IL: London House Press.

Jones, J. (1980b). *The Staff Burnout Scale for Police and Security Personnel*. Park Ridge, IL: London Press House.

Jones, J. (1981). *The Burnout Syndrome*. Park Ridge, IL: London House Press.

Judge, T. A. and Watanabe, S. (1993). Another look at the job satisfaction – life satisfaction relationship. *Journal of Applied Psychology* 78: 939–48.

Kabat-Zinn, J. *et al.* (1985). The clinical use of mindfulness meditation for the self-regulation of chronic pain. *Journal of Behavioural Medicine* 8: 163–90.

Kahill, S. (1988). Symptoms of professional burnout: A review of the empirical evidence. *Canadian Psychology* 29: 284–97.

Kalra, J. *et al.* (1987). Emotional strain on physicians caring for cancer patients. *Loss, Grief and Care* 1: 19–24.

Kaplan, C. A. (1986). Challenge of working with patients diagnosed as having a borderline personality disorder. *Nursing Clinics of North America* 21: 6–10.

Karasek, R. A. (1979). Job demands, job decision latitude and mental strain: Implications for jobs redesign. *Administrative Science Quarterly* 24: 285–307.

Karasek, R. and Theorell, T. (1990). *Healthy Work: Stress, Productivity and the Reconstruction of Working Life*. New York: Basic Books.

Katz, R. (1978). Job longevity as a situational factor in job satisfaction. *Administrative Science Quarterly* 23: 204–23.

Keane, T. M. (1995). The role of exposure therapy in the psychological treatment of PTSD. *National Centre for Post-Traumatic Stress Disorder: Clinical Quarterly* 5: 1–6.

Keane, T. M. (1997). Psychological and behavioural treatment for PTSD. In P. Nathan and J. Gorman (eds) *Treatments That Work*. Oxford, UK: Oxford University Press.

Keane, T. M. *et al.* (1994). Post-traumatic stress disorder. In M. Hersen and R. T. Ammerman (eds) *Handbook of Prescriptive Treatments for Adults*. New York: Plenum.

Keita, G. P. and Jones, J. M. (1990). Reducing adverse reaction to stress in the workplace: Psychology's expanding role. *American Psychologist* 45: 1137–41.

Kelly, J. E. (1992). Does job re-design theory explain job re-design outcomes? *Human Relations* 45: 753–74.

Kemeny, M. E. *et al.* (1989). Psychological and immunological predictors of genital herpes recurrence. *Psychosomatic Medicine* 51: 195–208.

Kennerly, H. (1997). *Managing Anxiety: A User's Manual and Tape On 'How to Relax'*. Oxford, UK: Oxford Clinical Psychology.

Kessler, R. C. *et al.* (1987). Unemployment and health in a community sample. *Journal of Health and Social Behaviour* 28: 51 9.

Kets de Vries, M. F. R. (1989). *Prisoners of Leadership*. New York: Wiley.

Khaleelee, O. (1994). The defence mechanism test as an aid for selection and development of staff. *Therapeutic Communities* 15: 3–13.

Kiecolt-Glaser, J. K. *et al.* (1984a). Psychosocial modifiers of immunoincompetence in medical students. *Psychosomatic Medicine* 46: 7–14.

Kiecolt-Glaser, J. K. *et al.* (1984b). Urinary cortisol levels, cellular immunocompetency and loneliness in psychiatric patients. *Psychosomatic Medicine* 46: 15–23.

Kiecolt-Glaser, J. K. *et al.* (1987a). Chronic stress and immunity in family caregivers of Alzheimer's disease victims. *Psychosomatic Medicine* 49: 523–35.

Kilpatrick, D. G. *et al.* (1982). Psychological sequelae to rape: Assessment and treatment strategies. In D. M. Doleys and R. L. Meredith (eds) *Behavioural Medicine: Assessment and Treatment Strategies*. New York: Plenum.

Kimble, M. O. *et al.* (1999). Cognitive behavioural treatment for complicated cases of post-traumatic stress disorder. In N. Tarrier *et al.* (eds) *Treating Complex Cases: The Cognitive Behavioural Therapy Approach*. Chichester, UK: Wiley.

Kirk, J. (2000). Cognitive behavioural assessment. In K. Hawton *et al.* (eds) *Cognitive Behavioural Therapy for Psychiatric Problems*. Oxford, UK: Oxford University Press.

Klaft, R. P. and Kleiner, B. H. (1988). Understanding workaholics. *Business* 38: 37–40.

Knapp, T. R. (1988) Stress versus strain: A methodological critique. *Nursing Research* 37: 181–4.

Knecht, T. (2004). What is Machievellian intelligence? Views on a little appreciated side of the psyche. *Nervenartz* 75: 1–5.

Kobasa, S. C. (1979). Stressful life events, personality and health: An inquiry into hardiness. *Journal of Personality and Social Psychology* 37: 1–11.

Kobasa, S. C. *et al.* (1982). Hardiness and health: A prospective study. *Journal of Personality and Social Psychology* 42: 168–77.

Koeske, G. F. and Koeske, R. D. (1989). Construct validity of the Maslach Burnout Inventory: A critical review and reconceptualization. *Journal of Applied Behavioural Science* 25: 131–44.

Koss, M. P. (1990). Changed lives: The psychological impact of sexual harassment. In M. Paludi (ed) *Ivory Power: Sexual Harassment on Campus*. Albany, NY: State University of New York Press.

Kotter, J. P. (1990). *A Force for Change: How Leadership Differs from Management.* New York: Free Press.

Kotter, J. P. (1996). *Leading Change.* Boston, MA: Harvard Business School Press.

Krakowski, A. J. (1985). Medicine and physicians: Rewards and burdens. *Psychiatria Fennica* 16: 73–83.

Kram, K. E. (1985). *Mentoring at Work: Developmental Relationships in Organizational Life.* Glenview, IL: Scott Foresman.

Krantz, S. E. (1985). When depressive cognitions reflect negative realities. *Cognitive Therapy and Research* 6: 595–610.

Kronfol, Z. and House, J. D. (1989). Lymphocyte mitogenics, immunoglobulin and complement levels in depressed patients and normal controls. *Acta Psychiatrica Scandanavica* 80: 142–7.

Kronfol, Z. *et al.* (1986). Depression, urinary free cortisol excretion and lymphocyte function. *British Journal of Psychiatry* 148: 70–3.

Kulka, R. A. *et al.* (1990). *Trauma and the Vietnam War Generation: Reports of Findings from the National Vietnam Veterans Readjustment Study.* New York: Brunner/Mazel.

Kushnir, T. and Melamed, S. (1991). Workload, perceived control and psychological distress in type A/B industrial workers. *Journal of Organizational Behaviour* 12: 155–68.

Kuyken, W. *et al.* (1998). The psychological adaptation of psychologists in clinical training: The role of cognition, coping and social support. *Clinical Psychology and Psychotherapy* 5: 238–52.

Kuyken, W. *et al.* (2000). A longitudinal study of the psychological adaptation of trainee clinical psychologists. *Clinical Psychology and Psychotherapy* 7: 394–400.

L'Abate, L. and L'Abate, B. L. (1981). Marriage: The dream of the reality. *Family Relations* 30: 131–6.

Lakein, A. (1984). *How to Get Control of Your Time and Your Life.* Aldershot, UK: Gower.

Lakein, A. (1991). *How to Get Control of Your Time and Life.* New York: New American Library.

Lally, R. (1997). Getting results for the hands-on manager. *Office Edition* 42: 8.

Lang, D. (1992). Preventing short term strain through time management coping. *Work and Stress* 6: 169–76.

Lau, F. L. (2000). Can communication skills workshops for emergency department doctors improve patient satisfaction? *Journal of Accident and Emergency Medicine* 17: 251–53.

Lavanco, G. (1997). Burnout syndrome and type A behaviour in nurses and teachers in Sicily. *Psychological Reports* 81: 523–8.

Lawler, E. E. and Finegold, D. (2000). Individualizing the organization: Past, present and future. *Organizational Dynamics* 29: 1–15.

Lazarus, A. (1975). A cognitively oriented psychologist looks at biofeedback. *American Psychologist* 30: 533–61.

Lazarus, R. S. (1966). *Psychological Stress and the Coping Process.* New York: McGraw-Hill.

Lazarus, R. S. (1976). *Patterns of Adjustment.* New York: McGraw-Hill.

Lazarus, R. S. (1977). Cognitive and coping processes in emotion. In A. Monat and R. S. Lazarus (eds) *Stress and Coping: An Anthology.* New York: Columbia University Press.

Lazarus, R. S. (1982). The psychology of stress and coping. In N. A. Milgram (ed) *Stress and Anxiety*, Vol. 8. New York: Hemisphere Publishing.

Lazarus, R. S. (1993). From psychological stress to the emotions: A history of changing outlooks. *Annual Review of Psychology* 44: 1–21.

Lazarus, R. S. and Folkman, S. (1984). *Stress, Appraisal and Coping*. New York: Springer.

Lazarus, R. S. and Folkman, S. (1989). *Manual for the Hassles and Uplifts Scales*. Palo Alto, CA: Consulting Psychologists Press.

Lazarus, R. S. and Launier, R. (1978). Stress related transactions between person and environment. In L. A. Pervin and M. Lewis (eds) *Perspectives in Interactional Psychology*. New York: Plenum Press.

Leather, P. *et al.* (1998). Exposure to occupational violence and the buffering effects of intra-organizational support. *Work and Stress* 12: 161–78.

Lee, C. W. *et al.* (1999). Factor structure of the schema questionnaire in a large clinical sample. *Cognitive Therapy and Research* 23: 441–51.

Lee, R. S. and McGrath, P. (1995). Dealing with time pressure. *International Journal of Stress Management* 2: 79–86.

Lee, S. and Crockett, M. S. (1994). Effect of assertiveness training on levels of stress and assertiveness experienced by nurses in Taiwan. *Issues in Mental Health Nursing* 15: 419–32.

Lehrer, P. M. and Woolfolk, R. L. (1993). *Principles and Practice of Stress Management* (2nd edn). New York: Guilford Press.

Leiter, M. P. and Maslach, C. (1988). The impact of interpersonal environment on burnout and organizational committment. *Journal of Organizational Behaviour* 9: 297–308.

Lemkau, J. P. *et al.* (1988). Correlates of burnout among family practice residents. *Journal of Medical Education* 63. 682–91.

Leonard, C. *et al.* (1998). The effect of fatigue, sleep deprivation and onerous working hours on the physical and mental well-being of pre-registration house officers. *Irish Journal of Medical Sciences* 167: 22–5.

Levi, L. (1990). Occupational stress: Spice of life or kiss of death? *American Psychologist* 45: 1142–5.

Levine, S. and Ursin, H. (1980). *Coping and Health* (Nato conference series 111: Human Factors). New York: Plenum Press.

Levine, S. *et al.* (1979). Inhibition of adrenal-pituitary activity as a consequence of consummatory behaviour. *Psychoneuroendocrinology* 4: 275–86.

Levy, M. S. (1998). A helpful way to understand re-enactments. *Journal of Psychotherapy Practice and Research* 7: 227–35.

Levy, M. S. (2000). A conceptualization of the repetition compulsion. *Psychiatry* 63: 45–53.

Leymann, H. (1992). Vuxenmobbning pa svenska arbeidsplatser. In H. Hoel *et al.* (eds) *The Costs of Violence/Stress at Work and the Benefits of a Violence/Stress-Free Working Environment*. Geneva: International Labour Organization.

Leymann, H. and Gustafsson, A. (1996). Mobbing at work and the development of post-traumatic stress disorders. *European Journal of Work and Organizational Psychology* 5: 251–75.

Lin, Y. *et al.* (2004). Evaluation of an assertiveness training program on nursing and medical students' assertiveness, self-esteem and interpersonal communication satisfaction. *Nurse Education Today* 24: 656–65.

Locke, S. and Colligan, D. (1986). *The Healer Within: The New Medicine of Mind and Body*. New York: E. P. Dutton.

Locke, S. E. *et al.* (1984). Life change stress, psychiatric symptoms and natural killer cell activity. *Psychosomatic Medicine* 46: 441–53.

Loher, B. T. *et al.* (1985). A meta-analysis of the relation of job characteristics to job satisfaction. *Journal of Applied Psychology* 70: 280–9.

Lomas, B. (2000). *Easy Step by Step Guide to Stress and Time Management*. Hayling Island, UK: Rowmark.

Lowman, R. L. (1991). *The Clinical Practice of Career Assessment: Interests, Abilities and Personality*. Washington, DC: American Psychological Association.

Lowman, R. L. (1993). The inter-domain model of career assessment. *Journal of Counselling and Development* 71: 549–54.

Lowman, R. L. (1997). *Counselling and Psychotherapy of Work Dysfunctions*. Washington, DC: American Psychological Association.

Lowman, R. L. and Schurman, S. J. (1982). Psychometric characteristics of a vocational preference inventory short form. *Educational and Psychological Measurement* 42: 601–13.

Lucock, M. P. and Morley, S. (1996). Health Anxiety Questionnaire (HAQ). *British Journal of Health Psychology* 1: 137–50.

Lundberg, U. and Frankenhaeuser, M. (1980). Pituitary-adrenal and sympathetic-adrenal correlates of distress and effort. *Journal of Psychosomatic Research* 24: 125–30.

Macan, T. H. (1994). Time management: Test of a process model. *Journal of Applied Psychology* 79: 381–91.

Macan, T. H. (1996). Time management training: Effects on time behaviours, attitudes and job performance. *The Journal of Psychology* 130: 229–37.

Machlowitz, M. (1980). *Workaholics: Living with Them, Working with Them*. Reading, MA: Addison-Wesley.

MacLeod, A. K. *et al.* (1993). Components of hopelessness about the future in parasuicide. *Cognitive Therapy and Research* 17: 441–55.

MacLeod, A. K. *et al.* (1997). Parasuicide, depression and the anticipation of positive and negative future experiences. *Psychological Medicine* 27: 973–7.

Marks, I. M. (1981). *Cure and Care of Neuroses*. New York: John Wiley and Sons, Inc.

Marks, I. M. (1986). *Behavioural Psychotherapy: Maudsley Pocket Book of Clinical Management*. Bristol, UK: Wright.

Marks, I. M. (1987). *Fears, Phobias, and Rituals: Panic, Anxiety and Their Disorders*. Oxford, UK: Oxford University Press.

Maslach, C. (1976). Burned out. *Human Behaviour* 5: 16–22.

Maslach, C. (1982). *Burnout: The Cost of Caring*. Englewood Cliffs, NJ: Prentice-Hall.

Maslach, C. and Florian, V. (1988). Burnout, job setting and self-evaluation among rehabilitation counsellors. *Rehabilitation Psychology* 33: 85–93.

Maslach, C. and Jackson, S. E. (1981). *The Maslach Burnout Inventory: Research Edition*. Palo Alto, CA: Consulting Psychologists Press.

Maslach, C. and Jackson, S. E. (1984). Burnout in organizational settings. *Applied Social Psychology Annual* 5: 133–53.

Maslach, C. and Jackson, S. E. (1986). *Maslach Burnout Inventory Manual*. Palo Alto, CA: Consulting Psychologists Press.

Maslow, A. H. (1954). *Motivation and Personality*. New York: Harper.

Matsumoto, M. and Smith, J. C. (2001). Progressive muscle relaxation, breathing exercises and ABC relaxation theory. *Journal of Clinical Psychology* 12: 1551–7.

Matteson, M. T. and Ivancevich, J. M. (1987). *Controlling Work Stress: Effective Human Resource and Management Strategies*. San Fransisco, CA: Jossey Bass.

Matthews, D. B. (1990). A comparison of burnout in selected occupational fields. *Career Development Quarterly* 38: 230–9.

Matthews, K. A. and Haynes, S. G. (1986). Type-A behavior pattern and coronary disease risk. *American Journal of Epidemiology* 123: 923–61.

Maultsby, M. C. (1975). *Help Yourself to Happiness through Rational Self Counselling*. Oxford, UK: Herman.

Mazur, P. J. and Lynch, M. D. (1989). Differential impact of administrative, organizational and personality factors on teacher burnout. *Teaching and Teacher Education* 5: 337–53.

McAlpine, A. (2000). *The Ruthless Leader: Three Classics of Strategy and Power*. Chichester, UK: John Wiley and Sons.

McCranie, E. W. and Brandsma, J. M. (1988). Personality antecedents of burnout among middle aged physicians. *Behavioural Medicine* 14: 30–6.

McGee, D. (1989). Burnout and professional decision making: An analog study. *Journal of Counselling Psychology* 36: 345–51.

McGinn, L. K. and Young, J. E. (1996). Schema focused therapy. In P. Salkovskis (ed) *Frontiers of Cognitive Therapy*. New York: Guilford Press.

McGinn, K. L. *et al.* (1995). When and how to do longer term therapy without feeling guilty. *Cognitive and Behavioural Practice* 2: 187–212.

McGrath, J. E. (1970). *Social and Psychological Factors in Stress*. New York: Reinhart and Winston.

McLean, P. and Hakstian, A. R. (1970). Clinical depression: Comparative efficacy of outpatient treatments. *Journal of Consulting and Clinical Psychology* 47: 818–36.

McManus, I. C. *et al.* (1996). Career preference and personality differences in medical school applicants. *Psychology, Health and Medicine* 1: 235–48.

McPherson, F. (2004). Clinical work in occupational psychology. *Clinical Psychology* 42: 21–3.

Medical Workforce Standing Advisory Committee (1997). *Planning the Medical Workforce*. Leeds, UK: NHS Executive.

Meichenbaum, D. (1977). *Cognitive Behavioural Modification: An Integrative Approach*. New York: Plenum Press.

Meichenbaum, D. and Jaremko, M. E. (1983). *Stress Reduction and Prevention*. New York: Plenum.

Meier, S. T. (1984). The construct validity of burnout. *Journal of Occupational Psychology* 57: 211–9.

Merodoulaki, G. M. (1994). Early experiences as factors influencing occupational choice of counselling and psychotherapy. *Counselling Psychology Review* 9: 18–39.

Meyer, R. J. and Haggerty, R. J. (1962). Streptococcal infection in families. *Paediatrics* 29: 539–49.

Milgram, N. A. *et al.* (1988). The procrastination of everyday life. *Journal of Research in Personality* 22: 179–212.

Miller, L. (1995). Tough guys: Psychotherapeutic strategies with law enforcement and emergency services personnel. *Psychotherapy* 32: 592–600.

Miller, R. J. (1984). *Relaxation and the Management of Stress and Anxiety*. Psychological Counselling Services.

Millon, T. (1981). *Disorders of Personality: DSM III Axis 11*. New York: Wiley.

Mimura, C. and Griffiths, P. (2003). The effectiveness of current approaches to work place stress management in the nursing profession: An evidence-based literature review. *Occupational and Environmental Medicine* 60: 10–5.

Minirth, F. *et al.* (1981). *The Workaholic and His Family: An Inside Look*. Grand Rapids, MI: Baker Book House.

Mintzberg, H. J. (1973). *The Nature of Managerial Work*. New York: Harper and Row.

Mintzberg, H. J. (1979). *The Structure of Organizations*. Englewood Cliffs, NJ: Prentice-Hall.

Mintzberg, H. J. and van der Heyden, L. (1999). Organigraphs: Drawing how companies really work. *Harvard Business Review* 77: 87–94.

Mitchell, E. (2000). Managing carer stress: An evaluation of a stress management programme for carers of people with dementia. *British Journal of Occupational Therapy* 63: 179–84.

Monet, A. and Lazarus, R. S. (1977). *Stress and Coping: An Anthology*. New York: Columbia University Press.

Moore, K. A. and Cooper, C. L. (1996). Stress in mental health professionals: A theoretical overview. *International Journal of Social Psychiatry* 42: 82–9.

Moore, R. and Garland, A. (2003). *Cognitive Therapy for Chronic and Persistent Depression*. Chichester, UK: Wiley.

Moos, R. (1990). *Coping Responses Inventory Manual*. Palo Alto, CA: Department of Psychiatry, Stanford University.

Morris, S. and Charney, N. (1983, June 18). Workaholism: Thank God it's Monday. *Psychology Today*: 88.

Moser, K. A. *et al.* (1987). Unemployment and mortality: Comparison of the 1971 and 1981 longitudinal study census samples. *British Medical Journal* 294: 86–90.

Moyle, P. (1995). The role of negative affectivity in the stress process: Tests of alternative models. *Journal of Organizational Behaviour* 16: 647–68.

Munz, D. C. *et al.* (2001). Effectiveness of a comprehensive worksite management program: Combining organizational and individual interventions. *International Journal of Stress Management* 8: 49–62.

Murphy, L. R. (1996). Stress management in work settings: A critical review of the research literature. *American Journal of Health Promotion* 11: 112–35.

Murphy, L. R. and Cooper, C. L. (2000). *Healthy and Productive Work: An International Perspective*. London: Taylor and Francis.

Murphy, L. R. and Hurrell, J. J. (1987). Stress management in the process of occupational stress reduction. *Journal of Managerial Psychology* 2: 18–23.

Nagy, S. and Davis, L. G. (1985). Burnout: A comparative analysis of personality and environmental variables. *Psychological Reports* 57: 1319–26.

Nakano, Y. *et al.* (1982). The effect of shift work on cellular immune function. *Journal of Human Ergonomics* 11: 131–7.

National Institute for Clinical Excellence (2004a). *Depression: Management of Depression in Primary and Secondary Care* (Clinical guideline 23). London.

National Institute for Clinical Excellence (2004b, November) NICE guidelines on depression and anxiety. *Health Summary* 21: 16.

Naughton, T. J. (1987). A conceptual view of workaholism and implications for career counselling and research. *Career Development Quarterly* 35: 180–7.

Newell, S. (2002). *Creating the Healthy Organization: Well-being, Diversity and Ethics at Work*. London: Thomson Learning.

Novaco, R. (1975). *Anger Control: The Development and Evaluation of an Experimental Treatment*. Lexington, MA: Health.

Novaco, R. W. (1978). Anger and coping with stress. In J. P. Foreyt and D. P. Rathjen (eds) *Cognitive Behaviour Therapy*. New York: Plenum.

Novaco, R. (1993). Clinicians ought to view anger contextually. *Behaviour Change* 10: 208–18.

Novaco, R. (1994). Anger as a factor for violence among the mentally disordered. In J. Monahan and H. R. Steadman (eds) *Violence and Mental Disorder: Developments in Risk Assessment*. Chicago, IL: University of Chicago Press.

Novaco, R. (1997). Remediating anger and aggression with violent offenders. *Legal and Criminological Psychology* 2: 77–8.

Nowack, K. M. (1988). Health habits, type A behaviour and job burnout. *Work and Stress* 1: 135–42.

Oates, W. (1971). *The Confessions of a Workaholic: The Facts about Work Addiction*. New York: World Publishing.

Obholzer, A. and Roberts, V. Z. (1994). *The Unconscious at Work: Individual and Organizational Stress in the Human Services*. London: Routledge.

O'Connor, R. C. and Sheehy, N. P. (2000). *Understanding Suicidal Behaviour*. Leicester, UK: BPS Books.

O'Connor, R. C. *et al.* (2000). Hopelessness: The role of depression, future directed thinking and cognitive vulnerability. *Psychology, Health and Medicine* 5: 155–62.

O'Leary, A. (1990). Stress, emotion and human immune function. *Psychological Bulletin* 108: 363–82.

Organ, D. W. (1988). *Organizational Citizenship Behaviour: The Good Soldier Syndrome*. Lexington, MA: Lexington Books.

Orpen, C. (1993). The effect of time management training on employee attitudes and behaviour: A field experiment. *The Journal of Psychology* 128: 393–6.

Ostell, A. (1991). Coping, problem solving and stress: A framework for intervention strategies. *British Journal of Medical Psychology* 64: 11–24.

Ostell, A. (1996a). Managing stress at work. In C. Molander (ed) *Human Resources at Work*. Lund, Sweden: Chartwell-Bratt.

Ostell, A. (1996b). Recruitment and selection. In C. Molander (ed) *Human Resources at Work*. Lund, Sweden: Chartwell-Bratt.

Ostell, A. and Oakland, S. (1999). Absolutist thinking and health. *British Journal of Medical Psychology* 72: 239–50.

Owen, I. (1993). The personalities of psychotherapists. *Counselling Psychology Review* 8: 10–4.

Padesky, C. A. (1994). Schema change processes in cognitive therapy. *Clinical Psychology and Psychotherapy* 1: 276–8.

Palmblad, J. *et al.* (1975). Stressor exposure and immunological response in man: Interferon-producing capacity and phagocytosis. *Journal of Psychosomatic Research* 20: 193–9.

Palmer, S. (1996). Developing stress management programmes. In R. Woolfe and W. Dryden (eds) *Handbook of Counselling Psychology*. Thousand Oaks, CA: Sage Publications.

Papez, J. W. (1937). A proposed mechanism of emotion. *Archives of Neurological Psychiatry* 38: 725–43.

Paris, J. (2000). Predispositions, personality traits, and posttraumatic stress disorder. *Harvard Review of Psychiatry* 8: 175–83.

Paris, J. and Frank, H. (1984). Psychological determinants of a medical career. *Canadian Journal of Psychiatry* 28: 354–7.

Parker, S. K. (1998). Role-breadth self-efficacy: Relationship with work enrichment and other organizational practices. *Journal of Applied Psychology* 83: 835–52.

Parker, S. K. and Wall, T. D. (1998). *Job and Work Design: Organizing Work to Promote Well-being and Effectiveness*. San Francisco, CA: Sage.

Parker, S. K. *et al.* (2001). Future work design research and practice: Towards an elaborated model of work design. *Journal of Occupational and Organizational Psychology* 74: 413–40.

Parle, M. *et al.* (1997). The development of a training model to improve health professionals' skills, self efficacy and outcome expectancies when communicating with cancer patients. *Social Science and Medicine* 44: 231–40.

Paterson, R. J. (2000). *The Assertiveness Workbook: How to Express Your Ideas and Stand Up for Yourself at Work and in Relationships*. Oakland, CA: New Harbinger Publications.

Patterson, G. T. (2001). The relationship between demographic variables and exposure to traumatic incidents among police officers. *The Australasian Journal of Disaster and Trauma Studies*, http://www.massey.ac.nz/~trauma/issues/2001–2/patterson2.htm

Paul, W. P. and Robertson, K. B. (1970). *Job Enrichment and Employee Motivation*. London: Gower.

Payne, R. L. (1979). Demands, supports, constraints and psychological health. In C. Mackay and T. Cox (eds) *Response to Stress: Occupational Aspects*. London: IPC.

Payne, R. (1988). Individual differences in the study of occupational stress. In C. L. Cooper and R. Payne (eds) *Causes, Coping and Consequences of Stress at Work*. New York: Wiley.

Payne, R. (2002). Organisations as psychological environments. In P. Warr (ed) *Psychology at Work* (5th edn). Harmondsworth, UK: Penguin Books.

Peck, E. C. (1987). The traits of true invulnerability and post-traumatic stress in psychoanalysed men of action. In A. J. Anthony (ed) *The Invulnerable Child*. New York: Guilford Press.

Pelletier, K. R. and Herzing, D. L. (1988). Psychoneuroimmunology: Towards a mindbody model: A critical review. *Advances* 5: 27–56.

Perris, C. (2000). Personality related disorders of interpersonal behaviour: A developmental-constructivist cognitive therapy approach to treatment based on attachment theory. *Clinical Psychology and Psychotherapy* 7: 97–117.

Pfohl, B. (1991). Histrionic personality disorder: A review of available data and recommendations for DSM-IV. *Journal of Personality Disorders* 5: 150–66.

Phelan, J. *et al.* (1991). Work stress, family stress and depression in professional and managerial employees. *Psychological Medicine* 21: 99–102.

Piaget, J. (1962). *Play, Dreams and Imitation in Childhood*. New York: Norton.

Pieper, G. and Maercker, A. (1999). Masculinity and avoidance of help seeking after job related trauma [*English abstract of German language article*]. *Verhaltenstherapie* 9: 222–9.

Pillemer, K. and Bachman-Prehn, R. (1991). Helping and nurturing: Predictors of maltreatment of patients in nursing homes. *Research on Aging* 13: 74–95.

Pines, A. M. (2000). Treating career burnout. *Psychotherapy in Practice* 56: 633–42.

Pines, A. M. and Aronson, E. (1981). *Burnout: From Tedium to Personal Growth*. New York: Free Press.

Pogrebin, M. R. and Poole, E. D. (1991). Police and tragic events: The management of emotions. *Journal of Criminal Justice* 19: 395–403.

Pollak, J. M. (1979). Obsessive compulsive personality: A review. *Psychological Bulletin* 86: 225–41.

Pollock, P. H. (2001). *Cognitive Analytic Therapy for Adult Survivors of Childhood Abuse*. Chichester, UK: Wiley.

Poole, A. D. *et al.* (1990). Power therapies: Evidence versus emotion. A reply to Rosen, Lohr, McNally and Herbert. *Behavioural and Cognitive Psychotherapy* 27: 3–8.

Power, K. G. *et al.* (1989). A controlled comparison of cognitive behavioural therapy, diazepam and placebo in the management of generalized anxiety. *Behavioural Psychotherapy* 17: 1–14.

Power, M. and Dalgleish, T. (1997). *Cognition and Emotion: From Order to Disorder*. New York: Erlbaum.

Pretzer, J. L. *et al.* (1989). Stress and stress management. *Journal of Cognitive Psychotherapy* 3: 163–79.

Price, J. P. (2002). *Occupation as Re-enactment: Adaptive or Maladaptive?* Unpublished doctoral thesis, University of Teesside, UK.

Price, V. (1982). What is Type A? A cognitive social learning model. *Journal of Occupational Behaviour* 3: 109–29.

Queen, J. A. and Queen, P. S. (2005). *The Frazzled Principal's Wellness Plan: Reclaiming Time, Managing Stress and Creating a Healthy Lifestyle*. Thousand Oaks, CA: Corwin Press.

Quick, J. C. and Quick, J. D. (1984). *Organizational Stress and Preventive Management*. New York: McGraw-Hill.

Quick, J. C. *et al.* (1992). *Stress and Well-being at Work: Assessments and Interventions for Occupational Mental Health*. Washington, DC: American Psychological Association.

Quine, L. (1999). Workplace bullying in NHS community trust: Staff questionnaire survey. *British Medical Journal* 318: 228–32.

Rabin, S. *et al.* (1999). Stress and intervention strategies in mental health professionals. *British Journal of Medical Psychology* 72: 159–69.

Rabinowitz, S. *et al.* (1996). Preventing burnout: Increasing professional self efficacy in primary care nurses in a Balint group. *American Association of Occupational Health Nursing Journal* 44: 28–32.

Rachman, S. J. and Hodgson, R. (1974). Synchrony and desynchrony in fear and avoidance. *Behaviour Research and Therapy* 12: 311–8.

Radeke, J. T. and Mahoney, M. J. (2000). Comparing the personal lives of psychotherapists and research psychologists. *Professional Psychology – Research and Practice* 31: 82–4.

Rahe, R. H. and Paasikivi, J. (1971). Psychosocial factors and myocardial infarction: An outpatient study in Sweden. *Journal of Psychosomatic Research* 15: 33–9.

Raskin, R. and Shaw, R. (1988). Narcissism and the use of personal pronouns. *Journal of Personality* 56: 393–404.

Rayburn, C. A. (1991). Counselling depressed female religious professionals: Nuns and clergywomen. *Counseling and Values* 35: 136–48.

Reed, J. (1993). *Teaching Interpersonal Skills*. London: Edward Arnold.

Rees, D. and Cooper, C. L. (1992). Occupational stress in health service workers in the UK. *Stress Medicine* 8: 79–80.

Reich, J. *et al.* (1989). Alprazolam treatment of avoidant personality traits in social phobic patients. *Journal of Clinical Psychiatry* 50: 91–5.

Resick, P. A. and Schnicke, M. K. (1992). *Cognitive Processing Therapy for Sexual Assault Survivors: A Therapist's Manual*. Newbury Park, CA: Sage.

Resick, P. A. *et al.* (1981). Social adjustments in victims of sexual assault. *Journal of Consulting and Clinical Psychology* 49: 705–12.

Richards, D. (1999). The eye movement desensitization and reprocessing debate: Commentary on Rosen and Poole *et al. Behavioural and Cognitive Psychotherapy* 27: 13–7.

Richman, J. A. *et al.* (1999). Sexual harassment and generalized workplace abuse among university employees: Prevalance and mental health correlates. *American Journal of Public Health* 89: 358–63.

Riggar, T. F. *et al.* (1984). Rehabilitation personnel burnout: Organizational cures. *Journal of Rehabilitation Administration* 8: 94–104.

Rippon, T. J. (2000). Aggression and violence in health care professions. *Journal of Advanced Nursing* 31: 452–60.

Rittenmeyer, G. J. (1997). The relationship between early maladaptive schemas and job burnout among public school teachers. *Dissertation Abstracts International* 58: 5-A, 1529.

Robbins, S. P. (1998). *Organizational Behaviour: Concepts, Controversies, Applications* (8th edn). Upper Saddle River, NJ: Prentice-Hall.

Robertson, I. T. and Makin, P. J. (1986). Management selection in Britain: A survey and critique. *Journal of Occupational Psychology* 59: 45–57.

Robertson, I. T. and Smith, M. (2001). Personnel selection. *Journal of Occupational and Organizational Psychology* 74: 441–72.

Robson, C. (1977). *Experiment, Design and Statistics in Psychology*. Harmondsworth, UK: Penguin Books Ltd.

Rodgers, L. M. (1998). A five year study comparing early retirement on medical grounds in ambulance personnel with those in other groups of health service staff. Part II: Causes of retirements. *Occupational Medicine* 48: 119–32.

Ronningstam, E. and Gunderson, J. (1988). Narcissistic traits in psychiatric patients. *Comprehensive Psychiatry* 29: 545–9.

Rose, J. *et al.* (1998). The impact of a stress management programme on staff wellbeing and performance at work. *Work and Stress* 12: 112–24.

Rose, M. (1982). *Industrial Behaviour: Theoretical Developments Since Taylor*. Harmondsworth, UK: Penguin.

Rosen, G. *et al.* (1999). Power therapies, miraculous claims and cures that fail. *Behavioural and Cognitive Psychotherapy* 26: 99–101.

Ross, C. E. *et al.* (1983). Dividing work, sharing work and in between: Marriage patterns and depression. *American Sociological Review* 89: 670–82.

Ross, R. R. and Altmaier, E. M. (1994). *Intervention in Occupational Stress*. London: Sage.

Roth, A. and Fonagy, P. (1996). *What Works for Whom? A Critical Review of Psychotherapy Research*. London: Guilford Press.

Rotter, J. B. (1966). Generalized expectancies for internal versus external control of reinforcement. *Psychological Monographs* 80: 1–28.

Rousseau, D. M. (1995). *Psychological Contracts in Organizations*. London: Sage.

Rush, M. C. *et al.* (1995). Psychological resiliency in the public sector: 'Hardiness' and pressure for change. *Journal of Vocational Behavior* 46: 17–39.

Safran, D. J. (1990a). Towards a refinement of cognitive therapy in the light of interpersonal theory: 1. *Clinical Psychology Review* 10: 87–105.

Safran, J. D. (1990b). Towards a refinement of cognitive therapy in the light of interpersonal theory: 2. *Clinical Psychology Review* 10: 107–21.

Safran, J. D. and Segal, Z. V. (1990). *Interpersonal Process in Cognitive Therapy*. New York: Basic Books.

Safran, J. D. and Segal, Z. (1996). *Interpersonal Process in Cognitive Therapy*. Northvale, NJ: Jason Aronson.

Salkovskis, P. M. (1989). Cognitive behavioural factors and the persistence of intrusive thoughts in obsessional problems. *Behavioural Research and Therapy* 27: 677–82.

Salkovskis, P. M. (1991). The importance of behaviour in the maintenance of anxiety and panic: A cognitive account. *Behavioural Psychotherapy* 9: 6–19.

Salkovskis, P. M. (1994). Somatic problems. In K. Hatton *et al.* (eds) *Cognitive Behaviour Therapy for Psychiatric Problems: A Practical Guide*. Oxford, UK: Oxford University Press.

Salkovskis, P. M. (1996). The cognitive approach to anxiety: Threat beliefs, safety-seeking behaviour and the special case of health anxiety and obsessions. In P. M. Salkovskis (ed) *Frontiers of Cognitive Therapy*. New York: Guilford Press.

Salkovskis, P. M. (1999). Understanding and treating obsessive-compulsive disorder. *Behaviour Research and Therapy* 37: 429–52.

Salkovskis, P. M. and Bass, C. (1997). Hypochondriasis. In D. M. Clark and C. G. Fairburn (eds) *Science and Practice of Cognitive Behaviour Therapy*. Oxford, UK: Oxford University Press.

Salkovskis, P. M. and Warwick, H. M. C. (1986). Morbid preoccupations, health anxiety and reassurance: A cognitive-behavioural approach to hypochondriasis. *Behaviour Research and Therapy* 24: 597–602.

Salmon, P. (1992). Performance anxiety. In A. Freeman and F. M. Dattilio (eds) *Comprehensive Casebook of Cognitive Therapy*. New York: Plenum Press.

Salz, C. (1983). A theoretical approach to the treatment of work difficulties in borderline personalities. *Occupational Therapy in Mental Health* 3: 33 6.

Sargent, L. and Terry, D. J. (1994, August). *The Effects of Work Control and Job Demands on Employee Adjustment and Work Performance*. Paper presented at the Annual Convention of the Academy of Management, Dallas, TX.

Saul, L. J. (1947). *Emotional Maturity*. Philadelphia, PA: Lippincott.

Savickas, M. L. (1990). Work and adjustment. In D. Wedding (ed) *Behaviour and Medicine*. St Louis, MO: Mosby.

Scandell, D. J. *et al.* (1997). Personality of the therapist and theoretical orientation. *The Irish Journal of Psychology* 18: 413–8.

Schekelle, R. B. *et al.* (1981). Psychological depression and 17-year risk of death from cancer. *Psychosomatic Medicine* 43: 117–25.

Schleifer, S. J. *et al.* (1983). Suppression of lymphocyte stimulation following bereavement. *Journal of the American Medical Association* 250: 374–7.

Schleifer, S. J. *et al.* (1985). Depression and immunity: Lymphocyte function in ambulatory depressed, hospitalized schizophrenic patients and hospitalized herniorraphy patients. *Archives of General Psychiatry* 42: 129–33.

Schmidt, N. B. *et al.* (1995). The Schema Questionnaire: Investigation of psychometric properties and hierarchical structure of a measure of maladaptive schemas. *Cognitive Therapy and Research* 19: 295–321.

Schneider, B. (1987). The people make the place. *Personnel Psychology* 40: 437–53.

Schroeder, R. E. (1998). Using time management to achieve a balance. *Medical Group Management Journal* 45: 21–8.

Schuler, R. S. (1979). Managing stress means managing time. *Personnel Journal* 58: 851–85.

Schwartz, H. S. (1982). Job involvement as obsession-compulsion. *Academy of Management Review* 7: 429–32.

Scott, A. J. (1992). Editorial: House staff = shift workers? *Journal of Occupational Medicine* 34: 1161–3.

Seiwert, L. (1991). *Time is Money*. London: Kogan Page.

Sekaran, U. (1986). *Quality of Life in Dual Career Families*. San Francisco, CA: Jossey-Bass.

Seligman, M. E. P. (1975). *Helplessness*. San Francisco, CA: W. H. Freeman.

Selye, H. (1936). A syndrome produced by diverse nocuous agents. *Nature* 138: 32.

Selye, H. (1946). The general adaptation syndrome and disease of adaptation. *Journal of Clinical Endocrinology and Metabolism* 6: 117–30.

Selye, H. (1952). *The Story of the Adaptation Syndrome (Told in the Form of Informal, Illustrated Lectures)*. Montreal: ACTA Inc.

Selye, H. (1974). *Stress Without Distress*. Philadelphia, PA: Lippincott.

Selye, H. (1975). *The Stress of Life*. New York: McGraw Hill.

Selye, H. (1976). *The Stress of Life* (rev edn). New York: McGraw Hill.

Selye, H. (1983). *The Stress Concept, Past, Present and Future*. Chichester, UK: Wiley.

Shah, R. and Waller, G. (2000). Parental style and vulnerability to depression: Role of core beliefs. *Journal of Nervous and Mental Disease* 188: 19–25.

Shapiro, F. (1989). Eye movement desensitization procedure in the treatment of traumatic memories. *Journal of Behaviour Therapy and Experimental Psychiatry* 20: 199–223.

Shapiro, F. (1995). *Eye Movement Desensitization and Reprocessing. Basic Principles, Protocols and Procedures*. New York: Guilford Press.

Shapiro, F. and Forrest, M. S. (1997). *EMDR: The Breakthrough Therapy for Overcoming Anxiety Stress and Trauma*. New York: Basic Books.

Shapiro, J. P. (1979). Fear of success imagery as a reaction to sex role innappropriate behaviour. *Journal of Personality Assessment* 43: 33–8.

Shekelle, R. *et al.* (1983). Hostility, risk of coronary heart disease and mortality. *Psychosomatic Medicine* 45: 59–63.

Shengold, L. (1989). *Soul Murder*. New Haven, CT: Yale University Press.

Sherman, M. D. (1996). Distress and mental impairment due to mental health problems among psychotherapists. *Clinical Psychology Review* 16: 299–315.

Shoestrom, E. (1967). *The Manipulator*. Nashville, TN: Abingdon Press.

Sieber, W. J. *et al.* (1992). Modulation of human natural killer cell activity by exposure to uncontrollable stress. *Brain, Behavior and Immunity* 6: 1–16.

Siegrist, J. (1996). Adverse effects of high effort/low-reward conditions. *Journal of Occupational Health Psychology* 1: 27–41.

Simons, A. D. *et al.* (1985). Predicting response to cognitive therapy for depression: The role of learned resourcefulness. *Cognitive Therapy and Research* 9: 79–89.

Sinatra, J. D. (2000). Relaxation training as a holistic nursing intervention. *Holistic Nursing Practice* 14: 30–40.

Singer, J. E. (1986). Traditions in stress research: Integrative comments. In D. C. Spielberger and I. G. Sarason (eds) *Stress and Anxiety*, Vol. 10. New York: Hemisphere Publishing.

Slade, P. D. and Owens, R. G. (1998). A dual process model of perfectionism based on reinforcement theory. *Behaviour Modification* 22: 372–90.

Smart, J. C. *et al.* (1986). Person–environment congruence and job satisfaction. *Journal of Vocational Behavior* 29: 216–25.

Smith, A. (2000). The scale of perceived occupational stress. *Occupational Medicine* 50: 294–8.

Smith, R. J. (1999). Psychopathic behaviour and issues of treatment. *New Ideas in Psychology* 17: 165–76.

Smoczyk, C. M. and Dedmon, R. E. (1985). Health management program: Kimberly Clark Corporation. *American Behavioural Scientist* 28: 559–76.

Smoot, S. L. and Gonzales, J. L. (1995). Cost effective communication skills training for state hospital employees. *Psychiatric Services* 46: 819–22.

Smucker, M. and Dancu, C. V. (1999). *Cognitive Behavioural Treatment for Adult Survivors of Childhood Trauma: Imagery Rescripting and Reprocessing*. London: Aronson.

Smucker, M. R. *et al.* (1996). *Imagery Rescripting: A Treatment Manual for Adult Survivors of Childhood Sexual Abuse Experiencing PTSD*. Milwaukee, WI: Cognitive Therapy Institute of Milwaukee.

Snapp, M. B. (1992). Occupational stress, social support and depression among black and white professional managerial women. *Women and Health* 18: 41–79.

Snyder, S. *et al.* (1986). Selected behavioural features of patients with borderline personality traits. *Suicide and Life Threatening Behaviour* 16: 28–39.

Solomon, G. F. (1990). Emotions, stress and immunity. In R. Ornstein and C. Swencionis (eds) *The Healing Brain*. New York: Guilford Press.

Solomon, G. F. *et al.* (1987). An intensive psychoimmunologic study of long surviving persons with AIDS: Pilot work, background studies, hypotheses and methods. *Annals of New York Academy of Sciences* 496: 647–55.

Somers, A. R. (1979). Marital status, health and use of health services. *Journal of the American Medical Association* 241: 1818–22.

Sparkes, K. *et al.* (1997). The effects of work hours on health: A meta-analytic review. *Journal of Occupational and Organizational Psychology* 70: 391–408.

Sparkes, K. *et al.* (2001). Well-being and occupational health in the 21st century workplace. *Journal of Occupational and Organizational Psychology* 74: 489–504.

Spector, P. E. (1998). Development of the work locus of control scale. *Journal of Occupational Psychology* 61: 335–40.

Speilberger, C. D. (1972). Anxiety as an emotional state. In C. D. Speilberger (ed) *Anxiety: Current Trends in Theory and Research*, Vol. 1. New York: Academic Press.

Speilberger, C. D. *et al.* (1988). The experience, expression and control of anger. In M. P. Jannise (ed) *Health Psychology: Individual Differences and Stress*. New York: Springer.

Spreitzer, G. M. (1995). Psychological empowerment in the workplace: Dimensions, measurement and validation. *Academy of Management Journal* 38: 1442–65.

Spruell, G. (1987). Work fever. *Training and Development Journal* 41: 41–5.

Spurgeon, A. and Harrington, J. M. (1989). Work performance and health of junior doctors – a review of the literature. *Work and Stress* 3: 117–28.

Srivastava, A. K. (1989). Moderating effect of self-actualization on the relationship of role stress with job anxiety. *Psychological Studies* 34: 106–9.

St. Yves, A. *et al.* (1989). Externality and burnout among dentists. *Psychological Reports* 65: 755–8.

Stallard, P. and Law, F. (1993). Screening and psychological debriefing of adolescent survivors of life-threatening events. *British Journal of Psychiatry* 163: 660–5.

Starrin, B. *et al.* (1990). A review and critique of psychological approaches to the burnout phenomenon. *Scandanavian Journal of Caring Sciences* 4: 83–91.

Stein, M. *et al.* (1988). Immune system: Relationship to anxiety disorders. *Psychiatric Clinics of North America* 11: 349–60.

Steiner, S. (2002, January 5). Bite by bite: Interview with Susie Orbach, celebrity psychotherapist. *The Guardian*, 30–34.

Steptoe, A. (1983). Stress, helplessness and control: The implications of laboratory studies. *Journal of Psychosomatic Research* 27: 361–7.

Steptoe, A. (1989). Stress, coping and stage fright in professional musicians. *Psychology of Music* 17: 3–11.

Stern, D. N. (1985). *The Interpersonal World of the Infant*. New York: Basic Books.

Stewart, R. (1967). *Managers and Their Jobs*. London: MacMillan.

Stopa, L. *et al.* (2001). Are the short and long forms of the Young Schema Questionnaire comparable and how well does each version predict psychopathology scores? *Journal of Cognitive Psychotherapy* 15: 253–72.

Storr, A. (1990). *The Art of Psychotherapy*. New York: Routledge.

Sutherland, V. J. and Cooper, C. L. (2000). *Strategic Stress Management: An Organizational Approach*. London: Macmillan Press.

Tait, M. *et al.* (1989). Job and life satisfaction: A re-evaluation of the strength of the relationship and gender effects as a function of the date of the study. *Journal of Applied Psychology* 74: 502–7.

Taylor, F. W. (1947). *The Principles of Scientific Management*. New York: Harper and Row.

Temoshok, L. *et al.* (1987, November) *An Intensive Psychoimmunologic Study of Men With AIDS*. Paper presented at the first Research Workshop on the Psychoneuroimmunology of AIDS, Tiburon, CA.

Terr, L. (1991). Childhood traumas: An outline and overview. *American Journal of Psychiatry* 148: 10–20.

The Sunday Times (2004, March 7). Best companies to work for 2004.

Theorell, T. and Rahe, R. H. (1971). Psychosocial factors in myocardial infarction: An inpatient study in Sweden. *Journal of Psychosomatic Research* 15: 25–31.

Theorell, T. and Rahe, R. H. (1972). Behaviour and life satisfactions: Characteristics of Swedish subjects with myocardial infarction. *Journal of Chronic Diseases* 25: 139–47.

Thorne, P. (1987). Workaholism – the acceptable face of addiction? *International Management* 42: 71.

Thwaite, R. and Freeston, M. H. (2005). Safety-seeking behaviours: Fact or function? How can we clinically differentiate between safety behaviours and adaptive coping strategies across anxiety disorders? *Behavioural and Cognitive Psychotherapy* 33: 177–88.

Topf, M. (1989). Personality, hardiness, occupational stress and burnout in critical care nurses. *Research in Nursing and Health* 12: 179–86.

Totman, R. *et al.* (1980). Predicting experimental colds in volunteers from different measures of recent life stress. *Journal of Psychosomatic Research* 24: 155–63.

Tremblay, J. M. *et al.* (1986). Relation between therapeutic orientation and personality in psychotherapists. *Professional Psychology: Research and Practice* 17: 106–10.

Trimpy, M. and Davidson, S. (1994). Chaos, perfectionism and sabotage: Personality disorders in the workplace. *Issues in Mental Health Nursing* 15: 27–36.

Trist, E. L. and Bamforth, K. W. (1951). Some social and psychological consequences of the long-wall method of coal-getting. *Human Relations* 4: 3–38.

Tulloch, R. (1991). Anger and violence. In W. Dryden and R. Rentoul (eds) *Adult Clinical Problems: A Cognitive Behavioural Approach*. London: Routledge.

Unterberg, M. P. (2003). Personalities, personal style and trouble getting along. In J. P. Kahn and A. M. Langleib (eds) *Mental Health and Productivity in the Workplace: A Handbook for Organisation and Clinicians*. San Francisco, CA: Jossey-Bass.

Ursin, H. *et al.* (1978). *Psychobiology of Stress*. New York: Academic Press.

Valko, R. J. and Clayton, P. J. (1975). Depression in the internship. *Disease of the Nervous System* 36: 26–9.

Vallis, T. M. (1998). When the going gets tough: Cognitve therapy for the severely disturbed. In C. Perris and P. McGorry (eds) *Cognitive Psychotherapy of Psychotic and Personality Disorders*. Chichester, UK: Wiley.

Van Dixhorn, J. J. (2001). Breathing and relaxation therapy: A complete treatment. *Nederlands Tijdschrift Voor Fysiotherapie* 111: 4–10.

Van Maanen, J. (1975). Police socialization: A longitudinal examination of job attitudes in an urban police department. *Administrative Science Quarterly* 20: 207–27.

Vogal, C. *et al.* (1987). Exploring the concept of manipulation in psychiatric settings. *Archives of Psychiatric Nursing* 1: 429–35.

Wachtel, P. L. (ed) (1982). *Resistance: Psychodynamic and Behavioural Approaches*. New York: Plenum Press.

Waddington, P. A. J. (1999). Police (canteen). sub-culture: Testing conventional and contemporary wisdom. *British Journal of Criminology* 39: 287–309.

Wallace, J. E. and Brinkeroff, M. B. (1991). The measurement of burnout revisited. *Journal of Social Service Research* 14: 85–111.

Waller, G. *et al.* (2001). Psychometric properties of the long and short versions of the Young Schema Questionnaire: Core beliefs among bulimic and comparison women. *Cognitive Therapy and Research* 25: 137–47.

Warr, P. (1987). *Work, Unemployment and Mental Health*. London: Oxford University Press.

Warr, P. (1990). The measurement of wellbeing and other aspects of mental health. *Journal of Occupational Psychology* 63: 193–210.

Warr, P. *et al.* (1979). Scales for the measurement of some work attitudes and aspects of psychological wellbeing. *Journal of Occupational Psychology* 52: 129–48.

Warshaw, L. J. and Messite, J. (1996). Workplace violence: Preventive and Interventive Strategies. *Journal of Occupational and Environmental Medicine* 38: 993–1006.

Warwick, H. M. C. and Salkovskis, P. M. (1989). Hypochondriasis. In J. Scott *et al.* (eds) *Cognitive Therapy in Clinical Practice*. London: Gower.

Warwick, H. M. C. and Salkovskis, P. M. (1990). Hypchondriasis. *Behaviour Research and Therapy* 28: 105–17.

Warwick, H. M. C. and Salkovskis, P. M. (1985). Reassurance. *British Medical Journal* 290: 1028.

Warwick, H. M. C. *et al.* (1996). A controlled trial of cognitive-behavioural treatment of hypochondriasis. *British Journal of Psychiatry* 169: 189–95.

Watkins, C. E. (1983). Combatting student burnout: A structured group approach. *Journal for Specialists in Group Work* 8: 218–25.

Wegner, D. M. *et al.* (1987). Paradoxical effects of thought suppression. *Journal of Personality and Social Psychology* 53: 5–13.

Weissman, A. N. (1979). The Dysfunctional Attitudes Scale: A validation study. *Dissertation Abstracts International* 40: 1389b–90b.

Wells, A. (1997). *Cognitive Therapy of Anxiety Disorders: A Practice Manual and Conceptual Guide*. Chichester, UK: Wiley.

Wells, A. (2000). *Emotional Disorders and Metacognition*. Chichester, UK: Wiley.

Wells, A. and Matthews, G. (1994). *Attention and Emotion. A Clinical Perspective*. Hove, UK: Erlbaum.

Wells, A. and Papageorgiou, C. (1998). Social phobia: Effects of external attention in anxiety, negative beliefs, and perspective taking. *Behavior Therapy* 29: 357–70.

Wells, A. and Papageorgiou, C. (2001). Social phobic interoception: Effects of bodily information on anxiety, beliefs and self-processing. *Behaviour Research and Therapy* 39: 1–11.

Wells, A. *et al.* (1998). How do I look with my mind's eye? Perspective-taking in social phobia imagery. *Behaviour Research and Therapy* 36: 631–4.

Wiley, P. L. (1968). Manipulation. In L. T. Zderad and H. C. Belcher (eds) *Developing Behavioural Concepts in Nursing*. Atlanta, GA: Southern Regional Educational Board.

Willey, B. (2003). *Employment Law in Context: An Introduction for HR Professionals* (2nd edn). London: Pearson Education Limited.

Williams, R. (1999). Personality and post traumatic stress disorder. In W. Yule (ed) *Post-Traumatic Stress Disorders. Concepts and Therapy*. Chichester, UK: Wiley.

Williams, S. *et al.* (1998). *Improving the Health of the NHS Workforce*. London: The Nuffield Trust.

Wilson, M. G. *et al.* (2004). Work characteristics and employee health and well-being: Test of a model of healthy work organization. *Journal of Occupational and Organizational Psychology* 77: 565–88.

Witt, L. A. *et al.* (2003). When conscientiousness isn't enough: Emotional exhaustion and performance among call center customer service representatives. *Journal of Management* 277: 1–12.

Wolpe, J. *et al.* (1973). The current status of systematic desensitization. *American Journal of Psychiatry* 130: 961–65.

Woods, S. M. *et al.* (1966). Medical student's disease: Hypochondriasis in medical education. *Journal of Medical Education* 41: 785–90.

Woolfolk, R. and McNulty, T. (1983). Relaxation treatment for insomnia: A component analysis. *Journal of Consulting and Clinical Psychology* 51: 495–503.

World Health Organisation (1992). *The ICD-10 Classification of Mental and Behavioural Disorders*. Geneva.

Worrall, L. and Cooper, C. L. (1997). *IM-UMIST Quality of Working Life Survey*. London: Institute of Management.

Wizesniewski, K. *et al.* (1987). Type-A behaviour pattern and illness other than coronary heart disease. *Social Science and Medicine* 27: 623–6.

Wycherley, R. J. (1989). *The Living Skills Handbook* (4th edn). St Leonards on Sea, UK: Outset Publishing.

Young, J. E. (1994a). *Cognitive Therapy for Personality Disorders: A Schema Focused Approach*. Sarasota, FL: Professional Resource Exchange.

Young, J. E. (1994b). *Young Parenting Inventory (YPI)*. New York. Cognitive Therapy Centre of New York.

Young, J. E. (1994c). *Young Compensation Inventory (YCI)*. New York: Cognitive Therapy Centre of New York.

Young, J. E. (1998). *Young Schema Questionnaire Short Form (YSQ-S1)*. Available at http://home.sprynet.com/sprynet/schema/ysqs1.htm

Young, J. E. (1999). *Cognitive Therapy for Personality Disorders: A Schema Focused Approach* (3rd edn). Saratosa, FL: Professional Resource Press.

Young, J. E. and Behary, W. T. (1998). Schema focused therapy for personality disorders. In N. Tarrier *et al.* (eds) *Treating Complex Cases. The Cognitive Behavioural Approach*. Chichester, UK: Wiley.

Young, J. E. and Brown, G. (1994). Young Schema Questionnaire (2nd edn). In J. E. Young (ed) *Cognitive Therapy for Personality Disorders: A Schema Focused Approach*. Sarasota, FL: Professional Resource Press.

Young, J. E. and Brown, G. (2001). Young Schema Questionnaire special edition. New York: Schema Therapy Institute.

Young, J. E. and Klosko, J. S. (1993). *Reinventing Your Life*. New York: Plume Penguin.

Young, J. E. and Rygh, J. (1994). *Young-Rygh Avoidance Inventory (YRAI)*. New York: Cognitive Therapy Centre of New York.

Young, J. E. *et al.* (1993). Depression. In D. H. Barlow (ed) *Clinical Handbook of Psychological Disorders* (2nd edn). New York: Guilford.

Young, J. E. *et al.* (2003). *Schema Therapy: A Practitioner's Guide*. New York: Guilford Press.

Yung, P. M. B. *et al.* (2004). Relaxation training methods for nurse managers in Hong Kong: A controlled study. *International Journal of Mental Health Nursing* 13: 255–61.

Zahourek, R. P. (1988). *Relaxation and Imagery: Tools for Therapeutic Communication and Intervention*. Philadelphia, PA: WB Saunders.

Zaleznick, A. *et al.* (1977). Stress reactions in organizations: Syndromes, causes and consequences. *Behavioural Science* 22: 151–62.

Zigmond, A. S. and Snaith, R. P. (1983). The hospital anxiety and depression scale. *Acta Psychiatrica Scandinavica* 67: 361–70.

Index

Page numbers for main entries which have subheadings refer to general aspects of that topic.
Page numbers for figures appear in *italic*. Page numbers for tables appear in **bold**.